VERSAILLES

VERSAILLES

Jean-Marie Pérouse de Montclos

Translated from
the French by John Goodman

ABBEVILLE PRESS PUBLISHERS

New York • London

THE SPIRIT OF A PLACE

There is a magic in the burnished effervescence and the golden reflections of a tapered glass of champagne, and there is magic in the photographs, masterfully capturing the play of light on the stones of the château of Versailles.

Connivance and complicity are the words that spring immediately to mind when one looks at these admirable photographs. Nothing is less objective than what emerges from an artist's lens (in French, "objectif"). He can breathe life into a legend and make the spirit of a place comprehensible.

The first mission assigned by the king to the château of Versailles was that of transmitting a message to its visitors. Such an ambassadorial role has also been played by the celebrated firm Champagnes Veuve Clicquot Ponsardin. One cannot help but reflect, while turning the pages of this book, on how the king's example was emulated, somewhat later, in the Hermitage and Pavlovsk palaces and in all the courts of Europe, where Veuve Clicquot champagne flowed freely.

There were, then, many reasons underlying our support for this project, and our aid to an artist able to exploit his technique without becoming enslaved to it. Very few painters have attained this level of mastery.

JOSEPH HENRIOT

FRONT COVER: *The Hall of Mirrors, executed by Hardouin-Mansart and Le Brun between 1678 and 1686 (see pages 240–241).*
BACK COVER: *The Apollo Fountain, executed by Tuby in 1668–70*

English-language edition

Editor: Jacqueline Decter
Text Designer: Patricia Fabricant
Jacket Designer: Celia Fuller
Copy Chief: Robin James
Copy Editor: Clifford Browder
Production Supervisor: Hope Koturo

Copyright © 1991 Editions Mengès, Paris
English translation copyright © 1991 Abbeville Press, Inc.

First edition
10 9 8 7 6 5 4

Library of Congress Cataloging-in-Publication Data

Pérouse de Montclos, Jean-Marie.
[Versailles. English]
Versailles/Jean-Marie Pérouse de Montclos ; photography by Robert Polidori.
p. cm.
Translated from the French.
Includes bibliographical references and index.
ISBN 978-1-55859-228-5
1. Château de Versailles (Versailles, France)—History. 2. Gardens—France—Versailles.
3. Classicism in art—France—Versailles. 4. Interior decoration—France—Versailles—History—17th century.
5. Architecture and state—France—Versailles. 6. Louis XIV, King of France. 1638–1715—Art patronage.
7. Versailles (France)—Buildings, structures, etc.
I. Polidori, Robert. II. Title
NA7736.V5P4713   1991
725'.17'0944366—dc20   91-23802

For bulk and premium sales and for text adoption procedures, write to
Customer Service Manager, Abbeville Press, 137 Varick Street, New York, NY 10013 or call 1-800-ARTBOOK.

Visit Abbeville Press online at www.abbeville.com.

CONTENTS

THE POWER OF A SYMBOL

by Olivier de Rohan, President of the Society of the Friends of Versailles

Versailles is the consummate symbol of sovereign power. Everything about it was calculated and realized with this end in mind. From the crown of a hill with a view extending into infinity, a king whose power was bestowed by God governed a France that was then the preeminent European power.

In this new Olympus he was surrounded by images of antique divinities and heroes painted and sculpted by the greatest artists of his era. One autumn day in 1789, when the extensive greenery of the park had begun to turn color, the king of France left Versailles under the pressure of a revolution that wanted France to be governed from Paris. Immediately upon his departure laborers, tapestry weavers, and gardeners set about making the palace yet more beautiful for his anticipated return. But destiny intervened. The king was beheaded and Versailles, symbol of his inherited power, seemed doomed to destruction.

Fortunately, the residents of the town of Versailles managed to prevent this. A few years later Napoleon, having founded a new dynasty, wanted to set up residence there, as did King Louis XVIII after him, having spent his youth there, and his brother Charles X during his short reign that followed — as if occupation of the throne and residence at Versailles were intimately related. The sovereign rulers who came after them never contemplated returning to Versailles, which indicates the extent of their deference to the symbolic power of the place.

Was it for this or other reasons that at Versailles the Third Republic was established and the sovereignty of the German Empire proclaimed; that presidents of France were elected by the assembled chambers there until the Fifth Republic; that the treaties ending the First World War were signed there; that even now modifications of the French constitution must be decided there, and contemporary French heads of state prefer to receive the leaders of the great nations there, when such summit meetings are mandated?

But if power and history have continued, and still continue, to reside in the palace in the absence of kings, a more regular use for the domain, which would justify its conservation and maintenance, remains to be found. We should be grateful to King Louis-Philippe for reviving the idea, born during the Revolution, of creating a museum in the château of Versailles. His was a museum devoted "To All the Glories of France," as inscribed on a pediment of the château.

But what attracts crowds from all over the world to Versailles is, above all, the grandiose manifestation of the power and history, allied with beauty, of a civilization at its apogee, rendered accessible through its architecture, painting, sculpture, furniture, and gardens.

Restoration work proceeds apace in all these areas. Whether it is a question of extensive preservation campaigns or the reconstruction of buildings, of attempts to reassemble the furnishings dispersed during the Revolution or to enrich the museum's collections, or of work undertaken to restore the gardens' original harmony, Versailles today is marked by various and incessant creative endeavors. Thanks to the good will and assistance of public agencies? Yes, but none of this would have been possible, either yesterday or today, without the passionate commitment of all those throughout the world who love Versailles. One would like to mention all the generous donors who have lent their moral and material support to this enterprise of restoration, but space limitations prohibit this; one example, perhaps the most striking one, the contribution of the Rockefeller family, will have to stand for all.

The admirable photographs in this book, realized by that passionate lover of Versailles, the artist Robert Polidori, evoke very nearly all the pleasures enjoyed by those who, like himself, might wish to prowl about Versailles at all hours and in all epochs. He lends us his eyes and his sensitivity, revealing an infinite variety of marvels: from the surprise of unexpected discoveries, always beautiful, to fresh views of consecrated but eternally vital masterpieces.

To guide us through this spellbinding world, Jean-Marie Pérouse de Montclos here offers a magisterial synthetic text that, like the design of a French garden, opens vast horizons and lays out byways inviting exploration, with new perspectives at each crossroads.

Without doubt, all those fortunate enough to hold this book in their hands will, like its authors, find it impossible to resist the charms of Versailles.

CHRONOLOGY

1610 Accession of Louis XIII.

1623 **Construction of the hunting lodge at Versailles.**

1624 Richelieu is given a seat on the king's council.

L'Architecture françoise des bastimens particuliers by Louis Savot.

Louis XIII spends his first night in the Versailles hunting lodge (March 9).

1628 Capture of La Rochelle.

1631 **Construction of the château of Versailles by Philibert Leroy (1631–34).**

Construction of the château of Richelieu begins.

1632 **Louis XIII acquires the seigniory of Versailles.**

1635 Establishment of the French Academy.

1636 *Le Cid* by Corneille.

1637 André Le Nôtre succeeds his father as first gardener to the king in the large garden at the Tuileries.

1638 Birth of Louis XIV.

Louise de La Fayette, beloved of Louis XIII, enters a convent.

1642 Death of Richelieu.

Construction of the château of Maisons by François Mansart (1642–48).

1643 Death of Louis XIII.

Victory of Rocroi.

1648 Treaty of Westphalia.

Establishment of the Royal Academy of Painting and Sculpture.

1649 Louis XIV flees Paris and takes refuge at Saint-Germain-en-Laye (January 5).

1652 Ceremonial entry of the king into Paris. End of the Fronde.

1654 Le Vau appointed first architect.

1656 Construction of the château of Vaux-le-Vicomte.

1659 Treaty of the Pyrenees.

1660 Marriage of Louis XIV.

Death of the sculptor Jean Sarrazin.

1661 Death of Mazarin.

Beginning of Louis XIV's personal reign.

Fall of Fouquet.

Beginning of Louis XIV's first building campaign at Versailles.

1662 **Construction of the Menagerie (1662 or 1663).**

Acquisition of the property known as the Gobelins in view of establishing a royal manufactory of tapestries.

The History of the King tapestry series is begun.

1663 **Construction of the first Orangery by Le Vau.**

La Vallière is officially presented at court.

Establishment of the Royal Academy of Inscriptions and Belles-Lettres.

Fêtes mounted at Versailles, featuring a performance of Molière's *Impromptu de Versailles* **(September).**

Letter from Colbert to Louis XIV advocating construction at the Louvre rather than at Versailles (September 28).

1664 Colbert is appointed overseer of the king's buildings (January 1).

Construction of the Grotto of Thetis.

Molière's *Tartuffe.*

The fête known as the "Plaisirs de l'île enchantée" is mounted at Versailles.

Establishment of the Beauvais tapestry manufactory.

A.-F. Van der Meulen is appointed painter of the king's campaigns.

Formation of the Compagnie des Indes Orientales.

1665 Establishment of the manufactory of mirror glass.

Busts of Louis XIV by Warin and Bernini.

Bernini's sojourn in France.

1666 Establishment of the Royal Academy of Sciences.

Louis XIV passes his last night in Paris.

1667 **Excavation of the Grand Canal begins.**

Le Nôtre's first widening of the central walk.

1668 **Purchase of the village of Trianon (January).**

Beginning of Louis XIV's second building campaign at Versailles.

Treaty of Aix-la-Chapelle (May).

Construction of the Envelope begins (October).

Sculpture for the Grotto of Thetis (1668–72).

Sculpture for the Latona Fountain (1668–70).

Sculpture for the Apollo Fountain (1668–71).

Sculpture for the Pyramid Fountain (1668–70).

Construction of the Louvre colonnade.

Montespan becomes the royal mistress.

The fête known as the "Grand Divertissement royal" is mounted at Versailles.

1669 **Design competition for reconstruction of the château (June).**

Le Vau departs for the Nivernais (August).

Reversion to the Envelope design solution (October).

Promenade de Versailles by **Mademoiselle de Scudéry.**

Death of Henrietta of England. Funeral oration by Bossuet.

1670 Le Vau returns from Nivernais (February).

Death of Le Vau (October).

Construction of the Porcelain Trianon.

Installation of the fountains along the Water Walk or Infants' Walk.

Puget begins work on the *Milo of Crotona* and the *Perseus and Andromeda.*

1671 **Completion of basic structural work on the Envelope.**

Decoration of the Ambassadors' Staircase (1671–80).

The Apollo Fountain is installed.

Extension of the Grand Canal and excavation of its crossbar.

Construction of the New City of Versailles (Nôtre Dame quarter) (1671–72).

Competition for the design of a French architectural order.

Establishment of the Royal Academy of Architecture.

1672 **The Fountains of the Seasons are installed.**

Decoration of the Room of the Hocquetons.

Louis XIV crosses the Rhine.

1673 Death of Molière.

1674 **Publication of the** *Description de Versailles* **by Félibien.**

Le Nôtre widens the central walk again.

The sailors' community known as the Petite Venise is established.

The Great Commission of sculpture.

A fête is mounted at Versailles on the occasion of the conquest of the Franche-Comté.

La Vallière enters a convent.

Françoise d'Aubigné is named marquise de Maintenon and is given the château of that name.

1675 **The Bosquet of Fame by Le Nôtre.**

Winter, sculpture by Girardon (1675–86).

1676 **The Neptune Fountain is installed.**

Sculpture for the Enceladus Fountain.

1677 **Construction of the pavilions in the Bosquet of Fame, which becomes the Bosquet of the Domed Pavilions.**

Rape of Proserpina, sculpture by Girardon (1677–99).

Racine's *Phèdre.*

1678 Treaty of Nijmegen.

Beginning of Louis XIV's third building campaign at Versailles, directed by Mansart.

Transformation of the Marble Court.

Construction of the Ministers' Wings (1678–79).

Construction of the Southern Wing (1678–82).

Decoration of the Hall of Mirrors and the Salons of War and Peace (1678–80).

Creation of the Pool of the Swiss Guards.

1679 Decoration of the Queen's Staircase (1679–81).

Construction of the Large and Small Stables.

The first Bosquet of the Springs by Le Nôtre.

The king's kitchen garden by La Quintinie.

1680 Creation of the Tapis Vert by Le Nôtre.

The Bosquet of the Ballroom by Le Nôtre.

1681 Construction of the Marly machine (an elaborate water pump) on the Seine.

1682 The seat of government is formally transferred to Versailles.

Construction of the Grand Commun.

1683 Death of Queen Marie-Thérèse.

Death of Colbert.

Creation of the Salon of Abundance.

Installation of Puget's sculptural groups.

Acquisition of terms after designs by Poussin for Versailles.

De l'excellence de la langue française by F. Charpentier.

1684 Louis XIV marries Madame de Maintenon.

Louis XIV appropriates the balance of the Appartements Intérieurs for his own use. They are redecorated.

Creation of the Small Gallery.

Le Brun's disgrace.

Construction of the Orangery by Mansart. Mansart's Colonnade.

Destruction of the Grotto of Thetis.

Construction of the Eure Canal (1684–88).

1685 Reception of the Genoese ambassadors (May 15).

Construction of the Northern Wing begins.

Mignard paints the ceiling of the Small Gallery (1685–86).

Sculpture for the Water Terrace (1685–94).

Twenty-four terms are commissioned for the gardens.

Arrival at Versailles of Bernini's equestrian statue of Louis XIV.

Revocation of the Edict of Nantes.

1686 Mansart is named first architect.

Construction of the Tennis Court.

1687 Construction of the Large Trianon begins (June).

Death of Lully.

1688 Outbreak of the War of the League of Augsburg, which soon slows down and, at one point, interrupts construction at Versailles.

Completion of the Large Trianon (January).

Decoration of the Large Trianon (1688–91).

Bronze versions of the fountains along the Water Walk (or Infants' Walk) are cast.

Death of Gabriel Jacques IV.

1689 Work on the Northern Wing ceases as a result of the war.

The silver furniture is melted down.

James II, the dethroned king of England, is given the château of Saint-Germain-en-Laye as a residence.

1690 Death of Le Brun.

1697 Treaty of Ryswick.

1699 Mansart is named overseer of the king's buildings.

Beginning of Louis XIV's fourth building campaign at Versailles.

Construction of the Chapel (1699–1710).

Death of Racine.

1700 Death of Le Nôtre.

1701 The Appartement Intérieur is recast and redecorated.

1702 Completion of basic structural work on the Chapel.

1704 Death of Bossuet.

1708 Delivery of two commodes by Boulle for the king's bedroom at Trianon.

Death of Mansart.

De Cotte is appointed first architect.

The ceiling of the Chapel is painted (1708–9).

1710 Consecration of the Chapel. Its interior decoration remains unfinished.

1711 Death of the Grand Dauphin.

1712 Death of the duc and duchesse de Bourgogne.

Work begins on what will become the Salon of Hercules.

1714 Death of the duc de Berry.

1715 Death of Louis XIV.

The young Louis XV leaves Versailles.

1721 Death of Watteau.

Les Lettres persanes by Montesquieu.

1722 Louis XV returns to Versailles.

1723 Louis XV attains his majority.

1725 Marriage of Louis XV and Marie Leszczynska.

1729 Birth of the dauphin.

1733 Ceiling of the Salon of Hercules by Lemoyne (1733–36).

1734 *Les Lettres anglaises* by Voltaire.

1735 Death of de Cotte.

Jacques Gabriel V is named first architect.

Remodeling of the righthand portions of the Appartement Intérieur is begun.

Painted decorations for the Gallery of Foreign Hunts (1735–36).

1736 The Salon of Hercules is opened.

1738 Decoration of Louis XV's bedroom.

Sculpture of the Neptune Fountain.

1742 Death of Jacques Gabriel V.

Ange-Jacques Gabriel is named first architect.

1744 War of Austrian Succession begins.

1745 Louis XV is victorious at the battle of Fontenoy.

Jeanne Poisson, later the marquise de Pompadour, becomes the royal mistress.

1747 Marriage of the dauphin and Marie-Josèphe de Saxe.

The dauphin's rooms are remodeled.

1748 Treaty of Aix-la-Chapelle.

The decision is made to construct the Opera House.

1749 Construction of the French Pavilion at Trianon.

Creation of the Menagerie at Trianon.

1751 First volume of the *Encyclopédie* of Diderot and d'Alembert.

Le Siècle de Louis XIV by Voltaire.

The pineapple arrives at Trianon.

1752 Destruction of the Ambassadors' Staircase and the Small Gallery.

L'Architecture française by J.-F. Blondel (1752–56).

1755 Death of Saint-Simon.

Death of Montesquieu.

Decoration of the Chamber of the King's Council.

1756 Beginning of the Seven Years' War.

1757 Damiens's attempt to assassinate Louis XV.

1759 Construction of the headquarters of the Department of War and that of the Departments of Foreign Affairs and the Navy (1759–61).

1760 Construction of the Small Trianon (1760–64).

9

Oeben receives a commission for the desk for the king.

1762 *Emile* by Rousseau.

1763 Treaty of Paris.

1764 Death of Rameau.
Death of the marquise de Pompadour.
Decoration of the Small Trianon (1764–68).

1765 **Final draft of a plan for the Opera House.**

1766 Lorraine annexed by France.

1769 **Louis XV reclaims Madame Adélaïde's apartment for his own use. She moves onto the ground floor.**

1770 Death of Boucher.
Marriage of the dauphin Louis and Marie-Antoinette.
Inauguration of the Opera House.

1771 **Louis XV approves implementation of the Grand Dessein (master plan).**
Construction of the Gabriel Wing.

1774 Death of Louis XV.
Decoration of Louis XVI's library.
A.-J. Gabriel retires.
Mique is named first architect.
Creation of the English garden at Trianon (1774–77).
The mature trees in the gardens and park are felled.

1776 **Mique's plan for completion of the château.**
Statuary for the Great Men of France series is commissioned.
The Baths of Apollo by Hubert Robert (1776–78).
Beginning of the war in support of the American Revolution.

1777 **The Temple of Love at Trianon by Mique (1777–78).**

1778 Death of J.-J. Rousseau.
Death of Voltaire.

1779 **The Queen's Theater at Trianon by Mique.**

1782 Death of A.-J. Gabriel.
Les Confessions by Rousseau.

1783 Treaty of Versailles.
Open competition for plans for completing the château.
Decoration of the Gilded Chamber of the queen.
Construction of the Hamlet (1783–85).

1784 Project for a cenotaph to Newton by E.-L. Boullée.

1785 David's *Oath of the Horatii* exhibited in Paris.

1787 **Jewelry cabinet for the queen by Schwerdfeger.**
The town of Versailles becomes a municipality.

1788 **Decoration of Louis XVI's dressing room.**

1789 Opening of the Estates General (May 5).
The Tennis Court Oath (June 20).
Parisians go to Versailles and escort the king back to Paris (October).

1791 **The king is arrested at Varennes while fleeing the country (June 22).**
David begins work on the *Oath of the Tennis Court.*

1792 Abolition of the monarchy (September 22).

1793 Execution of Louis XVI (January 21).
Sale of the furniture from Versailles (1793–94).
Opening of the Central Museum of the Arts in the Louvre.

1797 **Versailles becomes a museum for exhibiting works of the French school.**

1799 Bonaparte's coup d'état.

1801 **Opening of the Museum of Versailles.**

1814 First abdication of Napoleon.

1820 **Completion of the Dufour Pavilion, begun by Napoleon.**

1824 Death of Louis XVIII.

1830 Abdication of Charles X.

1833 **Redecoration of the château, now designated to house a Museum of French History (1833–37).**

1834 **Decoration of the Gallery of Battles.**

1837 **Inauguration of the Museum of French History.**

1839 **Decoration of the Rooms of the Crusades.**

1842 **Decoration of the African Rooms.**

1848 Fall of Louis-Philippe.

1871 **Proclamation of the German Empire in the Hall of Mirrors.**
The government withdraws to Versailles.

1875 **Construction of the Hall of Deputies.**

1879 **The government returns to Paris.**

1887 **Appointment of Pierre de Nolhac as conservator of the château.**

1925 **First gifts from the Rockefeller Foundation (1925–28).**

1953 **A law is passed safeguarding Versailles.**

1957 **Restoration of the Opera House is completed.**

1962 **The Debré decree, initiating the restitution of Versailles's furniture.**

1965 **Restoration of the Large Trianon is completed.**

1975 **Restoration of the queen's bedroom is completed.**

1978 **Legislation initiating regular subsidies for work at Versailles.**

1980 **Restoration of the king's ceremonial bedroom and the Hall of Mirrors is completed.**

1986 **Restoration of the ground-floor apartments of the royal family is completed.**

O*PPOSITE: View of the main axis, approximately east-west. From foreground to background: the forward court, the Royal Court, the Marble Court, the château, the Water Terrace, the Latona Fountain, the Apollo Fountain, and the Grand Canal. To the left, the Southern Terrace; to the right, the Northern Terrace.*

*B*ELOW: View along the main axis, from east to west. In the middle ground, the crow's-foot configuration, encompassing the Small Stables on the left (identifiable by the dome), the Large Stables on the right, and the Place d'Armes. Beyond, the château, the gardens, and the park.

*R*IGHT: View along the main axis, from east to west. In the foreground, the entrance gate, the forward court, and the Ministers' Wings. In the middle ground, the Northern Wing with the Chapel and the Opera House (right); the Southern Wing (left); and the Royal Court, the Marble Court, and the central block of the château (center). In the background, the Northern Terrace (right); the Southern Terrace with the beginning of the Stairways of the Hundred Steps (left); and the Water Terrace, the Latona Fountain, the Royal Walk, the Apollo Fountain, and the Grand Canal.

*B*ELOW: *The Large Trianon and the crossbar of the Grand Canal. Jules Hardouin-Mansart built the Marble Trianon (1687) in six months. The gardens were designed by Michel Le Bouteux under the direction of his uncle André Le Nôtre.*

*O*PPOSITE: *View along the transverse axis, approximately north-south. From foreground to background: a portion of the Neptune Fountain, the Dragon Fountain, the Water Walk or Infants' Walk, the Pyramid Fountain with the Fountains of the Crowns to either side, and the château.*

PART ONE

Geography and History

Chapter 1
EARTH, WIND, AND WATER

LEFT: The Nymphs' Bath, detail. OPPOSITE: Water, sculpture by Le Gros.

Versailles was a simple field from which would emerge one day, under the blade of a plow, a golden coin. *Versare*, to return, is the root of the word *Versailles*, which designates a cleared plot of land; in French, its ending affiliates it with a set of terms associated with cultivation and harvest (*semailles*).

Louis XIV inherited from his father a rather mediocre property situated in an agricultural valley; its topography necessitated extensive terracing and irrigation work to render it cultivable. But as the peasant in La Fontaine's *Fables* stated in bequeathing his own plot of land, a treasure was hidden within it. La Fontaine's volume appeared in 1668, the year in which extensive work was first undertaken at Versailles, work to which that author was a direct eyewitness. "Dig, shovel, probe, leave no place / that has not been worked and reworked by the human hand." A strange way indeed to till a field! And yet to be continually worked and reworked, made and remade, was to be the history of the château of Versailles.

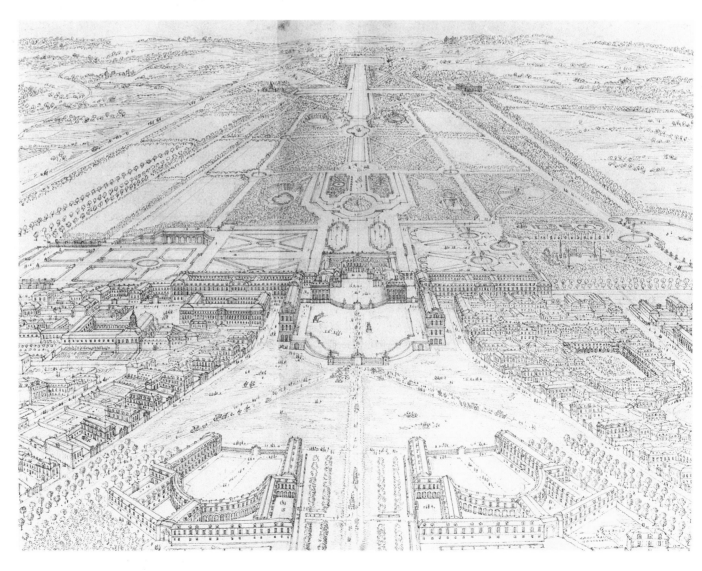

*T*he château circa 1668, as depicted by Pierre Patel (Versailles Museum). This painting shows the château immediately following Louis XIV's first building campaign. Note these features: the hills bordering the valley; the Grotto of Thetis and reservoirs, to the right of the accommodations for support services built by Louis XIV in front of Louis XIII's château; the crow's-foot with the pavilions stipulated by the first urbanization and development plan; and finally, the parish church of the old village.

THE NATURAL SITE

The Galie Valley was a low, marshy area through which ran several creeks, channels, and brooks. Its name derives from one of these, Galie Creek, whose source was located on the periphery of the present Grand Canal, where even today, at the end of one of the most celebrated perspectives in the world, the Galie farm is still to be found. The valley was punctuated with ponds, heaths, and pastures and was very uneven in many areas. The surrounding high ground rose above the Versailles hillock, the site of a windmill, a village, and a château in ruinous condition when it was acquired by Louis XIII in 1632.

The seigniory of Versailles, the first recorded mention of which dates back to 1038, then belonged to the

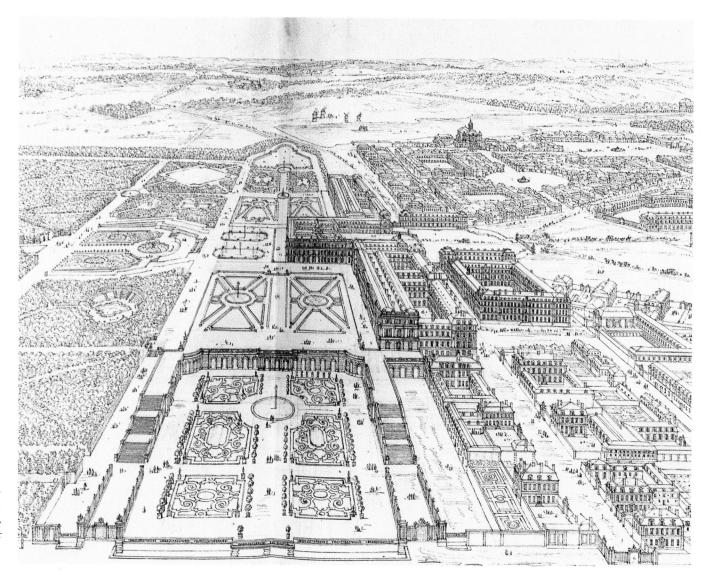

*B*ird's-eye view, drawing by I. Silvestre. The château circa 1690. In the foreground, the Orangery with the Stairways of the Hundred Steps.

Gondi family. Well before Louis XIII became its lord, he often frequented this valley, rich in game and conveniently located near the royal residence of Saint-Germain-en-Laye. Thanks to the *Journal* of Héroard, Louis XIII's doctor, in which the king's daily activities are recounted, we are well informed about the royal hunting parties in the Galie Valley. When the hunt was concluded too late to return to Saint-Germain for the night, the king had lodgings improvised in the old château or in the windmill, and on occasion even at the local inn, where he shared quarters with Norman cowherders driving their flocks through the valley on the way to Paris. It comes as no surprise, then, that Louis XIII soon conceived a desire for more suitable shelter in the area. Having constituted (with great difficulty, for the region was composed of many small plots) a property to be placed at his disposal, part of which he purchased outright and part of which he leased as life tenant, he had a hunting lodge constructed there in 1623, which was considerably enlarged in 1631. It was only the following year, however, that he purchased the seigniory of Versailles from the Gondi family. The 1632 instrument of transfer states explicitly that the ruined old château was to be conveyed along with the property. This indicates that the new structure had not been built on the site of the old one, but rather apart from it, where the windmill that shared the hillock's crown with the ancestral manse had been situated. Today nothing remains of the medieval château, but that of 1631, which subsequently came to be known as the Old Château, survives as the core of the great royal palace constructed by Louis XIV.

"Only one thing prevents this immense palace from being considered the most perfect in the world: its unfortunate site," wrote the architect Jacques-François Blondel in his *Architecture française* (1752–56). In fact, the site of Versailles has occasioned severe criticism from many quarters. This château, Blondel continued, is "constructed on a hillock that rises in the center of a valley surrounded by still higher hills, which gives it a rather diminished appearance." When Louis XIV made known his intention to enlarge his father's château, Colbert countered by observing that "it will be impossible to construct a large household complex in this space [the summit of the hill] . . . . The considerable incline . . . will preclude extensions and the use of more land, unless the whole site is to be recast,

which would entail enormous expense" (memorandum by Colbert entitled *Palais de Versailles. Raisons générales*, datable to 1669).

The east-west orientation of the valley meant that it acted as a wind tunnel, trapping the air flows that turned the windmills. The latter, of great utility while the region was being exploited agriculturally, would eventually be mobilized to pump the waters required for Louis XIV's pools and fountains. Indeed, some authors discern the etymological roots of the word *Versailles* in the Latin terms

The château circa 1690, by J.-B. Martin (Versailles Museum). This painting shows the crow's-foot with the new stables.

vertere and *alae*, or "turning sails." As already noted, the château itself was built on the site of a windmill. "You will recall, monsieur le maréchal," Louis XIV declared one day to the maréchal de Gramont, "that formerly a windmill was situated here." "Yes, sire," the marshal replied, "the mill no longer exists, but the winds do" (*Mémoires* of the maréchal de Gramont, published in 1716).

FAR FROM PARIS, FAR FROM THE PEOPLE

The political crises of his minority, which unfolded within the urban theater of Paris, had developed in the King a pronounced aversion [for the city] and had convinced him that continued residence there would be dangerous, and that installation of the court elsewhere would make plotting from a Parisian base less feasible, however small the distance from its limits, and simultaneously more difficult to hide, as absences would be easily remarked. He held a grudge against Paris for his forced flight from the city on King's Day eve (1649), and for witnessing the tears he shed at Mademoiselle de La Vallière's first entry into a convent. The awkwardness created by having mistresses, and the danger of provoking great scandals in the midst of so populous a capital, and one so full of independent thinkers, played no small part in encouraging him to move away. There he found himself importuned by the crowd when he went out, when he returned, and whenever he appeared in the streets, and he was no less frequently bothered there by another crowd, also from the city, that would have been discouraged from paying such assiduous court, had this entailed a bit of travel. His taste for walks and the hunt—much more convenient and accessible in the country than in Paris, which was far from woodlands and lacked appropriate areas for strolling—and that for buildings which came later and increased with the passage of time, made it difficult for him to amuse himself in a city where he was continually in the public eye. Finally he conceived the notion of making himself more venerable by removing himself from the gaze of the multitude and from being seen by it daily.

Saint-Simon

The persistent drafts plaguing the palace interiors would have been sufficient to evoke the site's background in the minds of the king's guests: their discomforting effects have entered the historical record along with the sighs of a chilly Madame de Maintenon. Even when these lines were being written, a ferocious storm destroyed a thousand trees in the gardens and the surrounding park.

There was no shortage of available water, but it was insufficient for the needs of the gardens and moreover disgustingly polluted. "There is an abundance of water extracted and pumped from all over, but these operations render it green, thick, and muddy; its omnipresence generates an evident and unhealthy humidity and an offensive odor," wrote the duc de Saint-Simon. Versailles was "the saddest, the most unpleasant of places, without attractive views, and effectively without woods, water, or land, because all that is there is unstable sand or marsh." One of the most surprising defects of the site, perhaps, was the lack of woodlands. The château of Versailles was not attached to one of the great forested domains in which the king could hunt. The nearest forest was situated on the highlands to the north, around Marly, where a rival château would eventually be built.

All that was lacking at Versailles was readily available at Saint-Germain-en-Laye. "A unique site in which were conjoined marvelous vistas, an immense, immediately adjacent forest, . . . and the charms and conveniences of the Seine" (Saint-Simon). The château of Saint-Germain, west of Paris, and that of Fontainebleau, to the southeast, had been the two most favored royal residences in the sixteenth century, but these were far from being the only ones of note: Francis I alone had built or transformed seven others in the vicinity of Paris. In the mid-seventeenth century a strong, apparently irreversible predilection for Saint-Germain became apparent. When, on the night of January 5, 1649, the king and court found themselves obliged to flee the Parisian mob, it was at Saint-Germain that they sought refuge. While it might be expected that the fear thereafter associated with residence in Paris would have tended to increase the attraction of Saint-Germain, it was in fact to be a crucial determinant of Versailles's future preeminence. The "young pretender" finally carried the day over the claims of the "legitimate heir," but the competition was to be fierce. Saint-Germain was sited in alignment with the royal axis emanating from

Paris, the one advancing from the Louvre toward the west that now culminates in the recéntly constructed Arche de la Défense. A curious effect of magnetic declination was to displace the pole of the monarchy to 48°48′ latitude and 22°17½′ longitude (the coordinates of Versailles recorded in Blondel's *Architecture française*, already cited). The longitudinal reading was clearly calculated in relation to the Paris meridian, as was current French practice, rather than that of Greenwich. The Versailles meridian passes directly through the château: its trajectory was given visible form in the floor of the Chamber of the Pendulum Clock (Cabinet de la Pendule), whose celebrated timepiece represented the passage of time at Versailles in the context of the turning stellar constellations. For an abstract point to be accorded a compelling material identity, it is necessary only to determine its precise position within the universe. Certainly the position of Versailles was emphatically plotted.

Eventually its gravitational dominance would become sufficient to force all the châteaux to the west of Paris into relative submission. Their configuration traced a great arc with Versailles at its center, encompassing, from north to south, Saint-Germain, Marly, Saint-Cloud, and Meudon, all of which boasted exceptional sites along the meandering Seine, while at a somewhat greater distance there were also Sceaux and Rambouillet. It could easily be argued that any one of these residences was to be preferred to Versailles. Only Marly was to be consistently favored by Louis XIV himself; Saint-Germain, which long remained the principal royal residence, would be ceded to James II, the unfortunate king of England, Louis's ally in exile. Saint-Cloud was the province of Monsieur, the French king's brother; Meudon, that of the Grand Dauphin, the king's son. Sceaux and Rambouillet were, respectively, the seats of the duc de Maine and the comte de Toulouse, the two legitimized bastard sons born of Madame de Montespan.

Within Versailles's sphere of influence there were, in addition to these subsidiary properties, still other affiliated sites such as any flourishing château tends to generate. Initially svelte and energetic like young hunters, with the passage of time châteaux tend to become gouty and tiresome; they fall into neglect and are avoided as younger rivals come to the fore. Thus in the era of Francis I the old château of Saint-Germain spun off the satellite hunting lodge in the forest at La Muette, which in turn soon fell into disfavor, and likewise, under Henry II, a new château that would be considerably expanded under Henry IV. In the beginning Versailles was but a by-product of Saint-Germain. But having become the largest château in France, it would in its turn prompt the creation, according to the same generative law, of Trianon and Marly, the one within and the other outside the boundaries of its park.

THE CREATION OF VERSAILLES

There was a swamp. And there were architects and gardeners. And there were lines, angles, triangles, rectangles, circles, and pyramids. And there was a park, and this park was born of the soul of Le Nôtre.

Jean Cocteau, Versailles aux lumières, *1954 (text written for a* Son et Lumière *spectacle)*

MAPS OF THE HUNT AND OF AFFECTION'S REALM

Fortunately, the remarkable state of the Paris basin at the end of the old regime, with its galaxy of royal residences and their surrounding parklands, has been recorded for posterity in a Hunting Map prepared at the king's order in 1765 by the engineer Jean-Baptiste Berthier. Like a map of the heavens, it is punctuated with "stars," namely the many crossroads that served as rallying points for hunting expeditions.

Inevitably, the pursuit of game entailed excursions beyond the boundaries of the royal forests, thus encouraging successive monarchs to acquire surrounding fields and pasture lands. In fact, the passion for the hunt, which remained a constant from the first Valois to the last of the Bourbon dynasty, placed the local wildlife in great ecological peril. Whether flying fowl or earthbound game, it was relentlessly pursued with firearms, every day and in every season. Whereas Louis XIV contented himself with a daily quota of a single stag, Louis XV required three, increasing the numbers of his horse and hound proportionately. To facilitate replenishment of the natural population through reproduction in the mating season, periodically the hunting parties moved elsewhere, to Fontainebleau, Compiègne, Chambord, or Rambouillet (purchased by Louis XVI in 1783), or even, on occasion, to the property of the Condé family at Chantilly or to the Orléans seat at Villers-Cotterêts. Nonetheless, by the end of the reign of Louis XIV the population of wolves in the Versailles region had been completely wiped out.

The domain of Versailles consisted of a hunting park enclosed by walls, a portion of which was appropriated to accommodate the château gardens and surrounding greenlands. In 1623 the park attached to the property consisted of forty hectares (about a hundred acres) acquired from seventeen different tract owners. In 1632, with the purchase of the seigniory, its size was more than doubled to about 250 acres. In 1636 this property, which corresponds to the area of the gardens we know today, was surrounded by walls. By 1662, when Louis XIV's marked predilection for Versailles was still fresh, the property had grown considerably, covering 2,471 acres. At the close of his reign the ensemble was composed of the gardens proper (235 acres); the so-called Small Park (Petit Parc, 4,200 acres), also enclosed by walls; and the extensive Hunting Park (Parc de Chasse, 14,827 acres, or about 23 square miles!), enclosed by yet another wall, this one some 27 miles in length. This vast precinct encompassed eight parishes and several châteaux, hamlets, and farm complexes, the whole being characterized by Saint-Simon as "one of the saddest, most wretched small provinces in the world." The property at Chambord was the next-largest royal domain (13,097 acres, enclosed by walls 22 miles in length). By the end of the seventeenth century the parks of Versailles and Marly were contiguous, their châteaux being joined by a wide avenue and the newly joined whole encompassing some 37,066 acres!

The plentiful supply of game in the Galie Valley, however, is not sufficient to explain the infatuation of successive French kings with so disadvantageous a site. The restless temperament of Louis XIII surely goes a long way toward explaining his initial interest; doubtless he saw in it the kind of rustic retreat that suited him. He was uncomfortable at the court of Saint-Germain; the women of the queen's entourage, above all, made him uneasy with their shrill laughter, precious conversation, elaborate fashions, and courtly demeanor. By design, the queen herself was not a presence at the "first" Versailles. In November 1626 she made a one-day excursion to examine the new residence, as she would do once again in April 1635, to view the new additions. When there was an outbreak of smallpox at Saint-Germain, Louis XIII tried to convince Richelieu to send the royal children to

*H*unting Map drafted as of 1765 by J.-B. Berthier. Around Versailles, tracing a broad arc intersecting the Seine at several points, was a network of royal residences devoted to the hunt. The countryside to the west of Paris was punctuated by "stars" formed by converging roadways opened for the hunt.

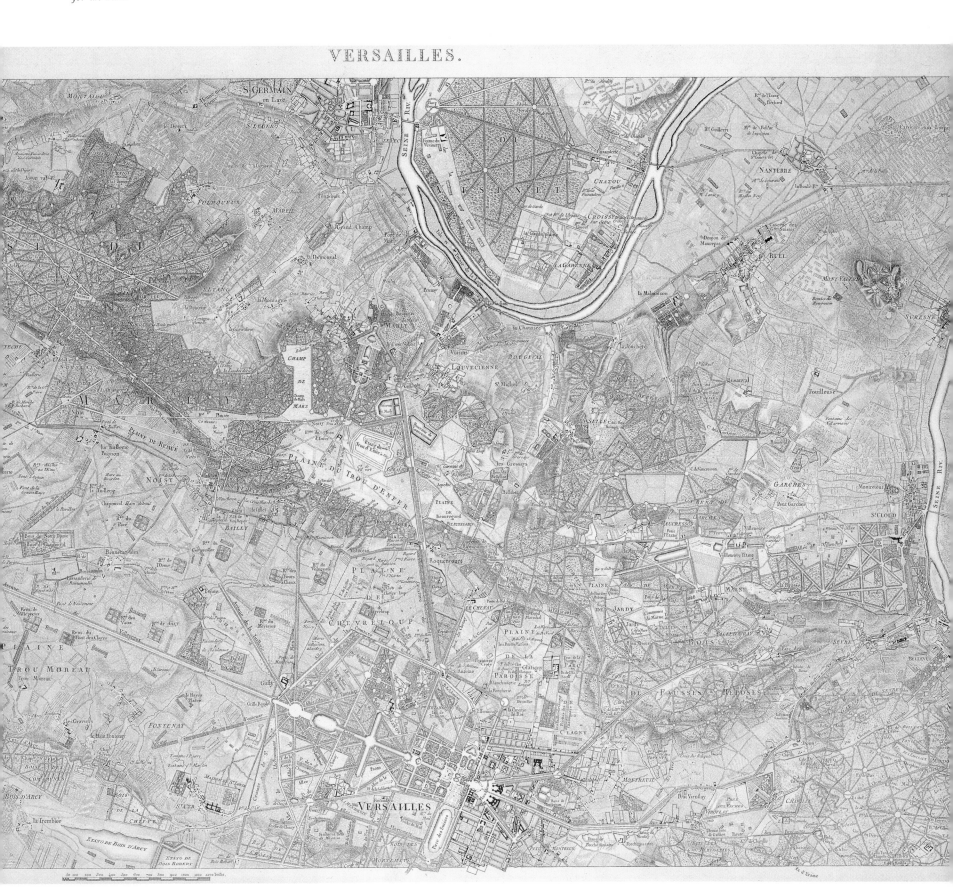

Versailles for safe haven; but he made it clear that the queen and her retinue would not be welcome there: "I suppose that the queen could be lodged at Versailles with my children," he wrote to his minister, "but I fear her numerous female entourage, whose presence here would spoil everything for me" (correspondence of Louis XIII with Richelieu). However, within this retinue Louis XIII had noticed a woman in whom he was singularly interested, Louise de La Fayette, for whom he cultivated a marked passion; he entreated her "to consent to reside at Versailles, there to be subject to his orders and at his disposal" (Madame de Motteville, *Mémoires*, published in 1723). In the end, the pious girl had no choice but to take the veil to escape the king's advances. A court circular of 1638 announced that the king had left Saint-Germain for Versailles: "The same day the *demoiselle* La Fayette, one of the queen's ladies-in-waiting, took the vows in the convent of the Daughters of the Visitation, to the great chagrin of the king, the queen, and the entire court." Before his departure, the king had announced his intention to pass the remainder of his days in stoical seclusion at Versailles and to abdicate in favor of his son. If this project had been implemented, the appropriateness of the site for such an austere purpose would have become proverbial.

The frustrated love of Louis for Louise is easily inscribed on the *carte du Tendre* (the Map of Affection's Realm), to employ the title of a chapter from *Clélie*, the novel by Mademoiselle de Scudéry, another eyewitness of early construction work at Versailles, which she described in her *Promenade de Versailles* (1669). In the subsequent chapter of her novel, another Louise says to another Louis: "I pronounce you a citizen of the Realm of Affection / But, by the grace of God, keep this to yourself." The new love Louis XIV conceived for Louise de La Vallière drew the young king to Versailles, where occasionally he had previously come to hunt without having evinced any particular interest in the place. "The liaison with Madame de La Vallière, initially a guarded secret, prompted frequent excursions to Versailles," wrote Saint-Simon. Louis XIV used Versailles "to progressively advance his intimacy with his mistress." Versailles served the same function for this royal couple as did barns and haylofts for less exalted, more rustic lovers.

So many dubious claims have been made about the role of women in the history of Versailles that it is tempting to bypass the subject altogether. This would be a mistake, however, for in this story construction and seduction amount to the same thing. A new mistress? Why then, a new house. The amorous adventures of kings made the fortunes of architects, above all under Louis XIV. Louis XV had more modest tastes; he simply rented a house in the Deer Park (Parc aux Cerfs), a walled precinct to retain does caught in the hunt, which was created under Louis XIII and subsequently parceled into lots.

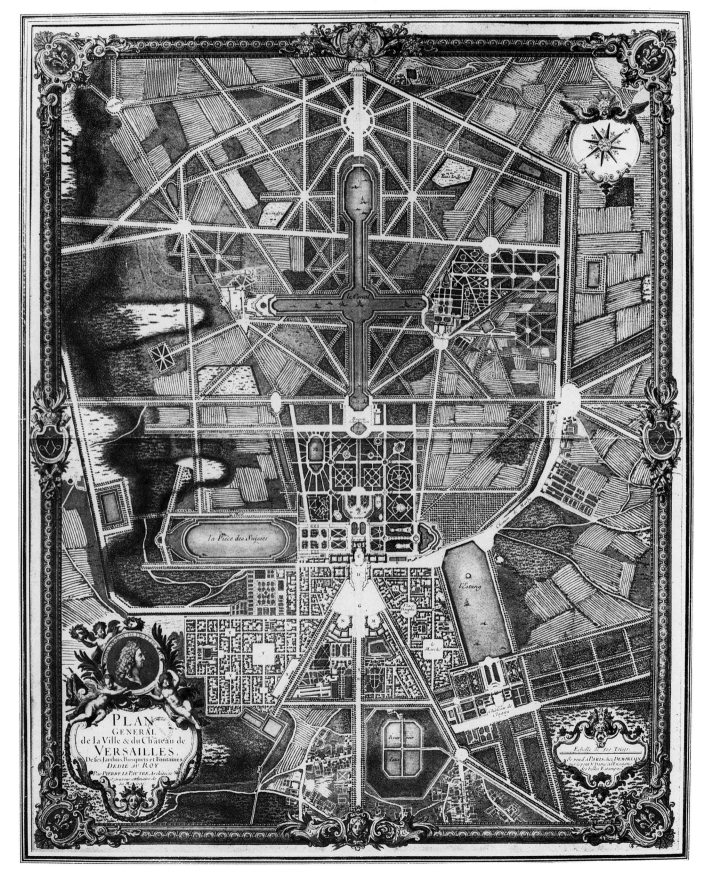

Map of Versailles by Pierre Le Pautre, late seventeenth century. Note especially these features: the irregular polygon delineating the Small Park; within this, the cross configuration of the Grand Canal and, to the left, the Pool of the Swiss Guards; at either end of the Grand Canal, the Menagerie to the left and Trianon to the right; the crow's-foot separating the Saint Louis quarter at the left from the Notre Dame quarter at the right; and still farther to the right, the château of Clagny and its reservoir. The ornamental compass is placed to the north, in the upper right corner: the north-south axis forms a diagonal with the perpendicular axes of the composition.

31

NATURE MASTERED

Thus Versailles was born of a marriage of love and the hunt. But having decided to establish a residence in the Galie Valley, Louis XIII could easily have chosen a location more amenable than the crown of the hill, with its ancient château. But doubtless it was precisely the presence of this structure there that shaped the decision. "It is always preferable to build on a site that has been inhabited previously than on one that has not," wrote the doctor Louis Savot in his *Architecture française des bastimens particuliers* (1624), published a year after the birth of Louis XIII's Versailles: "For one thing, one is thus assured of its fundamental suitability and wholesomeness." Without his realizing it, however, Savot's remark reveals the remarkable contemporary propensity for building on the sites of preexisting medieval châteaux; for better or worse, Versailles itself also embodies this tendency.

However, its initial placement would not necessarily have been definitive, if Louis XIV had not spent an enormous sum to modify the site—principally, to effect earthworks of all kinds. Blondel writes of "vast constructions hidden underground whose expense, while unknown to most, effectively equals that more easily visible to observers in the decoration, disposition, and magnificent appointments of the gardens" (*Architecture française*).

Manipulation of the terrain went hand in glove with that of the water supply. Louis XIV would never fully master this problem. The *Grandes Eaux* (as the spectacle

Clagny Lake. View by I. Silvestre (1674). At the beginning of Louis XIV's reign the lake was the main water source. Farther back, from right to left: the château, with the Envelope in its initial phase; the water pump, built in 1663 by Le Vau, situated on the roadway that would become the rue des Réservoirs; and the residences and pavilions of the town.

of the waterworks in full operation came to be known) required about 220 gallons of water per second. By the end of the reign the available supply sufficed only to deploy the works for two hours at a time, with the various fountains being operated in succession.

Clagny Lake, which disappeared in the eighteenth century to make way for the Versailles neighborhood known by this name, was initially the principal water source, and the only one under Louis XIII. It was in part artificial, having been enlarged by construction of a dam on Clagny Stream. The Galie Valley boasted no other bodies of water, with the exception of the Stinking Lake (Etang Puant), whose name suggests its unsuitability for most purposes; eventually this would be transformed into the Pool of the Swiss Guards (Pièce d'Eau des Suisses). Very early on, of course, plans were made to recover the waters that had completed one circuit through the fountain system for successive recyclings. Nonetheless, the ongoing development of the gardens would necessitate

forays in search of additional water farther and farther away, to the north as well as the south, in neighboring highlands as well as valleys, whose pools and lakes would be interconnected to create a single, immense network. In 1681 the Seine, to the north, would be plugged into this network, but the water thus made available would soon be earmarked for the gardens at Marly. In 1684, to the south, after having resorted to the Bièvre and Yvette rivers and exploited the lakes in the vicinity of Rambouillet, some twenty-one miles from Versailles, a partial diversion of the Eure River, in the Loire basin, was projected; work on this plan was begun but never completed.

The force necessary to pump these waters was generated by horse-driven mills or windmills. In 1663 the mill pump built beside Clagny Lake under Louis XIII was replaced by a water tower containing an elevated reservoir and flanked by two mill pumps. This tower, designed by Louis Le Vau, is clearly indicated in old engravings of the château; it was located close to the lake, adjacent to a roadway subsequently known as the rue des Réservoirs.

Three windmills punctuated the course followed by the water during its forced ascent from the far end of the Grand Canal to Clagny Lake. Five additional windmills on the hillocks to the south drew water from that direction. These mills, with their large, multicolored sails, were a singular addition to the landscape. The celebrated Marly machine, built on a curve of the Seine near this residence, was nothing more than a huge water mill generating the energy needed to pump water up from the valley floor. To construct a mechanism capable of overcoming the 532-foot difference in elevation between the banks of the Seine and Versailles, two experts were summoned from Liège, the engineer Antoine Deville and the carpenter Rennequin Sualem, who in 1681 fabricated what would become one of the century's most famous machines.

Conveyance of these vast quantities of water presupposed an extensive system of aqueducts. If completed, that from the Eure would have been sixty-nine miles long; at its origin, it would have been eighty-five feet lower than the height necessary for entry into the château's system of waterworks. The most spectacular and difficult constructions were those needed to "overleap" the intervening valleys. As a result of the successive campaigns of this unrelenting search for water, the bridging of valleys whose sources had themselves previously been tied into the system became a necessity. Thus the Bièvre, whose riverbed closely parallels the Galie Valley, was traversed by an aqueduct at Buc (constructed in 1683–84) that transported water from the south. The most remarkable of these structures was undoubtedly the Maintenon aqueduct, which crossed the Eure at the elevation of Maintenon, site of the famous château that Louis XIV gave to the celebrated marquise, his last amorous companion. In fact the Eure conduit, begun in 1684, was intended to draw water from a point considerably upstream from Maintenon, whose elevation was markedly lower than that of Versailles: owing to a meander in the river's course, the conduit was obliged to encounter it a second time, crossing it further downstream. In principle, a siphon would have been sufficient to cross the Maintenon Valley. But Louis XIV, who had admired the Pont du Gard during his marriage journey in 1660, insisted that a structure rivaling the most audacious of Roman aqueducts be built

instead. He entrusted this project to Vauban, his most renowned engineer, placing at his disposition some thirty thousand enlisted men under the command of the maréchal d'Uxelles. Work was begun, but the plan was definitively abandoned with the outbreak of the War of the League of Augsburg. In the spring of 1688 the marshal's men were at Maintenon; that fall they found themselves deployed on the battlefield at Neustadt.

From the perspective of the court at Versailles, it was easy to overlook these ongoing projects, despite their titanic scale: such undertakings held little appeal for the courtiers, who tended to confound the continuous intrigue in which they lived with the affairs of the world at large. They spoke of the diversion of a river's course as of that of a young girl. "Never have I heard anything more agreeable than what you told me of this great beauty soon to appear at Versailles, fresh, pure, and unaffected, and who will put all others to shame," Madame de Sévigné wrote to Madame de Grignan. "Be assured that I was most curious as to her name and that I was anticipating the arrival of some great female beauty who had been adopted by the court; but I find instead that you referred to a river diverted from its course by an army of forty thousand men. So demanding is she, that no less than such a number will prove necessary to make a satisfactory bed for her."

Having reached Versailles, the waters were channeled into one of several reservoirs, some open to the sky and others underground and invisible, prior to being conveyed through the royal waterworks for the king's pleasure. It would be difficult, if not impossible, to list these reservoirs exhaustively, but those of which traces remain today can be inventoried: under the Water Terrace (Parterre d'Eau), for example, those constructed in 1673 by the architect François d'Orbay; on the surface, along the rue des Réservoirs, the three large rectangular basins first constructed in 1667, subsequently altered and reworked several times; nearby, on the rue du Peintre-Le-Brun, a water tower hidden behind an illusionistic façade simulating a conventional residence, dating from 1684; and on Montbauron Hill, one of the natural eminences bordering the Galie Valley, the large reservoir into which the waters drawn from the Seine were stored. Yet another network emanated from these reservoirs, conducting the water to the fountains and their pools. Most

*B*ELOW AND FOL-
*LOWING PAGES: The reservoirs
constructed by d'Orbay under the
Water Terrace in 1673. Still in
good repair, they are emptied for
several days each autumn for
cleaning.*

of its conduits consisted of pottery or lead pipes, but
some were made of wood. The first cast-iron pipes used
in France were fabricated for Versailles in 1672, in the
forges of Normandy.

The extent of these undertakings is astonishing, and
they were intended to evoke precisely this response. The
monarchy understood that realization of such projects
would enhance its prestige considerably. The proposed
route of the Midi Canal, which would have united the
Atlantic with the Mediterranean by way of a channel cut
through the northern Pyrenees, was disseminated through
an engraving intended as royal propaganda, as were similar images of more conventionally prestigious architectural undertakings. It is useful to dwell momentarily on

this information to emphasize that Versailles, while an artistic masterpiece, was also a huge reservoir, a site at which waters drawn from many sources converged. And it would soon pull many of the realm's nonliquid resources into its orbit as well.

SPLENDORS AND MISERIES

It will be forever regrettable that this gigantic canal was never finished: its waters, carried to Versailles, would have nourished its fountains and created another marvel by rendering their operation forceful and continuous. It is troubling, without a doubt, that so many soldiers perished at the camp established for the work at Maintenon, in 1685; it is troubling that so many millions should have been spent on an enterprise that was left incomplete. But surely it is more troubling still that Louis XIV, under force of necessity, astonished by those cries for economy with which the loftiest projects are subverted, should have been so lacking in patience; otherwise, the grandest monument on the face of the earth would today belong to France.

François-René de Chateaubriand,
Mémoires d'outre-tombe, *1841*

THE SITE RECAST

The principal axis passing through the center of the château. The Latona Fountain (foreground) and the Grand Canal (background). By convention, it is assimilated to an east-west axis (its true orientation is from southeast to northwest).

The château, which had assumed something very close to its present form by the close of Louis XIV's reign, was carefully oriented in relation to a principal axis that also served as such for the town and the gardens. This was intersected by several secondary, transverse axes, and culminated at either end in clusters of roadways heading off in different directions. The three avenues of the ceremonial approach constitute the celebrated *patte-d'oie* ("goose's foot" or, in more colloquial English, "crow's-foot"), whose organizing lines determined the plan of the town. This arresting sign, which marked the precise location of Versailles on the earth's surface, was the idea of André Le Nôtre, Louis XIV's garden de-

signer. Its originality lay not in the conception per se, but rather in the emphasis with which it was impressed on the landscape: in effect, Le Nôtre simply gave permanent, prominent form to the ephemeral cross that every architect traces in the soil to indicate the main axes of a projected building.

The principal axis of Versailles is somewhat out of cartographic alignment. The town is more southeast than directly east of the château, and the gardens more northwest than directly west, while the brass meridian marker in the floor of the Chamber of the Pendulum Clock traverses it on a diagonal. This discrepancy is rarely discussed because the solar symbolism so central to the tradition of Versailles interpretation presupposes that the sun rises in the forecourt and sets in the gardens. But it should not be forgotten that Vitruvius, as well as many subsequent French theoreticians, advocated such "misalignment," recommending that structures be oriented

diagonally in relation to the four points of the compass. Many French châteaux illustrate this precept, Chambord being a notable example. But, whether by design or by oversight, none of the classic discussions of Versailles acknowledges its real orientation. The present author has no intention of challenging this convention, a tacit assumption underlying discussions of the château over the years.

The use of converging roadways was no more novel a concept than that of the main axis whose trajectory they dispersed. Earlier, Le Nôtre himself had designed such a crow's-foot configuration to mark the principal entry of the château of Vaux-le-Vicomte. There too he had employed a longitudinal axis extending into the horizon, around which the entire complex was organized. To grasp something of the genius of Le Nôtre, one has only to compare his procedures at Vaux and Versailles with those of his predecessors—at Richelieu, for example, where the château proper and the village were cast as two separate, uncoordinated complexes. Other examples still earlier in date demonstrate that prior to Vaux and Versailles such integration, subordinating the component parts to a general design concept, was not an option

open to architects. It is widely known that Vaux, which was built for the royal minister Fouquet in 1656 (and played a role in his disgrace), served as a model for Versailles. But Richelieu, constructed for the cardinal in 1631 and the largest château in France prior to the creation of Versailles, was also a point of reference. Louis XIV had visited it on the same marriage trip during which he had been so impressed by the Pont du Gard. The arrangement of the Sun King's château around progressively larger open courts is distinctly reminiscent of the similarly incremental unfolding of the wing extensions at Richelieu.

Within the prongs of the crow's-foot, which was introduced early on in the building campaigns undertaken by Louis XIV, the royal stables were located. To the north, beside the lake, was situated the château of Clagny, now destroyed but once renowned for its architecture. Clagny was an offspring of Versailles, but an "illegitimate" one, having been built for one of the king's mistresses, Madame de Montespan. The town itself quickly took on the character of a kind of garden city: configurations of buildings constructed for use by members of the court, spaced at regular intervals and surrounded by gardens, were disposed along its streets and avenues. The subsequent,

The transverse axis passing in front of the château's façade. Viewed from the Southern Terrace. On the horizon, the hills bordering the valley.

rather haphazard development of the intervening spaces has somewhat obscured this pattern, but it is clearly evident in old engravings, while a few surviving structures whose façades incorporate both stone and brick provide further clues as to the original architectural character of this urban environment. Surprisingly, two of these structures were designated the King's Pavilion and the Queen's Pavilion, suggesting that they were intended for the royal couple. In several respects, then, the garden city of Versailles was a prefiguration of the château of Marly.

To house staff as well as construction workers and craftsmen engaged to work at Versailles, the king created the New Town (la Ville Neuve) to the north (1671–72), while to the south he sponsored the tract development of the Deer Park; these symmetrically complementary neighborhoods would come to be known as the Quartier Notre-Dame and the Quartier Saint-Louis, after their respective parish churches. As a consequence of the relative isolation of these neighborhoods at their creation, the city plan now has the appearance of a set of unrelated fragments. Between 1740 and 1789 its physical extent doubled while its population rose to 70,000, making it the sixth largest city in the realm.

Versailles is perhaps unique in the extent to which phenomena typical of cities in this period were not to be encountered there: promiscuity, municipal bureaucracy (Versailles officially became a township only in 1787), fixed boundaries, and enclosing walls. Even newly founded towns (and perhaps they above all) tended to have

clear boundaries if not walls, as did Richelieu. But at Versailles the plow used by Romulus to establish the perimeter of the future city of Rome would find use only in the gardens.

These gardens were composed of terraces (*parterres*) and groves or glades (*bosquets*). As the first of these names suggests (*terre* = "earth"), the terraces were open spaces adorned, for the most part, only by design elements close to the ground, while the bosquets were small rectangular forested tracts. The pools, fountains, statues, and ornamental pavilions were, however, distributed through both of these component elements. Directly in front of the central body of the château building was the Water Terrace, with its two large pools. A secondary, transverse axis was placed so as to cross this terrace on the perpendicular, thereby connecting it with two others (the Northern Terrace or Parterre du Nord and the Southern Terrace or Parterre du Midi). The main, longitudinal axis ran from the center of the château through the Latona Fountain, down the Royal Walk (Allée Royale) to the Apollo Fountain and the Grand Canal. Like the Pool of the Swiss Guards, which was an extension of the Southern Terrace, technically the Grand Canal was not part of the gardens proper but rather of an intermediary band of parkland long designated as the Small Park, so as to distinguish it from the much larger Hunting Park extending out from the far end of the Grand Canal.

The Grand Canal itself was built in the shape of a cross. At either end of its crossbar were two structural complexes of considerable significance in the history of Versailles: to the south, the Menagerie, of which almost nothing remains; to the north, a small constellation of châteaux constructed near the village of Trianon—the Large or Grand Trianon built under Louis XIV, the Small or Petit Trianon of Louis XV, and farther on, the latest of these constructions, the thatch-roofed cottages of the Hamlet or Hameau, built for Marie-Antoinette. It was in this rustic environment that the waning monarchy, seeking escape from the splendor of its usual surroundings, found a last refuge, much like a laborer seeking repose at the close of a long day of plowing and sowing.

The transverse axis passing in front of the château. In the foreground, the Northern Terrace.

Chapter 2
TIME, IDEAS, AND MEN

LEFT: *Equestrian statue of Louis XIV. The figure of Louis XIV is by L. Petitot and the horse by P. Cartellier. The statue was commissioned by Louis-Philippe.* OPPOSITE: **The Oyster Luncheon** *by Jean-François de Troy (1737; Musée Condé, Chantilly). This painting was executed for Louis XV's private apartments. Louis XV admired what his predecessor had accomplished at the château; the transformations he ordered, though carried out very slowly, resulted in interior decors of remarkable refinement.*

*T*he chronology of the construction at Versailles is extremely complex, but for a very simple reason, namely, the exceptional length of the reign of Louis XIV, who took pleasure in constantly altering his château to suit his evolving tastes and needs. Louis XIV died in 1715 at the age of seventy-seven, having ruled for seventy-two years, one of the longest reigns in history. We have seen that even Louis XIII, who did not have a strong taste for building, built and rebuilt at Versailles. For some time historians failed to distinguish the château of 1631 from the hunting lodge of 1624—rather, they were unaware of the existence of the first of these, revealed only by the discovery of the construction contracts. Happily, Louis XIV was possessed of a strong sense of time, of its eddies and flows. Did this contribute to the development of the rigorous self-discipline for which he became known? "One could readily specify what the king was doing at any given hour of any given day," wrote Saint-Simon. Could this not also derive in part from his belief that his was a divinely sanctioned authority, one that made him Time's master, rather like his Oriental counterpart the emperor of China, who withdrew into the House of the Calendar to decree, at his will, the incremental divisions and close of each new year? Or yet again, could it be that the history of this ruler, who adopted the sun for his emblem, was especially sensitive to the natural order of things, to the mysterious temporal rhythms that determine the periodic arrival of years of crisis?

In any case the king's personal reign, which commenced with the death of Mazarin (1661), seems to have been ruled by ten-year rhythms, establishing chronological markers convenient for the historian. Every ten years, counting from the anniversary of his birth (1638), the king signed a victorious treaty, launched a new construction program, and took a new mistress. In 1659 the twenty-year-old king concluded the Peace of the Pyrenees; in 1668, at age thirty, the Peace of Aix-la-Chapelle; in 1678, at forty, the Peace of Nijmegen. The decade 1678–88 was the only peaceful one of the reign, of which it was the climactic moment, but it also seems to have disturbed its previously settled rhythms. The decade beginning in 1688, Louis's fiftieth year, was marked by war with the League of Augsburg, the most formidable coalition the king had ever confronted. In 1697 the Peace of Ryswick was concluded, just in time for his seventieth birthday, but its terms were those of a compromise without glory; soon after its conclusion another coalition was formed that aimed to force the matter of the Spanish royal succession, in the process bringing France to the edge of a precipice.

For the most part, construction work was undertaken between these wars, with the various peace treaties occasioning the commencement of new projects. There were three main construction campaigns, and another supplemental one toward the reign's close. "Campaign" is a term still used in two fields of endeavor, those of war and construction; in the past it referred to projects undertaken in the season of fair weather, it being customary for soldiers as well as stonemasons to "hibernate" during the inclement winter months. By extension, however, the word can be used to apply to a complex of construction initiatives ruled by a master plan and pursued over an extended period of many years.

The château under construction, circa 1679, as depicted by Van der Meulen (collection of the Queen of England). The Ministers' Wings are in progress. The Northern Wing is still to come.

THE CONSTRUCTION CAMPAIGNS

The first building campaign, initiated in the king's twentieth year, followed the Peace of the Pyrenees (1659). Like Louis XIII, Louis XIV began to come to Versailles at a very young age, but apparently he had no work done there prior to his personal reign. In 1661 Fouquet, the finance minister who hoped eventually to occupy Mazarin's post, organized at his château Vaux-le-Vicomte a lavish entertainment that has not been forgotten; that same year, Louise de La Vallière became the royal mistress. The king, having grown jealous of his ambitious minister, had him arrested shortly thereafter and appropriated his fortune, simultaneously assuring that of his favorite. For La Vallière, officially presented at court in 1663, he was to create a new Versailles conceived along the lines laid down at Vaux, then the most strikingly modern château in France; for Louis had also appropriated the celebrated design team of André Le Nôtre, Charles Le Brun, and Louis Le Vau, which had worked there for Fouquet. It was not the individual gifts of these men that were revealed to the king at Vaux, but rather the cohesion and mutual complementarity of their respective visions. Le Vau had been first architect to the king since 1654. Le Brun had been engaged to work for him prior to Fouquet's disgrace; although his status as first painter to the king was formalized only in 1664, he is already so described in a contract dating from 1660. As for Le Nôtre, although his work prior to Vaux is unknown to us today, surely this masterpiece was not his first project; he had succeeded to his father's post as first gardener to the king overseeing the Tuileries Gardens as early as 1637. The Vaux design team would win fame through works undertaken simultaneously at Versailles and the Tuileries palace in Paris.

By contrast, Mazarin's political legacy was to escape Fouquet's grasp and fall instead to Colbert, who was ap-pointed controller general of finances; in addition, on January 1, 1664, he was named overseer of the king's buildings, artistic enterprises, and manufactories, which accorded him authority over the undertakings at Versailles. He would be given valuable support by the Perrault brothers: Charles, author of the famous tales, whom he named his administrative assistant, and Claude, a doctor and architect. Most of the work undertaken in this first campaign was focused on the gardens and interior decoration. One larger project was also launched, however; construction of two parallel subsidiary buildings in front of the château of Louis XIII, to define a new entry court.

The second campaign, begun in the year marked both by the king's thirtieth birthday and by the Peace of Aix-la-Chapelle (1668), was crucial to the large-scale evolution of Versailles. It was during this campaign that the New Château (or, as it was dubbed, the Envelope) was constructed. These additions "enveloped" the château of Louis XIII in a new structure, so that only those façades facing the central court remained visible. Further, the subsidiary buildings, now designated to serve as lodgings, were connected to the main complex. The result was a U-shaped plan that branched forward to encompass a larger open space, thus defining two successive courts, the small one of the old château, known as the Marble Court (Cour de Marbre), and a larger one embraced by the former subsidiary buildings, known as the Royal Court (Cour Royale). Yet another entry court was created by the construction of four pavilions intended to house four government ministers, the secretaries of state. Most of the decoration of the so-called Grands Appartements, or Ceremonial Rooms, and the elaboration of the gardens dates from this second campaign.

This work was conceived by the same design team as that of the first campaign. But Le Vau died in 1670; his collaborator François d'Orbay replaced him, but without being named first architect, a post left vacant. Colbert, jealous of his prerogatives as overseer, was unwilling to bestow this title, which would have accorded a practicing

The château under con-
struction, at Louis XIV's death; by
P.-D. Martin (1722; Versailles
Museum). From foreground to
background: the Place d'Armes; the
forward court with its fence; the
Royal Court and its fence; the
Marble Court. Note the state of
the wings to either side of the
Royal Court prior to their transformation in the eighteenth and
nineteenth centuries.

architect an authority that, although technically subsidiary to his own, in reality would have imposed certain restrictions on it. Two things resulted from these changes so early in the campaign: first, it is difficult to distinguish the contribution of Le Vau from that of d'Orbay; second, Le Brun emerged as the real beneficiary of this change of personnel, assuming control of most of the design decisions pertaining to decoration both inside and out. The amplitude of the modified design vocabulary that he de-

ployed paralleled the bodily forms of the new favorite, the generously proportioned Montespan, who from 1668 on competed with the slender La Vallière for the king's attentions. La Vallière put an end to this rivalry only in 1674, when she entered a convent.

The next campaign, begun in the king's fortieth year, followed upon the Peace of Nijmegen (1678), which marked the emergence of France as a newly dominant European power, after which the monarch would be known as Louis le Grand. This third campaign was not accompanied by notable shifts in the king's affections: it is true that in 1674 Françoise d'Aubigné, the widow Scarron, was given the property of Maintenon as well as the title attending it, but this was in return for services she had rendered Madame de Montespan, the early education of whose children by the king she would oversee. By contrast, a master architect of considerable importance now appeared on the scene, Jules Hardouin-Mansart, who first attracted attention with his designs for Montespan's château of Clagny. He was soon charged with the difficult task of expeditiously increasing the available floor space in the wake of the king's decision to transfer the seat of government from Paris to Versailles, effected in 1682. The death of Colbert in 1683 and his replacement by Louvois occasioned Le Brun's disgrace but strengthened the position of Mansart, who was named first architect in 1686. The most notable projects he directed at Versailles were conversion of the four ministerial pavilions into two wings (thereafter known as the Ministers' Wings), the placement of the royal stables (effectively preventing further expansion toward the east, in the direction of the town), and finally, construction of the enormous Northern and Southern Wings along the transverse axis, the only viable emplacement for these much-needed additions.

After the extended peaceful interlude of 1678–88, which proved favorable to the arts, it was not peace but the outbreak of war that marked the king's fiftieth birthday. Louis still had before him thirty years as king, in the course of which he would be obliged to mobilize twice against a Europe united to oppose him. The king's honor was to be tainted by various misfortunes that successively plagued his realm; many would perish in the infamous winter of 1709, while death was to make several unwelcome appearances at Versailles as well, first claiming the Grand Dauphin, Louis's eldest son, in 1711. In 1712

the new dauphin, the duc de Bourgogne, and his duchess, the gracious Marie-Adélaïde of Savoy so beloved of Louis XIV, also died within days of each other, and in 1714 it was the turn of the duc de Berry, another son of the deceased Grand Dauphin. Over these thirty years the king found comfort in the company of Madame de Maintenon, whom he secretly married in 1684, one year after the death of his queen, Marie-Thérèse. Thereafter, Madame de Maintenon's austere tastes left their mark on religion, morals, and royal finance.

This decade of war, symbolically inaugurated by the sacrifice of the palace's solid-silver furniture, melted down in 1689 to pay for military campaigns, was not a favorable one for building. Conversely, and perhaps unexpectedly, the onset of the financial crisis seems to have stimulated the emergence of a new generation of talented practitioners of the decorative arts. The stylistic mutation effected during the 1690s, while conditioned by political circumstances, manifests the astonishing resilience so characteristic of this reign: while plunged into a twilight darkened by reaction, war, and the increasing poverty of the population at large, it sponsored the evolution of the stylistic language of Versailles into an idiom well suited to the century of the Enlightenment.

The king's sixtieth birthday coincided with a treaty, an unhoped-for surprise. With the negotiation of the Peace of Ryswick (1697), construction became feasible again. In 1699 Mansart was appointed overseer of the king's buildings, like Colbert and Louvois before him. The realization of a large chapel, a project long envisioned, was finally begun in earnest—the principal undertaking of this last campaign of the reign. It is difficult

General view of the entry courts, from the forward court. The brick buildings date from the seventeenth century. Construction of the Chapel (to the right) in the early eighteenth century was probably intended to launch implementation of the Grand Dessein, or Master Plan, which envisioned recasting all the façades of the courts in stone. This project would be taken up again at the end of the eighteenth century (the Gabriel Wing, next to the Chapel) and at the beginning of the nineteenth century (the symmetrical wing to the left), but was ultimately abandoned.

*T*he central block and the two forward wings, which define the Marble Court, retain the volume and basic structural work dating from the Old Château of Louis XIII. To either side are the extensions joining the Old Château to the wings bordering the Royal Court. These were built upon reversion to the Envelope plan.

to determine which portions of its design are due to Mansart and which to his closest collaborator, Robert de Cotte, who assumed sole responsibility for the building in 1708, after Mansart's death; the Chapel would be completed only after the king's own decease.

The reigns of Louis XV and Louis XVI were far less important in the development of Versailles than that of their predecessor. Louis XV was, however, on the throne for nearly sixty years (1715–74). No doubt persistent financial difficulties should be factored into any discussion of this question; nonetheless, these did not prevent the two later monarchs from launching building projects else-

where. The truth is that the revered ancestor, who had been transformed immediately into a formidable historical figure, remained the master of his residence. He who, on the threshold of death, could speak unaffectedly of "the age when I was king," would haunt Versailles as a kind of posthumous host until the end of the old regime. "Louis XIV's presence was still palpable there," wrote Chateaubriand of his presentation at Versailles in 1786. Under the Regency (1715–23) the government moved to Paris only because the regent himself detested Versailles. Contemporary chroniclers left several accounts describing how the young Louis XV, upon returning to the château

The Marble Court. This court's name derives from its marble paving. This paving, the columns, and the busts supported by consoles were added during alterations effected under Le Vau's direction. The attic level, the sculpture on the cornices, the balustrades, and the roofs were overseen by Hardouin-Mansart. But the brick and stone treatment of the façade and the Doric pilasters date from Louis XIII's château.

LEFT TO RIGHT: Central block; right wing of the Old Château; structure joining the Old Château to the wing bordering the Royal Court.

of his great-grandfather, was overcome with emotion and enthusiasm. The first works subsequently undertaken there involved completion of several projects left unfinished at Louis XIV's death. Around 1730, however, a period of extensive modification of the interior decoration began; it continued, with occasional fallow spells, until the Revolution. During this period many celebrated features of the seventeenth-century château were destroyed. A revivifying stimulus was provided by the birth of a male heir in 1729: in acknowledgment of his debt to the young queen, Maria Leszczynska, Louis XV had the principal reception room of her quarters completely redesigned. Thereafter, in piecemeal fashion, the quasi-

totality of the palace's private interiors would be recast in turn, with the last renovations being those ordered by Marie-Antoinette. The monarchs of the eighteenth century were not totally impervious to the dictates of changing taste, but they found ways to acknowledge its authority without sacrificing the imposing Grands Appartements of the seventeenth century.

Under Louis XV the Opera House was successfully completed and realization of a master plan was taken in hand. Both of these projects had been envisioned under Louis XIV but were now shaped into viable designs by Ange-Jacques Gabriel, whose work is all but indistinguishable from that of Mansart's studio. With the revival of

Detail, façade facing the Marble Court: brick and stone treatment and pilasters dating from Louis XIII; busts added by Le Vau; dormer windows and their crowning elements added by Hardouin-Mansart.

large-scale building projects, the pendulum-like alteration between peace and war once more became a key factor in the history of Versailles. The decision to build the Opera House was taken in 1748, the year of the second Treaty of Aix-la-Chapelle, but its construction was actually begun only after the Treaty of Paris in 1763. No sooner had the Opera House been inaugurated, on the occasion of the marriage of the dauphin and Marie-Antoinette (1770), than Louis XV resolved to complete

the Envelope of the château and thereby realize the principal goal of the long-standing master plan, known as the Grand Dessein (Great Design). All the additions to the side of the château facing the entry courts dated from the reign of Louis XIV and deferred to the château of Louis XIII. With its façade of brick and stone and its mansard roof, this portion of the building was regarded as archaic even during the lifetime of Louis XIV, but it had been allowed to remain for reasons of convenience. The Grand Dessein called for closure of the open side of the entry courts by building a seemingly flat-roofed addition with a stone façade; thus it would have made the entry façade consistent with the enveloping additions previously built on the side facing the gardens. Reconstruction of the right wing of the Royal Court was the only portion of the Grand Dessein realized prior to the Revolution, for the expense entailed by support of the American War of Independence (1776–83) was a death blow for this project. The Peace of Versailles (1783) made possible a competition for a master plan to replace that of Gabriel, now regarded as overly respectful of tradition; architects known for ingenuity and innovation were invited to submit designs, and many obliged, eager for the post left vacant by Gabriel's recent retirement. The Revolution put a stop to this undertaking, which otherwise could have resulted in another campaign of large-scale construction.

In 1814, with hope of realizing the Grand Dessein not yet abandoned, the projecting wing now visible to the left of the Royal Court was constructed by the architect Alex Dufour, duplicating the other one across the courtyard.

ACTORS AND EXPENDITURES

Le Vau, French school (Versailles Museum).

This overview of the history of Versailles leaves a strong impression of continuity. Without doubt, the principal architectural intervention dates from 1668, when the decision to erect the Envelope was taken. Subsequently, the main task falling to those working on the château, which included the most famous names in French architecture, was intelligent development of the implications of this initial move. It is not always easy to distinguish the various contributions of the many architectural collaborators. Le Vau and Mansart directed large studios where nothing was done by a single hand. The final development of any given project was the charge of a draftsman who was not, however, the author of its general concept. The master architects were occasionally absent at moments when crucial design decisions were taken, and at their deaths projected works were sometimes left incomplete. This state of affairs has lent credibility to the portrait of Mansart sketched by Saint-Simon: "A tall, amply built man of pleasant visage and rather common aspect, but naturally quick-witted, easy of manner, and disposed to please, never having purged himself of that coarseness deriving from his base origins.... He was ill informed about his craft; de Cotte, his brother-in-law, whom he named his first architect, was no better informed than he." Lassurance, one of the draftsmen-designers in the Mansart workshop, "whom he did his best to keep under lock and key," was proposed as the true author of all his designs. In reality, however, Mansart's oeuvre seems completely unified and consistent, betraying not a trace of the multiplicity of hands employed in working up his designs.

Transmission of a "house" style was facilitated by the fact that the title of first architect was handed down from generation to generation like a familial inheritance. Robert de Cotte served in the post from the death of Mansart, his brother-in-law (1708), until his own death in 1735. Exhausted and plagued with encroaching blindness, he trained Jacques Gabriel V to be his principal assistant. The latter was the son of Jacques IV (who died in 1688), a cousin of Mansart who had worked at Versailles. Jacques V succeeded de Cotte and in turn passed on the position to his son Ange-Jacques, who had already served as his assistant for several years. Ange-Jacques held the post of first architect from 1742 until his retirement in 1774, the year of Louis XV's death. The appointment as Gabriel's successor of Richard Mique, who was not a member of this family network, represented a significant shift, but timing dictated that it would come to nothing.

Just as one should guard against overestimating the contributions of the master architects' assistants, care should be taken not to overlook the importance of suggestions made by a more exalted master, namely the client. Louis XIV held the true author of his château to be none other than himself, and not without reason. His "Manière de montrer les jardins de Versailles," written between 1689 and 1705 (six manuscript copies are known, one in his own hand), is no more than a reasoned guidebook, but it nonetheless provides useful information regarding the intentions behind the conception of the gardens. Louis XIV is known to have followed the progress of his works closely, on a day-to-day basis. When obliged to be absent from Versailles, he insisted that memoranda recounting "everything in detail" be prepared and brought to him—which provoked one observer to remark to Saint-Simon that the king was possessed of an "intelligence preoccupied with minor matters, one that takes pleasure in all kinds of detail."

The celebrated anecdote of the window in the Large Trianon, recounted by Saint-Simon, demonstrates the degree to which concern with detail is indistinguishable from basic competence and is worth retelling. The Trianon "had scarcely emerged from the soil when the king perceived a miscalculation in one of the newly completed window casements. . . . Louvois, who was brusque by nature and, what is more, so spoiled as to find it difficult to be corrected by his master, resolutely denied the error, maintaining that the casement was impeccable. Whereupon the king turned his back on him and continued his promenade through the building site." Encountering Le Nôtre, he asked him to measure the window in question. "The king readily perceived that [Le Nôtre] was reluctant to engage in an exercise that would either prove the king wrong or incriminate Louvois. Louis XIV got angry and commanded him to appear at Trianon the following day." The next day, while Le Nôtre measured the window, Louvois, "furious at being obliged to submit to this verification, grumbled out loud, maintaining that this window was identical to all the others. The king kept his counsel and waited, but he was clearly anxious." Le Nôtre was obliged to acknowledge that the king was correct, and the monarch upbraided Louvois for his obstinacy. "In a word, he gave him a good dressing down." Louvois believed his disgrace was imminent. Saint-Simon imagined him reflecting to himself as follows: "The only resource at my disposal that might divert the king's attention from these building projects and render me again invaluable

Hardouin-Mansart by de Troy (Versailles Museum).

is war, and by ———— he will have one!" According to Saint-Simon, the origins of the League of Augsburg should be traced not to the occupation of the Rhine kingdoms, but rather to this argument over a window, which provoked Louvois to alarm all Europe by seizing and occupying these territories! Here again we see how many and various are the ties binding war and architecture together.

The idea for the peristyle of the Large Trianon came from the king himself, who, having ordered Robert de Cotte to execute working drawings, proceeded directly with its construction—contrary to the advice of Mansart, absent at the time but whose reactions had been solicited by letter. According to the duc de Luynes (1738), he had found "that the design was worthless, but neither his views nor his reasoning were accepted by His Majesty, and the design was executed as one sees it today." Perhaps this

*J*ean-Baptiste Colbert *by Claude Lefèvre (Versailles Museum). Appointed overseer of the king's buildings in 1664, Colbert supervised construction work at Versailles until his death in 1683.*

SO MUCH MONEY!

Hundreds of millions. . . . From the seventeenth century to the present, a tradition has developed of stigmatizing Louis XIV's extravagant expenditures at Versailles. On the eve of the Revolution, the figures were exaggerated without restraint: 500 million, proposed Voltaire. Mirabeau casually put forward the figure of 1,200, and Louis-Sébastien Mercier, future representative to the Convention from the department of Seine-et-Oise, concluded his 1771 pamphlet L'an 2440: rêve s'il en fut jamais *(The Year 2440: A Dream If Ever There Was One) with a prophetic scene: an old man seated on a pile of ruins, the ghost of Louis XIV amid the remains of Versailles, muttering through his tears, "It is here that all the realm's money was consumed."*

Jules Michelet, La Cité des Eaux

---

report should be taken with a grain of salt, since the duc de Luynes obtained his information from Robert de Cotte, who would have been tempted to cast his own role in a favorable light. But the basic architectural competence of Louis XIV is not to be doubted. Strong evidence for it is provided by surviving memoranda sent by him to Mansart from the period 1699–1702.

The architectural expertise of Louis XIV's successors was no less impressive, although (fortunately, perhaps) they abstained from showing it off at Versailles. The marquise de Pompadour wrote to d'Argenson that "the one thing that [Louis XV] finds unfailingly entertaining is architectural drawings"; presumably, as overseer of the king's pleasures, she knew whereof she spoke. "He is unhappy if there are no plans and drawings on his work table." In 1739 d'Argenson himself noted that "the king is always asking people to work on designs in his presence, especially young Gabriel." In the words of the duc de Luynes, "On those days when the king does not go hunting, he is often to be found working in the design studio with young Gabriel." Similar accounts concerning Louis XVI are far less numerous but, to take one example, corrections in his own hand were made on drawings for the Provence Stairway, built in the Southern Wing in 1788.

The restraint of Louis XIV's successors was due in part to the financial problems he bequeathed to them. The construction expenses he had incurred were all the higher because of his insistence on both quality and rapidity of execution. "Work on the new buildings must still be hastened to assure that they will be finished by the prescribed date," he wrote to Colbert in 1678. Between 1661 and 1663, 1.5 million livres were spent on Versailles. The château of Louis XIII had cost only 300,000 livres, including 213,000 for the building and 82,000 for the gardens. In 1660 the state revenues came to 80 million livres, but because of the nature of the tax-collection system then employed, which left much of these monies in the hands of intermediaries, only 26 million would be placed at the disposition of the king. In 1665 the financial administration of Colbert managed to place at the king's disposal only 63 of the 94 million needed to underwrite the projected budget. Through the 1680s, during which the annual budget vacillated between 100 and 110 million livres, each year 3 to 5 million were allocated for royal building projects. After the Peace of Nijmegen, annual budgetary allocations for construction rose as high as 15 million livres, falling back to 1.5 million upon the resumption of hostilities. On average, between 1664 and 1688 about 1 million livres were spent annually on Versailles, and this without figuring in the expenses of the Eure Canal, which alone, between 1685 and 1688, amounted to 2 million a year. This canal, which was never completed, nonetheless absorbed 9 of the roughly 80 million livres expended in construction of the château complex and its gardens.

Statistics regarding the manpower deployed to realize these projects are equally impressive: in 1684, 22,000 men were at work on Versailles; by 1685 the number had risen to 36,000. In 1684 some 30,000 were mobilized to dig the Eure Canal, two-thirds of them soldiers. The Pool of the Swiss Guards was so called after the regiment that built it. Work on these last two projects was particularly strenuous and unwholesome, exhausting the armies that were subsequently summoned to the field of battle to bring the "affair of the Trianon window" to a bellicose conclusion.

Many lives were lost: Madame de Sévigné wrote of the "prodigious death rate of the workers, wagonloads of whose bodies are brought away each night, as if from the Hôtel-Dieu" (i.e., a charity hospital, then infamous for a high mortality rate; letter of October 12, 1678). In fact, over a twenty-year period there were 227 recorded deaths. The family of each of those who perished was awarded an indemnity of between 40 and 100 livres. But these figures tend to sanitize the reality faced by these workers and their families on a daily basis, the full horror of which is conveyed by a famous anecdote: "A woman who had lost her son as the result of a fall suffered while working on the machines at Versailles . . . presented a petition in hopes of attracting the king's attention; at the same time, she muttered insults against the king, calling him a whoremonger, the king of machinists, and a tyrant, in response to which the king, surprised, asked her if she spoke of him. She answered that she did, and continued. Whereupon she was seized and condemned on the spot to be whipped" (Oliver Lefèbvre d'Ormesson, *Journal*, entry for 1668).

A Tour of the Gardens with Louis XIV. *Painting by P.-D. Martin (early eighteenth century; Versailles Museum). In the background, the Apollo Fountain and the Grand Canal.*

THE PROGRAM

What did it matter if a laborer died while sinking the foundations of the State? In effect, it was in such terms that Louis XIV gradually came to conceive of Versailles. The successive additions, above all those of 1668 and 1678, were accompanied by parallel amplifications of the overall program; initially the mere renovation of a hunting lodge, this would eventually be expanded to entail its transformation into the principal royal residence, which is to say the capital of the realm,

for in the words of Louis XIV himself, "in France the nation has no existence as an independent body; it resides integrally in the person of the king."

By tradition, the French monarchy had a nomadic character. This migratory tendency bore a resemblance to livestock herds that was more than superficial. Like a flock of sheep, the court exhausted the resources wherever it momentarily sojourned. It found itself obliged to move on so that the surrounding forests, parklands, and châteaux, damaged by this sudden overpopulation, could be replenished and repaired. Further, the royal tour of France played a significant role in actual governance, facilitating the consultation and/or control of public opinion, much as a convocation of the Estates General. The elaboration of Versailles did not exactly signal the end of governmental displacements, for the carriages of ministerial envoys and other members of the court continued to ply across the Isle-de-France. But the marriage journey of 1660, which took Louis XIV as far afield as the Pyrenees, was to be the last of the royal tours of France. Some 120 years later contemporaries would react to Louis XVI's journey to Cherbourg with wonder, as if it were an extraordinary event.

The notion of a French capital had no legal foundation, but there had always been a de facto principal residence. During Louis XIV's minority this had been located either at Paris or at Fontainebleau. From 1666 to 1681 it was situated at Saint-Germain, save in 1674, 1675, and 1677, when more time was spent at Versailles. The king's intention to eventually settle the court at Versailles was general knowledge as early as 1675; the decision was officially announced in 1677 and was carried out in 1682. Even at this late date the intention may not have been irrevocable, for during 1681–85 Louis XIV oversaw execution of the most extensive renovations ever undertaken at the château of Saint-Germain. But when, in 1689, he granted it to the exiled Stuart King James II as a residence, the die was cast.

Saint-Germain was not so much victimized by the emerging prominence of Versailles as it was complicit in

---

THE PIETY OF LOUIS XIV

Aside from once in the field on a day of forced marching, the King never neglected to attend Mass, nor did he fail to observe fast days, save on rare occasions and under unusually compelling circumstances. Some days prior to Lent, he delivered a brief public statement on awakening in which he made clear his marked disapproval of consumption of meat in this period, under whatever pretext, and charged the provost marshal to enforce this prescription and to inform him of any violations.

. . . During Advent and Lent he rarely missed a sermon and never failed to make his devotions through Holy Week and on the great feast days, nor did he miss the two processions of the Holy Sacrament, nor those of the feast of the Order of the Holy Spirit, nor that of the Assumption.

. . . At Mass he recited his rosary (he hardly knew to do otherwise) and always while kneeling, except during the reading of the New Testament. At Mass on the principal religious holidays, he refrained from seating himself in his armchair save when this was customary. At jubilee Masses he performed his devotions before the Stations of the Cross on foot and observed all fast days, as well as those during Lent when he refrained from eating meat and had only light meals.

Saint-Simon

this development. By "definitively settling the court in the country" (Saint-Simon), Louis XIV was doing much more than indulging his taste for exercise in the open air. He was creating a tool to be used by the monarchy against Parisian opposition as well as the high nobility, two power bases that had worked in alliance during the Fronde, the recent French civil war.

In 1666 Louis XIV spent the night in Paris for the last time. In 1668 the massive project of modernizing the Louvre, to which the famous colonnade had just been added, was abandoned in favor of a similarly vast undertaking to renovate Versailles, where construction of the

Envelope was begun. As early as 1663, Colbert had sensed that the recently launched work at Versailles would prove fatal to the Louvre project. On September 28 he wrote a celebrated letter to the king voicing his concern:

I implore [Your Majesty] to allow me to address to You a few words, repeating sentiments I have already expressed, and beseech You to indulge my insistence. This residence will prove better suited to advance Your Majesty's pleasure and entertainment than to enhance Your glory. . . . It is only fitting that, after having managed difficult affairs of state with such skill and aplomb as to incite general admiration, You should then

*L*ouis XIV in the Chapel. *Painting by A. Pesey depicting "Louis XIV accepting the oath of the marquis de Dangeau, grand master of the merged orders of Notre Dame of Mount Carmel and of Saint Lazare, December 28, 1685" (Versailles Museum). The scene takes place in the fourth chapel, later replaced by the Salon of Hercules.*

turn to such pleasures and amusements, but care must be taken that this not be done in such a way as to prejudice Your future glory. If Your Majesty should be inclined to seek out evidence at Versailles of the more than five hundred thousand écus spent there over the last two years, You would find the task difficult. . . . Posterity will discover in the account books of Your department of buildings that, while expending such considerable sums on this house, You neglected the Louvre, which is assuredly the most superb palace in the world and that most worthy of Your Majesty's grandeur.

If initially Colbert did not understand the extent to which the transfer to Versailles was a political maneuver, this was because the king himself had not so construed it at the beginning. He loved spending time at Versailles, as had his father; unlike him, however, he also enjoyed being surrounded by the world of the court. "For some it was considered a black mark . . . not to reside at court, for others to put in appearances there only occasionally; but never to appear there at all, or almost never, was sufficient to bring disgrace upon one's head. . . . The king was particularly irritated by those predisposed toward Paris. He could endure with relative ease those who were fond of the country, but even they were well advised to moderate their enthusiasm, or, preliminary to an extended absence, to find satisfactory reasons for their plans." However, Louis XIV soon sensed that by uprooting the nobility from its lands and from Paris he deprived it of its power. This was an accurate perception, for upon Louis XIV's death, when there was a notable antiabsolutist reaction, this manifested itself in the ephemeral return of the nobility to business and finance—which meant a return to Paris, and to the Palais Royal that the regent had made the seat of his government. The following passage from Louis XIV's *Mémoires* clearly reveals the political motivation underlying his fabrication of a royal amusement center at Versailles: "This pleasure-oriented way of life, which accords members of the court a selective familiarity with Our person, moves and charms them more than one can say. . . . By such means We gain a sway over their inclinations and their sentiments even greater, perhaps, than that won by bestowal of rewards and benefits."

Such dispensations were nonetheless given out and were all the more valuable a tool, as most of them cost the monarchy nothing. Elaborate protocols of precedence, governed by exacting considerations of etiquette to which all voluntarily submitted, sufficed to instill a suitably deferential sense of comportment in the courtiers. Double doors were half or fully opened according to the rank in the court hierarchy of those passing through them. Again in accordance with one's rank, one was authorized to sit on a folding stool, or on a more substantial one known as a *tabouret*, or on a conventional chair. At chapel the princes of the blood placed their *carreaux* or prayer-stool cushions squarely on their supports, while dukes and peers were obliged to orient them obliquely. At the nightly ritual of the king's retirement (the *coucher du roi*), special prestige was associated with carrying the king's candle stand. "Although the room in which [the king] undressed was very well lit, the almoner of the day charged with carrying a lighted candle during his evening devotions subsequently surrendered it to the first valet, who held it during the king's passage to his armchair. After surveying the room, the king pronounced the name of one of those present, so designating him as the evening's recipient of the candle. It was considered a great honor to be singled out in this way, thus revealing the extent to which the king had mastered the art of attaching significance to things trivial in themselves" (Saint-Simon). In the words of Louis XIV himself, "One of the most remarkable consequences of Our power is the capacity to attach, at Our pleasure, infinite value to something in itself quite without importance" (*Mémoires*).

Of these honorific privileges, the one most eagerly coveted was undoubtedly the bestowal of lodgings within the château. Here are Saint-Simon's reflections upon having been temporarily deprived of his quarters under the same roof as those of the king: "This entailed my being deprived . . . of the rooms in the château formerly occupied by the maréchal de Lorge, which I was obliged to surrender to the duc de Lorge, previously quartered in those of his father-in-law, and which the king now wished to be otherwise employed. . . . I implored [the king] to keep me in mind for another lodging, which would allow me to pay him court all the more assiduously. He replied that no others were then available."

Access to the king's bedroom was not indiscriminately accorded every woman of the court, but all could aspire to have their portrait hung in the Chamber of Beauties (Cabinet des Beautés). Seventeen such portraits

The Reception of the Genoese Ambassadors. *Painting by Claude-Guy Hallé. On May 15, 1685, Louis XIV received the emissaries of the doge of Genoa in the newly completed Large Gallery (the Hall of Mirrors). In this painting, contemporary with the event, the artist has represented some of the silver furniture, notably the silver throne created for the Grand Appartement of the king.*

in identical formats have survived (most of them the work of the Beaubrun brothers, who seem to have specialized in them), but it is not known where they were intended to be displayed. Decorative ensembles conceived around portrait galleries had been quite fashionable in the first half of the century. The room in question had perhaps been envisaged for the "first" Versailles; such is suggested, at least, by the advanced age of those represented, each of whom is duly identified by an inscription. Judging from these portraits, it would seem that wealth sometimes carried the day over beauty in the Miss Versailles competition!

It was a great hunter indeed who managed to assemble at Versailles the final descendants of the feudal wild beasts that had harried the royal authority for so long. In this instance domestication was deemed prefer-

able to systematic eradication such as that used against local wolves. Thus tamed, the nobility could bask in the illusion of participating in the government, whose center of operations Versailles had become. The King's Council now held its meetings in a room adjacent to the monarch's bedroom. Additional quarters needed to house the ministers and their staffs were located in the wings on either side of the forward entry court. It was at Versailles that the king officially received diplomatic envoys. Some of these ritual receptions have remained famous, most notably those of the Genoese ambassadors in 1685, of the Siamese in 1686, and of the Persians in 1715.

In fact it could be maintained, parodying Clausewitz, that architecture is the continuation of war by other means. For all intents and purposes this is what Colbert maintained in his famous letter of September 28, 1663:

"Your Majesty is well aware that, excepting brilliant military campaigns, there is nothing that signals the grandeur and intelligence of princes more strikingly than buildings; and posterity judges them in accordance with the splendor of the residences constructed by them during their reigns." Louis XIV's final utterance also acknowledged the connections between architectural enterprise and warfare: his dying words to the future Louis XV were, "Do not emulate me in my taste for building and war."

Louis XIV's successors administered his legacy astutely: not only were they less inclined than he to wage expensive wars, but they also wisely retained the elaborate rituals associated with Versailles that so fascinated observers. "The king of France has no gold mines like those of his cousin the king of Spain," wrote Montesquieu's perceptive Persian visitor, "but he is nonetheless far richer, given that he can draw upon the bottomless vanity of his subjects, a resource far more difficult to deplete than any mine" (*Lettres persanes*, 1721).

THE NOBILITY TAMED

Frequent festival entertainments, private walks at Versailles, and journeys were all tools that the King used to mark his favor or disfavor by naming those chosen to participate, thereby keeping everyone around him all the more attentive to his pleasure. He understood that he had at his disposal nothing like the number of real favors he would need to keep this dynamic in motion continually. So he substituted ideal for real ones, playing upon jealousy, carefully distributing gestures of preference through the day, thus manifesting his considerable artfulness in such matters. As to the expectations born of small preferences and distinctions, and the prestige attending them, no one was more ingenious than he in inventing this sort of thing. Marly, a little later, proved of great use to him in this regard, and Trianon too, where everyone was given access to pay him court, but where only ladies were accorded the honor of dining with him, having been carefully selected for each meal. At his retirement in the evening, he made similar use of the candlestick that he directed to be carried by a courtier whom he wished to honor, always one of the most distinguished of those in attendance, and whom he named in a strong voice upon rising from his prayers. The honorific jerkin was another of these inventions. It was quite handsome, lined in red with cuffs and vest also in red, embroidered with a magnificent design of gold and a bit of silver that was specific to this article of clothing. Among the few who were allowed to wear it were the King, members of his family, and the princes of the blood; but these latter, like the rest of the courtiers, were accorded this article only when one of their limited number became available. The most distinguished members of the court begged the King to grant this favor either to themselves or to those close to them, and it was held to be a great honor to have obtained it. Until the death of the King, as soon as one became available, there was considerable jostling among the most exalted members of the court as to who would be granted it, and if it went to a younger man, the honor was held to be particularly great. The various devices of this kind that were created one after another as the King grew older, and the alterations he effected in the festival celebrations to similar ends, and the gestures he made in view of keeping the court at his disposition—explanation of all these things would prove endless.

Saint-Simon

OPERATION

The Conquest of the Franche-Comté. Oil sketch by Le Brun for one of the ceiling compartments of the Hall of Mirrors (Versailles Museum). This ceiling is decorated with paintings of key episodes of Louis XIV's early reign, rendered more impressive by use of elements from classical mythology. Here, Louis XIV stands above a prostrate Franche-Comté (conquered in 1674); behind him Hercules and Minerva are seen fighting on his behalf.

At the end of the old regime the court and its supporting service staff consisted of about 10,000 persons. Of this number only a thousand were courtiers. As many as 5,000 people resided in the château itself. In 1789 it contained 288 lodging units, adding up to 1,252 rooms with fireplaces and more than 600 without. To these must be added the 152 rooms occupied by the king, the queen, and the royal princes. Accommodation for most of the necessary support services had to be found in the city. The so-called Grand Commun alone, built by Mansart behind the left Ministers' Wing, contained 1,000 rooms occupied by at least 1,500 people.

The first maître d'hôtel and the controller general of consumables (contrôleur général de la Bouche) together oversaw an impressive array of operations, culinary and other: the bakery, responsible not only for bread but also for eating utensils and table linen; the wine cellars, responsible for beverages; the kitchens; the *fruiterie*, charged not only with provision of fruit but also with illumination; and finally the furnace masters or *fourriers*, who handled matters pertaining to heating. And all this was for the exclusive use of the royal family. The army of courtiers had no canteen (*commun*) at their disposition in the Grand Commun!

The set of buildings erected by Mansart within the prongs of the crow's-foot consisted of the Large Stables to the north, where saddle horses were kept, and the Small Stables to the south, which housed carriage horses. At the close of the reign of Louis XIV they sheltered a total of some 700 animals. This number would progressively increase, exceeding 2,000 under Louis XVI. And only the king's horses were housed here, the queen and the princes having separate stables elsewhere. These same buildings also provided space for other services more or less directly related to their principal function, notably the Royal Mounted Band (Ecuries du roi), composed of the king's trumpeters, oboists, and percussionists.

The Department of Menus-Plaisirs (literally, Lesser Amusements), quartered on the avenue de Paris behind the stables, was responsible for organizing and mounting entertainments and ceremonies. Numerous balls, ballets, dinners, fireworks, concerts, and theatrical presentations considerably enlivened the social life of Versailles. Such entertainments were sometimes given in series over several consecutive days, thereby constituting fêtes. The first such event dates from September 1663 and included a production of Molière's L'Impromptu de Versailles. By consensus the most magnificent fêtes were those of 1664, 1668, and 1674. The first of these, dubbed "Les Plaisirs de l'île enchantée," was organized for Madame de La Vallière; that of 1668, the "Grand Divertissement royal," was in honor of Madame de Montespan. The recent con-

quest of the Franche-Comté was the focus of the last in this series, whose apotheosis featured a tableau in which Condé presented Louis XIV with banners captured from the enemy. As nothing with a bearing upon the king's glory could risk historical oblivion, the fêtes of Versailles were all memorialized in published engravings.

These fêtes played an important role in the history of French art. Their ephemeral structures, scenery, decorative appointments, banquet halls, and tableaux consumed by rockets and flames were testing grounds for effects that would be given more permanent form in the various pavilions and fountains subsequently erected in the gardens. The mastermind responsible for these spectacular presentations was Carlo Vigarani, but the contributions of Molière and Lully were also considerable. These French monarchs had a genuine passion for music and the theater. Louis XIII composed, while Louis XIV played

the guitar and the harpsichord and had an excellent ear: the day after the first performance of Lully's *Atys* he was heard to hum several of its more striking melodies. The motets of Delalande and François Couperin ("le Grand") were composed for performance in the Chapel, and Rameau was appointed royal composer of chamber music. It was at Versailles that the famous *querelle des Bouffons* raged, with the king's entourage preferring French opera and the queen's, Italian opera buffa. Several musical instruments preserved in the Versailles storerooms attest to the musical proclivities of Louis XV's daughters as well as of Marie-Antoinette. All of which might seem rather banal. After all, was it so rare in this period for women to make music? The pageantry of Versailles and its court no longer takes us by surprise, so proverbial has it become. But we should bear in mind that many reigns have not boasted courtly arts comparable to those of Versailles,

The fête of 1764, celebrating the conquest of the Franche-Comté. Performance of Lully's Alceste *in the Marble Court; engraving by Le Pautre (1676). The court is seen as transformed by Le Vau, who added the marble paving, the colonnades, the antique busts, and the cast-iron aviaries in the corners, prior to Hardouin-Mansart's alterations.*

*T*he Large Reception Room of Madame Adélaïde. Note the salon organ, which may have belonged to Madame Adélaïde, the most musically accomplished of Louis XV's daughters. The painting by Nattier is a posthumous portrait of Madame Henriette, another of Louis XV's daughters, who died in 1752. In this work, commissioned by Madame Adélaïde, Nattier depicts her playing the bass viol.

whose enormous prestige would be unthinkable without these lavish manifestations. By the eighteenth century this prestige had become an all but irresistible force, making itself felt not only in other European courts but even among those same philosophes who dared to challenge absolutism's prerogatives, notably Voltaire, whose famous *Siècle de Louis XIV* (1751) is a case in point.

When not engaged in the periodic fêtes or daily hunting expeditions, the court turned its attentions to the games table. Louis XIV made billiards fashionable. At games of chance money was bet, and large sums could be made or lost on those evenings set aside for the parties known as *appartements*. These were occasions when "the entire court, from seven o'clock in the evening until ten, came to observe the king at the gaming tables in the Grand Appartement" (Saint-Simon). It is interesting to note the appropriation of the architectural terms "court" and "apartment" to describe the social life of the château. Beginning in 1682 these so-called *appartements* took place each Monday, Wednesday, and Thursday.

The strict ordering of manners and rigorous time management were anything but unique to Versailles. But what distinguished the French court from all others was the presence of the public, which had free access to the château. In the French tradition the king's life was held to belong to the nation, and this took foreigners by sur-

PLEASURES AND DIVERSIONS

Comedies were given three times a week, a ball every Saturday, and on the remaining three days all men and women of rank then at court gathered at six in the evening in the Grand Appartement of the king, which was magnificently appointed with silver furnishings worth over six million livres. The suite was very well lit, and all present were free to amuse themselves as they pleased. In one room there were musicians who sang from time to time, and a band of winds and violins played music to which one could dance. In another the queen played reversi, and the king played, too. In yet another, Madame la Dauphine played with the ladies; Monseigneur played at one table, and Monsieur and Madame at another; and in this same room there were many more tables covered with beautiful carpets on which one could play whatever game one wished, and many servants were present who were at the complete disposition of the guests. In the fourth room there was a billiard table on which the king played quite often with the best players in the court. In the fifth, a magnificent buffet was set from which any and all could eat and drink to their heart's content.

marquis de Sourches, Mémoires

prise. In the words of Arthur Young, "It was amusing to see the blackguard figures that were walking uncontrolled about the palace, and even his bed-chamber; men whose rags betrayed them to be in the last stage of poverty, and I was the only person that stared and wondered how the devil they got there. It is impossible not to like this careless indifference and freedom from suspicion" (*Travels in France during the years 1787, 1788, 1789,* first published in 1792.)

Two moments in the life of the palace were particularly dear to the public: the king's public meals (le Grand Couvert) and the queen's giving birth. As might be expected, there are many anecdotes about these events; we will report only one, an astounding story concerning Marie-Antoinette told by Madame Campan, an eyewitness.

When Doctor Vermond announced, "The queen is about to give birth," a flood of curiosity-seekers rushed into the bedroom; so many and boisterous were they that the queen was endangered. Luckily, during the night the king had taken the precaution of securing the large tapestry screens surrounding Her Majesty's bed with cords; otherwise they would surely have been knocked over onto her. Thereafter it became impossible to move about in the room, which was jammed with a crowd so motley that one would have believed oneself in a public square. Two observers from Savoy went so far as to climb up on the furniture to gain a better view of the queen. (Madame Campan, Mémoires, account of the birth of Madame Royale in 1778)

Free public access engendered serious problems of hygiene and security. In his book *La Police des Mendiants* (The Policing of Beggars) of 1764, La Morandière wrote: "One is revolted by the disgusting odors hanging over the park, the gardens, and even the château itself. Passageways, courtyards, . . . hallways, all are full of urine and fecal matter; . . . the lowest dregs of the population relieve themselves there before passersby, shamelessly and without constraint." These odors of Versailles have raised some doubts about the hygiene of the royal family and the court. This was better than has sometimes been claimed: later transformation of the château into a museum entailed the disappearance of many of its smaller spaces, notably its dressing rooms and water closets. The petty crimes of visitors were particularly damaging to the gardens, where

---

"THE KING IS WOUNDED!"

Toward six o'clock in the evening, under a sky that was overcast but rather bright, under the light of a full moon and flaming torches, King Louis XV set out to return to Trianon, where everyone had remained. As he descended the last step from the guardroom to enter his carriage, with the assistance of his principal squire the duc d'Ayen, followed by Monsieur the Dauphin and preceded by the Captain of the Hundred Swiss Guards in full regalia, a man hurled himself between two of the guards, causing one to turn to the left and the other to the right, while giving an officer of the guard a vigorous push; coming a bit from behind, he struck the king with all his strength on his right side with a penknife, using such force that the handle thrust the king forward, so that he said, "Duc d'Ayen, I have just been given a fist-blow!" The man did this with such speed that he escaped through the opening created before those whom he had all but knocked down could recover their balance, and no one saw the wound, because of the torchlight as well as the need to watch one's step on the stair. In response to the king's remark the maréchal de Richelieu, who was also behind him, said, "Who was this man with the hat?" The king turned his head and, feeling the side where he had taken the blow and finding his hand now covered with blood, said, "I am wounded! Arrest that man but do not kill him!" A footman opening the carriage door saw the king bleeding and cried out, "The king is wounded!" The man was brusquely seized and the king retraced his steps. It was proposed that he be carried, but he said, "No, I still have enough strength to go up." He proceeded to mount the stairs, having to that point manifested remarkable courage and presence of mind.

duc de Croÿ, Mémoires

---

theft of plumbing fixtures and mutilation of statuary was common. In 1730 a decision was taken to close off the bosquets with iron fences.

The king's very life was at risk. In his attempt to assassinate Louis XV, Damiens emerged from a crowd on the château grounds. In July 1789 it was discovered that the locks on the entry gates had fallen into disrepair and that the keys had been misplaced. Temporary padlocks were hastily improvised, but these proved insufficient to restrain the crowd of Parisians who descended on Versailles the following October intent on forcing a final public invasion of the château.

THE MONUMENT AND THE MUSEUM

*L*ouis-Philippe and His Sons before the Gates of the Château. *Painting by Horace Vernet (Versailles Museum). Transformation of the château into the Museum of French History served a political agenda designed to reinforce the legitimacy of the Orléans family line.*

*L*arge crowds would return to Versailles only on July 19, 1801, to view the operation of the fountains in the first *Grandes Eaux* since 1789. In the interim, the château had been designated a national monument and museum. Such a vocation was perhaps less novel in the history of Versailles than it might appear. For several years following the death of Louis XIV, the château, essentially abandoned but still furnished, was on the itinerary of visitors from all over Europe who came to admire its many

treasures. The behavior of the young Louis XV, who upon returning to Versailles lay down in the Hall of Mirrors to view its painted ceiling, is already that of a visitor to a renowned monument. Louis XIV had assembled an impressive array of collections. He inherited 150 paintings, but by 1710 he owned 2,300. Several rooms in the château were specially fitted out for the preservation and display of works of art. The idea of creating a museum for public exhibition of the royal collections was first proposed in the mid-eighteenth century. It would be realized only in 1793, with establishment of the Musée Central des Arts at the Louvre. Many works of art formerly housed at Versailles were transferred there, while the revolutionary government ordered the royal furniture auctioned off. However, a decree of 1794 stipulated that the château itself not be sold like other former royal properties, but be retained "to serve the pleasures of the people." In 1797 an agreement was made designating the château as a museum devoted exclusively to the French school, with the Louvre being set aside for exhibition of works from other nations. This museum opened in 1801 but was short-lived, for a policy calling for the return of art works previously removed from churches, implemented shortly thereafter, entailed its demise.

First Napoleon, then Louis XVIII dreamed of transforming Versailles into a residence once more. Louis-Philippe, who briefly entertained the same idea, converted it into a museum instead. All three rulers recoiled from the enormously high number of personnel its renewed operation would require, as well as, perhaps, from the ghosts of the past that were so palpable there. Napoleon and Louis-Philippe, for whom reinstallation within the château would have been political folly, made do with Trianon; as for Louis XVIII, his reign was too short to allow for implementation of such a plan.

The ambitions behind the Museum of French History, sponsored by Louis-Philippe and inaugurated in 1837, were altogether different. Seeking to rally all social classes to his dynastic rule, this "king of the French" dedicated the château "To all the glories of France." This undertaking was much admired by contemporaries, but the judgment of subsequent commentators has not been favorable. To do it justice, its several thematically coherent rooms, for which images and decoration were commissioned from contemporary artists, are among the most important such ensembles of the nineteenth century. On the other hand, adapting the building entailed the destruction of many superb older interiors.

In 1871 Versailles, yet again under the sway of wartime exigencies, reverted to its original function as the seat of government, Paris having been abandoned to the Commune. Only one physical trace was left by this episode, the assembly room built in the Southern Wing to accommodate the Chamber of Deputies; during this same period the Senate met in the Opera House. On June 18, 1879, the two legislative bodies voted to return once more to Paris.

In 1887 a young historian named Pierre de Nolhac was appointed chief curator. He initiated a new policy of restoring the interiors destroyed under Louis-Philippe. The example he set has been followed throughout the twentieth century, which has witnessed a sustained effort to return Versailles to its original state as a château.

The Rooms of the Crusades, decorated in a Gothicizing idiom in 1839. Paintings of episodes from the crusades encouraged the legitimist faction to support the Orléans line.

*T*he Gallery of Battles. Constructed by the architects Fontaine and Nepveu in 1833, decor executed in 1834. It contains paintings of thirty-three battles, from Tolbiac (1496) to Wagram (1809). Engraving published in Charles Gavard, Versailles, galeries historiques . . . , 1838.

LEFT: The Battle of Rivoli *by P.-H.-E. Philippoteaux. This painting was executed for the Gallery of Battles in 1842–44. Of the thirty-four battles represented in the gallery, five depict episodes from the Napoleonic wars (here, an event that took place in 1797). Such a choice is not surprising coming from Louis-Philippe, who organized the return of Napoleon's ashes to Paris in hopes of winning over that portion of public opinion still faithful to the emperor's memory.*

*B*ELOW OPPOSITE: The Battle of Bouvines *by Horace Vernet.* BELOW: *The Battle of Taillebourg by Eugène Delacroix.*

Two of the most significant paintings in the Gallery of Battles. Philip Augustus proposed to relinquish his crown, offering to bestow it upon anyone better equipped than he to carry the day. This painting was commissioned for the Tuileries (1827) prior to Louis-Philippe's accession; the latter chose to use it, as it recalled that royal power derived from an election among the barons. At Taillebourg Louis IX, the dynasty's canonized saint, defended the cause of national unity by confronting a rebel vassal. If similar messages are conveyed by these two paintings, their respective styles could hardly be more different. Delacroix is now much better known than Vernet. The latter was, however, one of Louis-Philippe's favorite painters, and his work has recently benefited from revisionist reassessments of the idiom known as art pompier, which is well represented in the Gallery of Battles.

PART TWO

The Architecture of the Buildings and the Gardens

Chapter 3 ⟨⟩
THE CHATEAU AND ITS SUBSIDIARY BUILDINGS

LEFT: One of the stairways of the Opera House, by Gabriel. OPPOSITE: The Rape of Proserpina, original by Girardon, commissioned for the center of the Colonnade, but recently removed to the Large Stables.

*I*n current usage, the word *château* most often designates not only a residential building but the entire precinct within which it is set, including its surrounding lands and various subsidiary structures. However, the château proper of Versailles is such a complex architectural organism, and the set of its supporting structures is so large, that it will be best to deal with these two entities separately. The structures constituting the château in the strictest sense of the word are all the easier to isolate as they are compact and literally of a piece, though the status of the Ministers' Wings flanking the forward entry court is somewhat ambiguous. Traditionally in châteaux the quarters of the various support services opened onto such forecourts. As we have seen, at Versailles the Royal Court was originally no more than such a courtyard, providing access to stables and rooms allotted for domestic servicing. Upon being accorded a more dignified role, it was fitted out with an impressive gated fence (now destroyed) that isolated it from the court between the Ministers' Wings. In the end, however, these latter structures must be regarded as part and parcel of the château itself, as they sheltered support services rather than offices; the courtyard they embrace is closed by an iron fence even today. The spacious Place d'Armes (Parade Ground) extending forward from this point establishes a respectful distance between the château and the stables, the only subsidiary structures readily visible from the royal apartments. All other support services were housed within the town.

THE BUILDING CAMPAIGNS OF LOUIS XIII

The proportions of the present Marble Court are essentially those established by the building constructed for Louis XIII in 1623. The contract executed by the master mason Nicholas Huau is dated September 15 of that year. The author of this building's design remains unknown. Given the structure's modest scale, it was probably a master mason rather than a famous architect, but it can be stated firmly that this was not Nicholas Huau himself, as he obtained the commission by submitting a competitive bid. It has been suggested that the designer was Philibert Le Roy, the royal engineer and architect responsible for the structure of 1631, but no proof supports this hypothesis. There is no documentation of Le Roy's presence at Versailles prior to 1629, when he and the hydraulics specialist Alexandre Francine were consulted regarding the water supply. Huau had died the preceding year, which suggests that Le Roy might have been called in to replace him. Although Huau was not the structure's designer, it seems clear that he was responsible for overseeing the site until his death.

The building was constructed of rough-textured stone and consisted of a central block and two projecting wings, somewhat lower, that defined a courtyard whose fourth side was closed by a gated wall. The king's apartments, where he first passed the night on March 9, 1624, were on the second floor of the central structure. There were other, less comfortable residential quarters in the building, but none of these was intended for use by the queen.

In June of that same year a moat was sunk; rather than being flush with the walls, it was placed somewhat forward from the building and thus allowed for an intervening terrace. In military fortifications such terraces were referred to as *fausses braies* or "false cuffs," and were used as cannon emplacements. Clearly such was not the in-tention at Versailles where, though replete with parapet-like projecting platforms at the corners, these elements functioned simply as straightforward evocations of military architecture. In all likelihood this hunting lodge had no additional, subsidiary structures outside the boundary traced by its moat, for at least a portion of the wings seems to have been used for support services.

Between 1631 and 1634 the king signed no fewer than eight different contracts relating to the almost total reconstruction of the building, which proceeded incrementally so as to allow use of the central block during the work. This central element was slightly extended and widened (its approximate width was expanded from six to eight meters), and the height of the wings was increased to equal that of the central structure, while culminating pavilions were built at the wings' extremities. In addition, four corner pavilions were erected on the projecting platforms of the "false cuff." The closing wall of the court was replaced by an arcaded entry portico. The plan of the central structure could hardly have been simpler, accommodating only a single series of rooms between its front and back façades. The central portion of the second floor was once more given over to the king's lodgings, which were divided in half by a central staircase. A gallery was situated on the second floor of the right wing. There were still no quarters envisaged for the queen. The original masonry facing was replaced by a mixture of brick and stone. The detailing, including Doric pilasters at the corners and blocklike elements punctuating the piers, was of stone. The result was quintessential Louis XIII architecture, although this mixture of materials was not new to the French tradition. It was a technique that tended to return to favor in moments of extensive building activity: it facilitated rapid construction, it was more sober of aspect and more attractive than soft construction stone, and its polychrome effect could be rendered even more seductive by "enlivening" the brick and mortar with red and white paint.

It was the château of 1631 that Saint-Simon described, with seeming irony, as a "house of cards" (*château de cartes*), although another of his comments—a suggestion that Louis XIII undertook to build at Versailles "so that thereafter he could avoid sleeping in the hay"—suggests a tendency on his part to confuse this later building with the more modest structure of 1623. Oft-cited expressions of contempt uttered by the Venetian ambassador and the maréchal de Bassompierre undoubtedly apply to this last. In 1624 the ambassador wrote of the "piccola casa . . . per recreazione" (very small pleasure house), and in 1627 the marshal spoke of the "paltry château of Versailles, a construction hardly worthy of a mere gentleman" (*Mémoires de ma vie*, published in 1877). The château of 1631 was far from grandiose, but it would not have evoked such mocking characterizations as these. This information should be borne in mind while interpreting Saint-Simon's later quip. With the phrase "house of cards" does he mean to designate a fragile, childish construct? Consider Tallemant des Réaux's remark that the château of Monbazon, "the most extravagant ever built," was "a house of cards with many small towers" (*Historiettes*, ca. 1660–70). And also Furetière's comment in his *Dictionnaire* (1690): "One terms a house of cards an elaborately appointed house that is in fact far more modest than it at first appears." True, the related phrase "king of cards" is intended to evoke a figure of ridicule. But Henri Sauval, the celebrated architectural specialist, maintained that "around 1620 brick and stone were considered to be the only materials suitable for prestigious buildings. . . . The combination of red bricks, white stone, and black slate roof created a variously colored effect so agreeable to contemporaries that it was used for all the great palaces. . . . Notice was taken of the fact that the alternating patterns thus created evoked houses of cards only upon this style's being adopted for middle-class residences" (*Histoire et recherches des Antiquités de Paris*, mid-seventeenth century). The taste for a mixture of brick and stone reached its peak in the 1620s, thereafter becoming much less pronounced. Of course the most prestigious buildings, notably the Louvre, the Tuileries, and the Luxembourg Palace, were constructed exclusively of stone, but as late as 1656 the first projects for Vaux-le-Vicomte still envisioned use of this mixture of materials. In the end, the main residential block at Vaux would be built of stone, and its service structures of mixed brick and stone. This solution would be much emulated, and it implied a stylistic hierarchy of genres that proved important in the subsequent evolution of Versailles.

*L*ouis XIII Crowned by Victory, *painting by Philippe de Champaigne (1635; Louvre Museum).*

LOUIS XIV'S FIRST CAMPAIGN

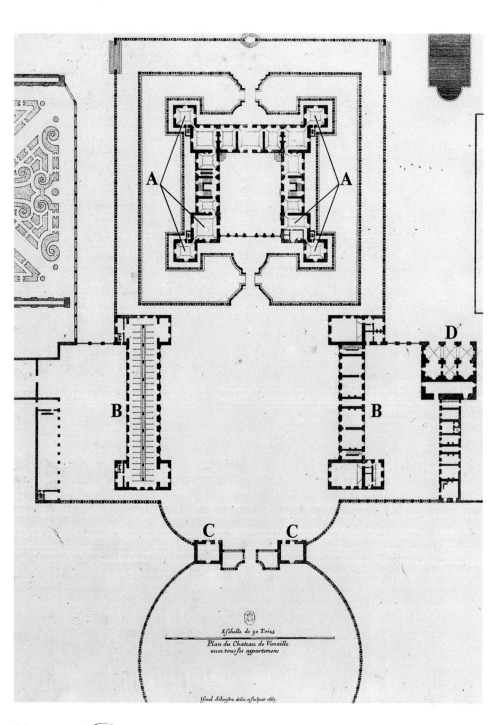

Efchelle de 30 Toises

Plan du Chateau de Versaille
avec touffes apartemens

Ifrael Siluestre delin et sculpsit 1667.

The most important large-scale modifications of Louis XIV's first campaign (in the 1660s) involved reconstruction of the subsidiary structures built by Louis XIII within the confines of the moat; thus it is not surprising that this work was realized in brick and stone. These two parallel blocks housed stables to the left and support services to the right. The form of the moat was altered, the projecting platforms of the "false cuff" being squared away in the process. Two small peak-roofed enclosures were built in the corners of the courtyard. A wide balcony with an ironwork railing was added, circling the entire perimeter of the second floor.

This balcony was strongly reminiscent of the one that Anne of Austria had added to the main façade of the Palais Royal, one that in the 1640s had been regarded as a splendid innovation. Doubtless Louis XIV explicitly intended the Versailles balcony to evoke this earlier structure; he had spent his youth at the Palais Royal and had inherited the tastes of his mother, whom he greatly admired. Such ironwork balconies would, within a few decades, come to be regarded as indispensable elements of any architectural design. For one thing they rendered basic, one-room-deep plans more practical by adding secondary circulation routes; true, these were exposed to the elements, but contemporary standards of comfort were far less rigorous than ours today and open passageways were quite common in the period. At Versailles such balcony circulation was kept under control by use of iron gates with locks at the junctures between lodgings.

Beginning with Louis XIV, the queen would be a welcome presence at Versailles. The queen mother was provided with quarters on the ground floor, while Marie-Thérèse was accorded rooms on the second floor symmetrically disposed to Louis's own; thus the queen's were to the left and the king's to the right, establishing a tradi-

LEFT AND OPPO-SITE: The château at the close of Louis XIV's first building campaign. A plan dated 1667, and a view of the château dated 1664, engraved by I. Silvestre. Note the pavilions added to the central block during Louis XIII's second campaign (at A); the two parallel structures containing the support services facilities (at B); the small pavilions (at C); and the Grotto of Thetis (at D), added in the course of Louis XIV's first campaign.

tion that would long be honored. The central stairwell was removed and replaced by two symmetrical stairs placed in the wings. Each of the royal suites extended from the center of the building to one of these new stairwells. This equitable, bipartite allocation of living space was unusual for the period and is in itself rather suggestive; in fact, it has been held to imply the legitimacy of the queen's claim to the Spanish crown! In the end this reading is untenable, but it nonetheless merits discussion. A clause in the Treaty of the Pyrenees concerning the anticipated marriage of Louis XIV and Marie-Thérèse, daughter of Philip IV of Spain, stipulated that the Infanta would renounce all claim to the Spanish throne in return for a dowry of 500,000 gold écus (a sum that would never in fact be remitted). In the history of French architecture there are several instances of equal distribution that might be deemed to carry political implications, the most remarkable of which is the earliest in date. The twin donjons at the château of Niort, built in the twelfth century by Henry II of England on lands over which his sovereignty was by indirect right, deriving from his wife, Eleanor of Aquitaine, have a profile that seems, to us at least, to suggest two crowns. Equal spatial allocation is less systematic at Amboise and Blois, but certainly the quarters there allotted to the reigning duchess of Brittany were more or less comparable to those of the king, her husband. By contrast, the palaces and châteaux built by the queen mothers (the Tuileries, the Luxembourg Palace) and by government ministers (Vaux-le-Vicomte) from the late sixteenth century on all conform perfectly to the law of symmetrical distribution; a suite of rooms designated for use by the visiting monarch, rarely occupied, was consistently counterbalanced by a similar suite for the master or mistress of the house.

Much about Louis XIV's first building campaign remains unknown. Records of the work at Versailles were kept only from Colbert's appointment as overseer of the king's buildings in 1664. Thus the start of the work terminated in March 1663 cannot be dated with certainty. Some authors refer to a 1664 architectural competition preliminary to an anticipated total reconstruction, which initially seems quite plausible. Louis Le Vau, the king's first architect, who was then simultaneously in charge of work at the Louvre and at Versailles, did not enjoy the full confidence of Colbert, who early in his tenure organized such a competition for the Louvre in hopes of marginalizing Le Vau. Colbert was surely tempted to resort to a similar tactic at Versailles. But the king kept a close watch on the work there, and he was a supporter of Le Vau. In all likelihood the authors in question simply confused a hypothetical 1664 competition with that of 1669, which is fully documented.

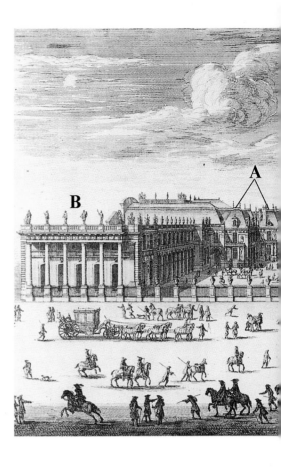

TOP LEFT: The entry court façades at the close of Louis XIV's first building campaign. Engraving by I. Silvestre, dated 1664. This engraving, contemporary with that on the preceding page, provides a closer view of the central block. Note the pavilions added during Louis XIII's second campaign (at A), and the subsidiary structures added by Louis XIV (at B). These last are still separated from the main building by Louis XIII's moat. The central block's second floor is now circled by a balcony. BOTTOM LEFT: The garden façade at the close of Louis XIV's second building campaign. Engraving by I. Silvestre (1674). In 1668–69 the decision was taken to construct the Envelope, including the garden façade that, though usually attributed to Le Vau, is perhaps the work of d'Orbay. The general disposition is bipartite: in the center is a terrace that will disappear with construction of the Hall of Mirrors. TOP CENTER: The château at the close of Louis XIV's second building campaign. Engraving by I. Silvestre (1674). In the 1670s Le Vau, with d'Orbay's assistance, joined the main building (at A) and the subsidiary structures (at B), which were remodeled as lodgings.

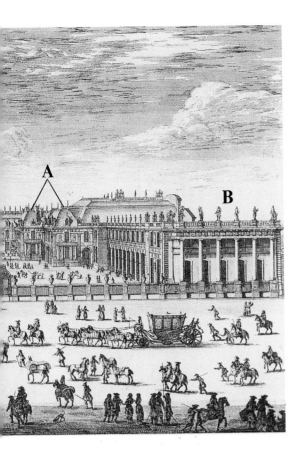

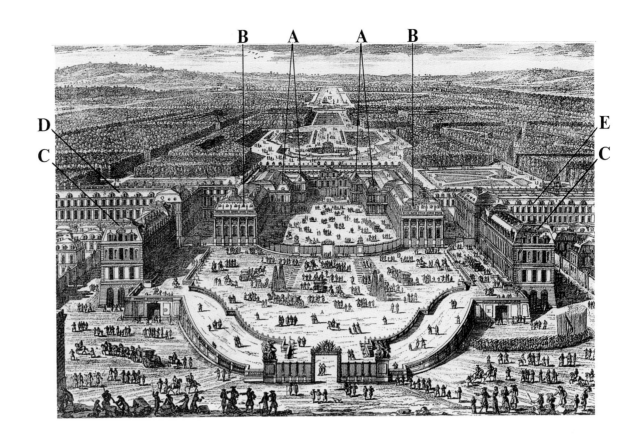

*T*OP RIGHT: The entry façades at the close of Louis XIV's third building campaign. Engraving by N. Langlois (1688). In the course of the 1680s Hardouin-Mansart recast the former support services wings, thereby defining the Royal Court (at B); built the Ministers' Wings, similarly defining the forward court (at C); built the Southern Wing (at D); and began construction of the Northern Wing (at E). But for the absence of the Chapel, this represents the château as it appeared at Louis XIV's death. BOTTOM RIGHT: The garden façade at the close of Louis XIV's third building campaign. Engraving by Pérelle. Hardouin-Mansart has filled in the central volume, redesigned the second-floor windows, and begun construction of the Southern Wing (to the right) and the Northern Wing (to the left, without the Chapel).

LOUIS XIV'S SECOND CAMPAIGN

*T*he competition of 1669 can be said to mark the beginning of Louis XIV's second campaign, which continued through the subsequent decade. There is no lack of documentation for these years, rather the contrary, but the archival records are not dated with sufficient rigor to enable us to establish a precise chronology of this eventful period, whose history grows quite complicated in tandem with the king's successive whims. Before beginning a detailed survey, it will be useful to provide a few chronological benchmarks. May 1668: the signing of the Peace of Aix-la-Chapelle. October: commencement of work on a "new" château to envelope the old one. June 1669: an open competition anticipating a complete reconstruction; preliminary work is quickly undertaken. October 1669: reversion to the Envelope design solution, with its retention of the Old Château. By 1671 the basic structural work has been completed.

In a memorandum titled *Palais de Versailles. Raisons générales*, probably drafted between June and October 1669,

Colbert laid out his view of the situation: "All the work projected so far is piddling. . . . It is true that uncertainty, perpetual changes of plan, and great cost do not make for royal actions of an impressive character. . . . There are, then, two options to consider: preservation of that which is extant, with worthless results; or destruction of this, with a new, small structure to be built in its place. Either way the outcome will be regarded by posterity as pitiable, so much so that one could only hope for the building's collapse upon the king's losing interest in it." Two questions are put by Colbert. First, should the Old Château be retained or demolished? "The king's conspicuous public announcement of his intent to raze the little château . . . renders reconsideration of this decision problematic." Second, if the château was to be enlarged, should it be done horizontally or vertically, by the addition of new floors? Colbert favored the second solution: "All fine residences should be of a certain height, and the greater their elevation the better." The site would not favor lateral extension. Fortunately, "it would seem that the king is resigned to accept the limitations imposed by the natural terrain." Further, the addition of wings of disproportionate length would create a "monster": "Any man possessed of taste in architectural matters, present

*V*iew from the gardens. *Mist obscures the Northern and Southern Wings, added by Mansart, highlighting the central block, known as the Envelope, built by Le Vau and remodeled by Mansart. Note the open view through the center, specifically requested by Louis XIV.*

or to come, would find that such a château resembled a man small of stature with long arms and an overlarge head, that is to say an architectural monster." Colbert made his peace with this solution, but in terms that are rather astonishing: "This course of action is consistent with the reasonable disposition that everything undertaken by the king during his reign should be proportionate with his grandeur, which is to say monstrous, though carefully judged as such."

This account, which ascribes to Louis XIV a desire to destroy the Old Château, is contradicted by another based on the testimony of Charles Perrault:

It was felt that the small château was ill conceived and ill proportioned in relation to the new additions. It was proposed to the king that this small château be demolished and replaced with a structure whose character and symmetrical disposition would be more consistent with the recent construction. But the king would not consent to this. While every effort was made to convince him that much of it was in a ruinous state and that considerable rebuilding would be necessary, he suspected a plot to exaggerate the little château's structural fragility so as to assure its demolition, and he said, with some emotion, that if it were razed to the ground he would have it rebuilt exactly as it was, without the slightest change. (Mémoires)

To reconcile the two accounts, both of which are reliable, it need only be allowed that the king changed his mind at least once regarding the fate of the Old Château. The king was conservative by nature, but not emphatically so: having summoned Bernini to complete the Louvre, he informed him that, although he would prefer to retain those elements erected by his ancestors, he was willing to sacrifice these if necessary. Note that the accounts of Colbert and Perrault imply a chronology for the king's changing views: prior to June 1669 he made known his intention to abolish the Old Château; after October 1669, with construction of the "new building" under way, he opposed its destruction.

The Envelope was a set of structural elements disposed in the shape of a U, encompassing the Old Château on the three garden façades while defining two symmetrical enclosed courts. Though substantially consumed by subsequent additions, the space originally occupied by these courts is still discernible today. With the exception

Southern façade of the Envelope.

of an open gallery at ground level adjoining the central block along the full extent of its length, the original Envelope was structurally connected to the Old Château at only a few points. Thus a decision to build it did not preclude the eventual demolition of the Old Château. With this removed, the Envelope would have constituted a distinctly bipartite château dominated by two separate, symmetrical structural blocks housing, respectively, the king's and queen's lodgings and united only by a low gallery. The château of Vincennes as rebuilt by Le Vau for Mazarin was similarly disposed and, with Vaux-le-Vicomte, Richelieu, and the Palais Royal, must be considered one of the successful buildings that Louis XIV aimed to surpass at Versailles. Use of such a bipartite plan here may well have had political implications. The War of Devolution, concluded by the Peace of Aix-la-Chapelle, was waged by Louis XIV in defense of Marie-Thérèse's claims to the Spanish throne, left vacant by the death of Philip IV.

This symbolic reading has been countered by another more function-oriented one. In the middle of the century Parisian architects introduced "double-depth" domestic plans featuring two parallel room sequences between the outer walls of the central block. Many advantages resulted from this strategy, most notably the multiplication of circulation routes. Le Vau himself used such a plan at Vaux-le-Vicomte. According to this view, the Envelope was a means of "doubling" the interior spaces of the Old Château, which thus had to be retained. But this reading is not convincing, for the original structural ties between the old and new buildings were few; if such had been the intent, it would have been better implemented by construction of volumes that doubled the extant ones more systematically. On the other hand, it is true that the Envelope facilitated expansion of the royal apartments. This design gave two suites of rooms to the king and two to the queen, one suite for each within the Envelope, intended for ceremonial use, and another in the Old Château consisting of more informal accommodations.

The ceremonial Grands Appartements of the king and queen were more separated than joined by the open arcade of the low gallery. An enclosed means of passage between the two suites would be introduced only with construction of the famous Hall of Mirrors (Galerie des Glaces) above, in the course of the third building campaign. The low gallery was no more than an open portico opening onto the gardens; its arcades were enclosed only by grillwork.

One need only describe the massing of the garden façade of the newly constructed Envelope to construe this structure as two distinct, paired châteaux: there were two structural blocks, each with its own central pavilion; between them extended the low gallery and terrace and, rising above them in the background, the redesigned façade of the Old Château with its own projecting central

*M*ain façade of the Envelope.

frontispiece. At ground level the elevation was very "French" in character: its bays inscribed within an arcade derived from Lescot's design for the Louvre, its continuous bands of rustication from Salomon de Brosse's Luxembourg Palace, and its French windows from earlier work by Le Vau himself. Initially the second-floor windows were rectangular, with ornamental relief plaques inset above as at Vaux-le-Vicomte; Mansart would subsequently suppress these reliefs to accommodate expanded arched windows. Portions of Le Vau's original elevation remain visible today on the northern and southern façades of the Envelope. As in Lescot's design for the Louvre, the façade was topped by an attic story. The absence of a visible roof was doubtless the most surprising aspect of the design: "It resembles a palace that has been burned out, or one whose final story and roofing have not yet been built," declared Saint-Simon, who was nonetheless familiar with the old château of Saint-Germain, whose flat roofs doubling as terraces dated from the reign of Francis I.

Use of these indigenous design features, however, does not suffice to make this design perfectly French. The horizontals are more strongly articulated than was the norm, easily prevailing over the vertical accents usually dominant in the French tradition—an effect that remained evident even after Mansart's redesign of the second-floor windows, which added vertical emphasis. It has been proposed that this façade elevation was influenced by Bernini's designs for the Louvre. It is difficult to reach any firm conclusions on this point, though it might be admitted that the Versailles façade resembles the work of a Bernini who had thoroughly adapted his style to suit French tastes.

In fact, the grand duke of Tuscany, who visited Versailles in August 1669, reported that a façade designed by Bernini was then being erected there! In the letter of July 15, 1667, in which Colbert informed Bernini, who had returned to Italy, of the king's decision to abandon his Louvre project, the minister proposed to compensate him with another commission, this one for an undertaking plagued with fewer potential pitfalls. During his 1665 sojourn in France Bernini had visited Versailles and been rather taken with it. Could Colbert have asked Bernini to submit designs for the 1669 competition? The consensus has been that Le Vau was author of the winning design, but what proof is there of this? It is widely

believed that this project is identical with that of a plan originating from the Le Vau workshop, now preserved in Stockholm. Excavations of the foundations of Versailles were made in 1949, but they were insufficient to determine whether or not the building that began to rise in June was that of the Stockholm design. A memorandum of Colbert records the names of six participants: Carlo Vigarani, Claude Perrault, Antoine Le Pautre, Thomas Gobert, Jacques Gabriel IV, and Louis Le Vau. This

Lateral frontispiece of the main façade of the Envelope, facing the gardens. The uppermost windows are false, opening onto the roofs above the Large Gallery and the other ceremonial rooms.

memorandum is uncompromisingly critical of the submitted designs, notably of Le Vau's. Could Bernini have been asked to contribute a project? Perhaps, but it would be most surprising for so important a fact to have been recorded only by the grand duke of Tuscany.

On a more general level, questions remain about the relative contributions of Le Vau and d'Orbay, Le Vau's assistant who later succeeded him. Le Vau was in Nivernais tending to his affairs from August 1669 to February 1670 and died the following October. This means that he left Versailles immediately after the competition of June 1669 and was still absent when the decision was taken to revert to the Envelope design concept. Does this imply that the project on which work had begun in October 1668 was revived without modification? If changes had been introduced and Le Vau was thus obliged to endure the humiliation of watching a design rise whose authorship was unclear, this would surely have resulted from the direct intervention of the king, with d'Orbay executing his orders, as de Cotte would do subsequently for the Large Trianon. Clearly many questions concerning the period 1668–70 remain unresolved.

Important changes were made in the entry courts during this second campaign. The Marble Court received its marble pavement and its name, and its surface was elevated three steps higher than before, thereby precluding carriage access. Such a disposition was not new, being encountered in the châteaux of Salomon de Brosse and François Mansart. A pool was sunk in the court's center, and the finial-roofed corner enclosures were replaced by iron bird cages. The Marble Court was thus fitted out as a kind of forward extension of the gardens, from which it was separated only by the open gallery; in fact, the three central doorways giving onto the court were closed only by iron grillwork. Classical busts supported by brackets were affixed to the walls. A portico of eight marble columns supported a central balcony-terrace whose railing was of ornamental ironwork. Similar elements, though somewhat more modest, were installed on the end walls of the wings of the Old Château as well as on those of new wings joining its corner pavilions to the subsidiary buildings constructed during the first campaign. Erection of these narrow connecting wings necessitated the elimination of the Louis XIII moat. These connecting elements did not remain narrow for long: beginning in 1674 d'Orbay enlarged them, so that their volume came to equal that of the structural masses they joined. The now-attached subsidiary buildings were modified in accordance with their new status: their culminating walls were fitted out with columned porticos echoing that of the Marble Court, albeit on a more monumental scale, and their upper reaches were changed to render them consistent with those of the garden façades. But all these alterations allowed for substantial retention of the brick-and-stone treatment of the exterior. At this point the subsidiary structures were designated as space for lodgings, and the court they enclosed was dubbed the Royal Court. Another forecourt was created between the four pavilions intended to house the secretaries of state, while accommodations for the support services were displaced into the town.

It was the second campaign that established the pointed dichotomy between the principal façade and the one facing the gardens that has been so widely criticized. On the front facing the entry courts, the old elevations were selectively modernized or, to be more precise, decked out with antique elements (busts, columns). Although somewhat exaggerated, Saint-Simon's assessment is not altogether devoid of truth: in his view, at Versailles Louis XIV had constructed "one thing after another without a general plan: the good and the bad, the vast and the constricted were here stitched together."

Lateral façade of the Envelope. The niches surmounted by reliefs recall the original elevation, before Mansart suppressed the corresponding plaques above the windows to accommodate their expansion into arches.

LOUIS XIV'S THIRD CAMPAIGN

Louis XIV's third campaign, which unfolded during a ten-year peace (1678–88), was at least as extensive as the second, but its history is less complex, largely owing to Mansart's clear emergence as overseer of the work.

However, the principal contributions of this gifted architect are to be sought in newly constructed secondary structures, for the choices made by his predecessors regarding the château itself were irreversible. This does not reflect the lack of a master plan. Like Colbert, Mansart felt that the château was of insufficient height: he advocated the construction of further floors to provide much-needed space within the main residence. Further, he favored introduction of stone facing for all of the entry court façades. The history of the so-called Grand Dessein must be held to commence here, with Mansart. Its evolution is documented in the archives by a series of drawings whose dating and attribution are sometimes problematic. To take but one example, it has just been discovered that one of these designs traditionally regarded as a product of Mansart's workshop can be dated no earlier than 1741! This redating demonstrates the extraordinary persistence of the style of Mansart; the overall disposition of his Grand Dessein would be retained through most of the eighteenth century. If ever there was a moment that favored realization of this master plan, it was in 1678. It is difficult to understand why the king did not seize it. It should be recalled that the opposition to destruction of the Old Château reported by Perrault could very well date from the period of Mansart's tenure. In any case, it is certain that the work begun in 1678 would render implementation of the Grand Dessein difficult, if not impossible.

Construction undertaken on the side of the château facing the gardens (1678) was particularly important. To allow for addition of an enclosed high gallery between the two Grands Appartements, Mansart simply filled in the void that Le Vau had defined there, advancing the wall of the Old Château, formerly recessed behind the central terrace, to a level flush with that of the end blocks. As already noted, he suppressed the relief plaques above the second-floor windows, which were extended upward and arched. The dimensions of all these windows were made to conform with those of the Hall of Mirrors and the new rooms that frame it, the Salons of War and Peace (Salon de la Guerre and Salon de la Paix). All three of these spaces were capped by vaulted roofs hidden behind the attic story—in reality not a story at all, but a false attic whose windows overlooked the wooden framework supporting the ceilings below.

To a certain extent, transformation of the Marble Court (1678) was rendered imperative by the changes effected on the garden façade. The central pavilion was given taller, arched windows, as if the outline of those facing the garden had penetrated the château. In fact, access between the Hall of Mirrors and the central room of the Old Château (later the bedroom of Louis XIV) was provided by three similar round-arched doorways. Thus it was obligatory to bring these various openings into mutual conformity. To facilitate a raising of the ceiling of this central room, the middle bays of the elevation facing the Marble Court were fitted with a false attic like that of the other façade; the attic's windows opened into the central room's upper reaches. Two monumental pilasters were introduced to frame this new central frontispiece, which was crowned by a sculpted group. With Mansart's removal of the corner bird cages, the number of bays making up the façade increased from five to seven. Mansart replaced the dormer windows punctuating the roof above these lateral bays with highly placed bull's-eye (oeil-de-boeuf) windows more consistent with the spirit of the new focal composition of the façade. These modifications occasioned a general reconsideration of the roofs and their ornament. The steeply pitched roofs were extended (1679) over the wings of the Royal Court, which had previously been flat-roofed; by contrast, the stone balustrade topping the façade of these wings was introduced into all adjacent façade elevations. In the new overall effect, this balustrade tended to dominate the larger dormer windows retained in the wings of the Old Château, which, while prominent in the French tradition for over three centuries, had been unfashionable for about fifty years. The pavilions of the secretaries of state were remodeled, each of the two facing pairs being fused (1678–79); from this point on they were

The Southern Wing. Mansart here reiterated the elevation of the Envelope façade.

*M*asks on the key-
stones of the Envelope's ground-
floor arches, representing the stages
of life from youth to maturity.

known as the Ministers' Wings. The Royal Court and the forecourt were closed by iron fences (that of the forecourt still exists).

Mansart's alterations to Le Vau's building failed to provide all the additional space needed. To address this problem, Mansart constructed two enormous buildings that—somewhat inappropriately, given their scale—were known as wings. These so-called Northern and Southern Wings, disposed along the north-south axis, had rather complex plans: each consisted of two parallel constructions, one bordering the gardens and another the street, while the intervening space was divided into several courts by transverse elements. The Northern and Southern Wings were as wide as those bordering the Royal Court were long. For their garden elevations Mansart adopted a treatment duplicating that of the Envelope. This solution has its admirers, who praise the resulting effect of unity and monumentality, and its detractors, who emphasize its elephantine quality and monotony. The Southern Wing was built between 1678 and 1682. The Northern Wing was begun only in 1685. Its construction was still under way in 1689, when war necessitated its abandonment before completion, leaving the projected street-side extension, the new Chapel, and the Opera House unrealized.

From the beginning the château had boasted a chapel. By this time it had already occupied three different sites, but none of these early structures had been large enough to satisfy the château's needs. It was intended that the Northern Wing finally include a fourth and definitive chapel for the *Roi Très Chrétien* (Very Christian King). Mansart's initial proposal, to be placed in the middle of the wing, featured a central plan topped by a dome. This project closely resembled the one he would build at the Invalides, but it also recalled, oddly, his great-uncle François Mansart's proposal for a Bourbon dynasty mau-

soleum at Saint-Denis. This latter design had been kept with the papers of the great-uncle's workshop, which the great-nephew inherited. This curious episode, which raised no eyebrows, tellingly demonstrates how problematic is application of our own notion of authorship to seventeenth-century France.

Having abandoned the rather modern central-plan project for reasons unknown, Mansart reverted to a more traditional axial disposition deriving from Gothic prototypes. Construction of the new Chapel was begun in 1689 but was immediately interrupted by the outbreak of war; it would not be taken up again for ten years.

The far end of the Southern Wing. In the background, a portion of the structure bordering the rue de l'Indépendance Américaine. To the right, the gardener's house and the beginning of the Stairway of the Hundred Steps.

In the background, the Southern Wing. In the foreground, the Borghese Faun, *after the antique original, and one of the door-windows of the Large Reception Room of the dauphin, who had unusual railings installed in these windows. This picturesque detail is rarely noticed.*

LOUIS XIV'S FOURTH CAMPAIGN

Construction of the Chapel was resumed in 1699, in the wake of the Peace of Ryswick, and would continue despite subsequent hostilities. Basic structural work was complete by 1702. The Chapel was consecrated in 1710, but its decorative elements were still incomplete at Louis XIV's death. Its construction was the sole event of the reign's fourth building campaign. Thus Louis XIV, whose piety had always been sincere

View of the lateral approach to the château, taken from the rue des Réservoirs. From left to right: the Gabriel Wing, the Chapel, the Northern Wing.

but who embraced the church with a new urgency once Madame de Maintenon had "converted" him, had but little time to exercise his devotions there.

The project of 1699 was notably different from that begun in 1689, although its basic plan was retained. In 1689 an interior elevation featuring three levels had been envisaged, with two superimposed ranges of arches of almost equal dimensions topped by high windows. The second of these arcades, level with the Grands Appartements, was to have been articulated with pilasters. Extensive use of multicolored marbles was envisioned in its interior. The subsequent abandonment of marble in favor of stone typifies the stylistic mutations at Versailles that marked the reign's final years. On the exterior, use of masonry marked a striking contrast with the brick and stone treatment of the entry courts; it is possible that this decision reflects a long-term plan to execute the Grand Dessein, which called for the entire building's encasement in stone. Certainly the prominence of the Chapel's high, peaked roof, which towered over the buildings facing the courts, would have been consistent with the eventual construction of additional stories envisaged by the master plan. But in truth, the Chapel's visual preeminence should be understood less as a failure to complete a project than as an expression of God's sovereignty over the king. Its considerable height was the result of a decision to extend upward the second range of arches, with its previously envisaged pilasters replaced by Corinthian columns. Thus while the Doric order dominated the court elevations from the time of Louis XIII and, since Le Vau, the Ionic order prevailed in those facing the gardens, the most perfect of the three orders was consecrated to God.

The Chapel is, in our view, the most accomplished single entity of the château complex, largely due to the success with which it blends advanced design elements with highly traditional ones. Its modern aspect is visible in the interior elevation, which recalls the Colonnade of the Louvre. This parallel was drawn by contemporaries, and it has even been proposed that the presumed author of the Colonnade as well as of another, quite innovative

design for a columned church, Claude Perrault, could well have had a hand in the Chapel's design. Perrault died in 1688; he is known to have formulated a design for the Versailles Chapel that is now lost, but its character is sufficiently well documented to preclude its having influenced the structure that was eventually built. True, the predilection for large columns indulged here was cultivated in Perrault's circle. But the only credible contenders for actual paternity of this masterpiece are Mansart himself and his collaborators. Certainly Mansart, appointed overseer of the king's buildings in 1699, would have been unable to monitor the Chapel's construction in close detail, and given Mansart's death in 1708, it seems probable that the task of formulating the decorative program fell to de Cotte. But as regards the general architectural concept, if the competition is limited to Mansart and de Cotte, the choice must be clear: one need only compare the oeuvres of these two men to discover which of them

was possessed of genius. In our view, authorship of the Chapel can be confidently ascribed to Mansart.

In numerous respects—its orientation (with choir to the east), its pronounced verticality, the prominence of its wall-dissolving windows, its use of flying buttresses to support the vault and of gargoyle drainage spouts, and the archaic construction of its steeply pitched wooden-frame roof—the Chapel proclaims its allegiance to the Gothic tradition. In plan it resembles the cathedral of Notre Dame de Paris. Its overall disposition was probably inspired by the Sainte-Chapelle, the influential palatine chapel built in Paris by Saint Louis, to whom the Versailles Chapel was dedicated. Both were composed of two stories corresponding to two hierarchical levels: in Paris the chapel's lower level was reserved for use by the service staff and the upper one for the king; at Versailles the king heard daily mass from a tribune on the same level as his apartments, descending to the lower floor only

The Chapel, viewed from one of the courtyards in the Northern Wing. To the left, the structure bordering the street; to the right, the structure facing the gardens. The latter structure includes, on the side facing the court, two levels of arcades that were originally open to the elements; these openings provide light for the so-called Stone Gallery. The tripartite organization of the Chapel's elevation is clearly visible here. Of particular interest is the projecting structure attached to the side of the Chapel, containing the Chapel of the Virgin and the Chapel of Saint Louis; it was apparently intended to serve as the base for a bell tower that was never built.

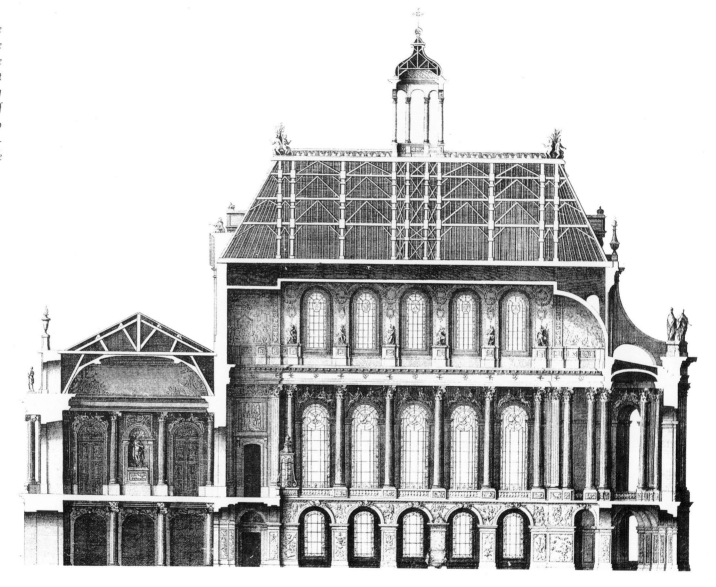
when he took communion, which is to say only on religious feast days.

The Chapel is flanked, to the north, by an isolated square structure visible only from a courtyard of the Northern Wing. This obscure placement is probably the cause of its having received so little attention. It consists of two superimposed rooms, one at the first-floor level housing an altar dedicated to Saint Louis, and another above with an altar dedicated to the Virgin. Given that numerous secondary altars were easily accommodated against the interior walls of the Chapel's perimeter, this appended structure cannot have been intended primarily to house subsidiary chapels. We believe that it was built

as the base of a belltower that was never completed, and that was provisionally covered by a roof that, as of about 1733, needed to be rebuilt. Instead of constructing an upper bell chamber, a less expensive, substitute solution seems to have been adopted, namely the erection of a simple campanile rising rather unceremoniously above this improvised roof. In 1765 it was dismantled because of structural instability, which demonstrates that it had not been built to last. Louis XV could well have been responsible for amputating the original project, for he detested the sound of bells. The stunted belltower of the church at Choisy, near the royal château there, bears further witness to this curious aversion. If our hypothesis

The flying buttress, invented by Gothic architects, was perfected by classical architects. The latter, by inverting its upper extension, allowed for reorientation of the thrust of the lower buttress, thereby facilitating its dissimulation behind crowning elements.

is correct, yet another "Gothic" trait was originally envisioned in the chapel design that, if executed, would have substantially altered the silhouette of the château.

The Versailles Chapel was very badly treated by eighteenth-century critics. Voltaire crudely dubbed it an "astonishing knickknack," and Saint-Simon, with somewhat greater subtlety, called it an "immense catafalque." Jacques-François Blondel, who never forgot that he was professor of architecture at the Academy, gave high marks to some points and low marks to others. But to a remarkable extent the Chapel at Versailles prefigures the "Greco-

Gothic" ideal that would be influential in ecclesiastical architecture in the second half of the eighteenth century. The neoclassical theorists were not mistaken: "in the interior of this chapel [Mansart] replaced the massive, heavy piers and arcades usually employed in church architecture with splendid, light Corinthian columns, adopting the majestic disposition of Perrault's Louvre façade to new ends. Mansart was even more daring than Perrault, making these columns actually bear the immense weight of the ceiling and of the wood-frame roof" (Julien David-Leroy, *Histoire . . . des temples*, 1764).

*B*ELOW AND OPPO-
SITE: *The Chapel. Its interior de-*
cor was executed by eminent
painters and sculptors under the di-
rection of Robert de Cotte. The
ceiling was painted (1708–9) by
Antoine Coypel, Charles de La
Fosse, Jean-Baptiste Jouvenet, and
Louis de Boullogne. The sculpture
is the work of a large team dom-
inated by the Coustou brothers,
Guillaume and Nicolas. The altar
is by Van Clève, perhaps with the
assistance of Antoine Vassé. The
pulpit and the tabernacle were de-
stroyed during the Revolution (the

tabernacle was reconstituted in the
nineteenth century). The Chapel
allies traditional with modern ele-
ments. Dedicated to Saint Louis,
it recalls the Sainte-Chapelle built
by this canonized monarch to
house the crown of thorns: another
chapel with a discreet floor desig-
nated for royal use and an icon-
ographic program focusing on the
Passion. The relief trophies deco-
rating the piers depict the Way of
the Cross. But the colonnade is a
splendid innovation: perhaps in-
spired by the Louvre colonnade, it
announces the idiom of neoclassi-
cal religious architecture.

*F*OLLOWING PAGES.
LEFT: *View of the left interior el-*
evation with the Chapel of the Vir-
gin and the Chapel of Saint Louis
in the background. RIGHT: *View*
of the ambulatory.

OPPOSITE: View of the main ceiling vault and of the ceiling of the tribune. God the Father by Antoine Coypel on the main ceiling; apostles by the Boullogne brothers on the tribune ceiling (1709).

RIGHT: The salon of the Chapel, leading to the royal tribune. In the spandrels, the Christian virtues; in the corners of the ceiling, the four continents, illustrating the universality of Christianity. BELOW: An organ, 1710. Instrument by Robert Clicquot, casing designed by de Cotte and sculpted by the team of Degoullons, Le Goupil, and Taupin. This is the earliest use at Versailles of the palm frond, a decorative motif that would subsequently proliferate there.

BELOW: *The ceiling of the Opera House by Louis Durameau. OPPOSITE: General view of the Opera House. Built by J.-A. Gabriel, realizing a plan dating from 1765. Inaugurated on the occasion of the marriage of Louis and Marie-Antoinette. The oval plan was borrowed from the most modern theaters in Italy; the colonnade, from the Teatro Olimpico in Vicenza by Palladio. Some elements, such as the royal tribune, are the work of Charles de Wailly. The sculpture is by Augustin Pajou.*

COMPLETION OF THE CHATEAU AFTER LOUIS XIV'S DEATH

The Opera House is the counterpart of the Chapel. Placed at the end of the same Northern Wing, it was originally envisioned by Mansart but was constructed only much later by Ange-Jacques Gabriel. A fortunate delay, for it facilitated the incorporation of many important innovations in theater design that emerged in the mid-eighteenth century. But this hiatus was nonetheless insufficient to deter negative criticism: the Opera House was the work of the elderly Gabriel, and a new generation had secured a monopoly on architectural modernity. This new generation attempted to make its mark at Versailles, and perhaps its influence is visible in some of the more advanced elements of the building's design. However, despite its handsome interior colonnade, it was not as widely admired as the theaters of Lyons and Bordeaux, and the Théâtre-Français in Paris, built respectively by Soufflot, Louis, and Peyre and de Wailly, standard-bearers of the new generation.

Few theaters were built in France during the first half of the eighteenth century, and these were often temporary structures perpetuating a tradition of long, narrow facilities improvised in enclosed tennis courts. A large theater at seventeenth-century Versailles, where many masterpieces of the classic repertory were produced, would have fulfilled a genuine need. Louis XIV had envisioned such a theater, but in the end he opted for a chapel instead. The first part of Louis XV's reign was, in the words of Jacques-François Blondel, "a period of languor." A decision to construct the Opera House was taken in 1748, after the second Peace of Aix-la-Chapelle. However, in 1745 Ange-Jacques Gabriel had sent his collaborator Nicolas-Marie Potain to Italy to study its most renowned theaters. In 1753 Soufflot, newly returned from an Italian trip with a similar purpose, constructed the theater in

Lyons, rich in innovative ideas but less resolved than that of Versailles. Working plans for the Opera House were drafted only in 1765, in the wake of the Peace of Paris. It was completed five years later, but only because the impending marriage of the dauphin Louis and Marie-Antoinette of Austria imposed a binding deadline. Thus it was built well before the theater in Bordeaux, the most celebrated French theater of the eighteenth century. The fame of this last was largely due to its monumental entry spaces, while at Versailles one gained access to the theater through a foyer that was rather cramped, so as to facilitate the overall structure's enclosure within the Northern Wing. However, the requirements of a private theater surrounded by domestic rooms differ somewhat from those of a public theater. The theater proper has the oval plan earlier employed in Lyons and a colonnade—a feature that would be imitated in Bordeaux, but to less elegant effect. This oval plan had become the norm in Italian theaters by virtue of its fine acoustics and sight lines. The colonnade, which creates such a monumental effect, was probably inspired by the antique theater in

Vicenza built by Palladio in the sixteenth century. Can responsibility for this allusion be ascribed to Gabriel, who had not made the trip to Italy and who, faithful to the French tradition, was untouched by the new generation's enthusiasm for the master of Vicenza? More likely this idea was suggested to him by Potain. It would seem that Charles de Wailly had no hand in it, although his collaboration on the Opera House is documented: he designed the classical, semidomed treatment of the focal element intended to serve as the royal loge. Louis XV, not partial to conspicuous public display of his person, preferred to use another, more discreet loge hidden by a grill that he had had installed beneath it. "Paradise"—the colloquial name for the highest seats—was hidden behind the springs of the ceiling vault, its occupants being obliged to view the proceedings through oculi. To improve the acoustics, all interior ornament was made of wood, but the structure itself was entirely of stone to minimize the risk of fire, always a concern in a theater lit by candles. This masonry work, especially that of the entrance corridors, perfectly exemplifies the superb mastery of such construction typical of the French tradition.

The financial difficulties that so delayed construction of the Opera House would have discouraged any attempt to realize the Grand Dessein. Unfortunately, Gabriel's ambition eventually overcame the prudent reservations of the king who, his reign almost at an end, in 1771 authorized construction on the east front "of an overall plan of decoration analogous to that of the façade facing the gardens." The picturesque character of the entry courts was no longer acceptable in an era partial to monumental neoclassical conceptions. Jacques-François Blondel had already called attention to the defects of the courts, which he characterized as "semi-Gothic", particularly deploring "the overly repetitious reiteration of peaked roofs"; in his view, "such prominent deployment of gable stories above the residence of a crowned head" was a "violation of decorum" (*Architecture française,* 1752–56). Gabriel's design clearly took such observations into account but did not effect a break with the tradition of Mansart, who in his royal squares had legitimized the use of façades with rusticated basements topped by giant classical orders uniting the two upper floors. The hidden roofs and lack of pediments in this project demonstrate that Gabriel was not totally immune to contemporary

*I*nterior of the Opera House. Engraving published in Charles Gavard, Versailles, galeries historiques . . . , 1838.

innovation. However, the death of Louis XV and the retirement of Gabriel (1774) opened the way to the new generation—one that, on Gabriel's death (1782), would characterize Louis XV's first architect as "mediocre and thoroughly ordinary" (*Mémoires secrets*, 1782). Richard Mique worked on a project of his own from 1776 on even while execution of Gabriel's design was under way. A competition was organized to solicit innovative proposals. It is not clear whether this was initiated in 1780 or 1783, though the second date seems more plausible, as it corresponds to the Peace of Paris. The project submitted in 1784 by Pierre-Adrien Pâris, architect of the Menus-Plaisirs, seems to have been selected the winner. Among other projects still preserved is that of the celebrated

Etienne-Louis Boullée, the immense horizontal mass of which would have blocked out two centuries of history.

The Revolution saved Versailles! Had it erupted earlier, it would have precluded Gabriel's modifications to the right wing of the Royal Court (1771), the only portion of his variant of the Grand Dessein to be built.

Napoleon inherited a château that was asymmetrical and architecturally unresolved. Pierre Fontaine, the emperor's favorite architect, and Jacques Gondouin, architect of the Arc de Triomphe in Paris, submitted their own version of the Grand Dessein. Finally Alex Dufour was placed in charge; in 1820 he added a culminating pavilion to the left wing of the Royal Court, thereby reestablishing a symmetrical disposition.

The last stage of large-scale work worth mentioning also concerns this wing, which was known as the Old Wing because it dated from the era of Le Vau. It had been so neglected during the first quarter of the twentieth century, owing to insufficient funds for its maintenance and preservation, that when the manna of the Rockefellers' substantial donation descended (11 million francs in 1925, 25 million in 1928, totaling U.S. $2,166,000), it was deemed necessary to reconstruct it entirely.

BELOW AND OPPO-SITE: The foyer of the Opera House, with decorative sculpture by Pajou. The theater proper is entered through a kind of interior façade (left) featuring interior windows providing secondary light to the small rooms to which the king could retire during intermissions. The foyer is narrow, being wedged between the theater itself, which occupies most of the width of the Northern Wing, and the garden façade (right).

FOLLOWING SIX PAGES: The access corridors and staircases of the Opera House. These were entirely of stone to minimize the risk of fire, a serious problem in the period. This precautionary measure provided Gabriel with an opportunity to exploit the full technical capacities of the stonemason's art, a key element in the French architectural tradition.

SUBSIDIARY FACILITIES IN THE TOWN

During the reign of Louis XIV, the increasing complexity of support services and the expansion of their accommodations gradually necessitated their displacement into the town. The kitchens and stables were ejected from the wings of the Royal Court when the Envelope was built; provisional quarters for the former were established on the far side of the left wing, and for the latter in the town (on rue Carnot, formerly rue de

la Pompe). The new kitchens were condemned in turn by construction of the Southern Wing. And the new stables, built in 1672 by Jacques Gabriel IV, would prove insufficient and be set aside exclusively for the queen's horses and equipages. A building housing administrative offices (the Hôtel de la Chancellerie) was built in 1670 by d'Orbay, with a façade of mixed brick and stone; this is one of the few extant traces of the early urbanization of Versailles (rue de la Chancellerie).

Most of the support facilities erected in the town date from the campaign of Mansart and evidence burgeoning spatial needs. Among the buildings constructed were the Stables on the Place d'Armes (1679); the new

*D*rawing by David dated 1791 (Versailles Museum), indicating the entire composition of his projected painting The Tennis Court Oath. The tennis court, which still exists in an altered form, provides the setting.

*T*he Chimay Attic in the
course of remodeling. Visible is a
fragment of J.-L. David's painting
of the Tennis Court Oath, begun
in 1790 and never completed.

Grand Commun, behind the left Ministers' Wing (1682); the Office of the Overseer of the King's Buildings (1683, rue de l'Indépendance Américaine, formerly rue de la Surintendance, at the corner of the rue de l'Orangerie); the Large Kennels, behind the Stables (1685); and the Tennis Court (1686). Additional subsidiary facilities, ever larger and more numerous, also rose in the château's vicinity. A tennis court or *jeu de paume* (actually, courts designed for an archaic form of racket ball no longer played) was considered a necessary complement to any aristocratic residence: under Louis XIII there were two at Versailles, an enclosed one for the version of the game known as *la courte paume* and another open-air court for *la longue paume*. These have now disappeared, like most such facilities. The one built under Louis XIV has survived by historical chance: it was here that the famous oath of 1789 was sworn. The Grand Commun, built of mixed brick and stone, is also well preserved, as are the Stables, which are likewise constructed, save for the façades facing the château, which are entirely of stone.

The ensemble composed of the Large and Small Stables is Mansart's masterpiece. No need to seek an emblematic reading of their horseshoe shaped plans, so admirably adapted to the encompassing crow's-foot. The generous use of cornices, the windows inscribed within an arcade, the horizontal rustication, the quality of the detailing, the handling of the vaults, the mansard roofs—all are in the best French tradition. But it might be argued that these components had never before been manipulated with such virtuosity. Particularly remarkable is the masterful use of cornice work to organize the elevations facing the courts and to emphasize their central portals.

Under Louis XV, in 1759–61, additional buildings were constructed between the Grand Commun and the Office of the Overseer of the King's Buildings, namely two *hôtels* intended to house the Ministry of Foreign Affairs and that of the Navy (rue de l'Indépendance Américaine). These buildings, the work of Jean-Baptiste Berthier, author of the Hunting Map discussed earlier, seem to have been the first such ministerial offices in the history of French architecture. Previously French administrators had improvised their accommodations in structures designed for other purposes, notably palaces. Here

Berthier solved a new problem with exceptional ingenuity. To assure proper conservation of state archives, he used brick partitions to divide the interior spaces and replaced the usual combustible floorboards with brick vaults, a form of construction used in the Mediterranean for centuries and known as Saracen or Catalan vaults. The exceptional interest of such vaulting had only recently been noted by the Academy of Architecture; Berthier was among the first to use it in northern France. In a building shared by two ministries (until 1789, when the Navy was transferred to the building on the Place de la Concorde in Paris where it remains to this day), the Ministry of Foreign Affairs disposed of the handsome second floor. Here were kept, in seven superbly decorated rooms, all the official correspondence, memoranda, treaties, agreements, and reports documenting the diplomatic life of the French monarchy.

The building housing the Menus-Plaisirs (1748), built under Louis XV on the avenue de Paris, rates only a summary mention, but such is not the case for the administration it housed, which assumed surprising importance under Louis XVI. It was responsible for ephemeral decoration of all kinds during a reign when the monarchy had few resources at its disposal for permanent building projects. The queen, whose appetite for new spaces and decors was insatiable, commissioned the fabrication of portable interior suites whose luxurious appointments were designed by the Menus-Plaisirs' most experienced artists. For the carnival of 1787, Versailles's last, a temporary wood-frame village was built on the Southern Terrace that included reception rooms, ballrooms, and theaters. One of these large interiors was subsequently installed, with minor modifications, in the Hôtel des Menus-Plaisirs to accommodate the recently convened Assembly of Notables and Estates General. It was within a space conceived for the queen's pleasure that representatives of the nation first signaled that the "fête" was at an end. And the collective oath by which that nation was reconstituted would be sworn in a tennis court, subsequently acknowledged as the "cradle of the new religion, its Bethlehem manger" (Michelet). Thus the events marking the old regime's end unfolded within jerry-built, temporary walls.

Courtyard of the Large Stables, built by Jules Hardouin-Mansart in 1679. Under Louis XIV the royal stables occupied two other sites before moving into these quarters within the crow's-foot. The semicircular disposition of the court skillfully solves the problem of integrating a monumental design into a triangular site.

The portal of the Large Stables is a masterpiece within a masterpiece. Hardouin-Mansart was highly skilled in the typically French art of detailing: here the play of moldings and projections creates a rich multileveled effect. The idea of having horses spring forth from the tympanum of the doorway, which would often be imitated in eighteenth-century stables, was probably born at Versailles.

*B*ELOW, OPPOSITE, AND FOLLOWING PAGES: *The Small Stables. It now shelters the plaster casts formerly in the Ecole des Beaux-Arts, acquired in the nineteenth century to serve as models for the school's students and removed in the wake of the student uprisings of May 1968. The horse is copied from the celebrated quadriga of San Marco in Venice.*

"REJECTION OF THE ABUSES ENTAILS REJECTION OF THE ENTIRE STRUCTURE"

I have before my eyes, in writing these lines, the great marvel of royal France, Versailles. In my mind's eye I summon up many of the figures from that vanished age. In the center, the king; here, Condé and the princes; over there in that walk, Bossuet and the bishops; here in the theater, Racine, Lully, Molière, and already a few freethinkers; there on the stairways of the Orangery, Madame de Sévigné and the great ladies; in the distance, within the melancholy walls of Saint-Cyr, Madame de Maintenon and her boredom. Here is a civilization vulnerable to criticism, certainly, but perfectly unified and complete; a manifestation of the human spirit like many another. After all is said and done, it would have been a great pity for it not to have existed. And of course it never could have, but in exchange for terrible sacrifices. The degradation of the people, arbitrary and capricious judgments, court intrigues and lettres de cachet, *the Bastille, the gallows, and the Great Days of ritual punishment are essential components of this edifice, such that rejection of the abuses entails rejection of the entire structure. . . . From the individual's perspective, absolute liberty and equality are natural rights. The species as a whole, however, comprehends that government and inequality are perpetual companions. It is preferable to have a brilliant manifestation of humanity, in the king and the court, than only a general mediocrity. Our little system of middle-class government whose fundamental aspirations are to guarantee the rights and procure the well-being of each and all is based on an individualist vision and is incapable of producing anything truly great. Could Louis XIV have built Versailles if he had been obliged to face off with surly deputies determined to prune his budgets?*

Ernest Renan, L'Avenir de la science, *1848,*
published in 1890

*B*ELOW AND FOL-
LOWING PAGES: *Sculpture
stored in the Large Stables. Many
original works from the gardens
are now kept here under protective
cover; some of these once adorned
bosquets that no longer exist, while
others have been replaced by copies.* OPPOSITE: *Cupid by
Tuby, designed for the Labyrinth
(destroyed).*

HYMN TO LIGHT

A hymn to light as the source of order, Versailles is truly the last palace of the sun, a poem composed in stone, greenery, and water, in every respect the most beautiful work, and the most significant, of our seventeenth century. A single idea is accorded clear dominance, but without becoming oppressive. Here chance plays no part in the expression of truth, or in the play of fancy. Not only the eyes are captivated, but also the soul, the heart, the imagination, and the intelligence. Its effects are achieved with a straightforward symbolism that our modern, technical, and urban-oriented culture should learn once more. Versailles is a poem that joins antiquity to the contemporary world, an admirable attempt at synthesis crowned by the glory of God.

Gérard Van der Kemp, Versailles, *1977*

BELOW: *Coronation
carriage of Charles X, fabricated
in 1825 by the carriage maker
Daldringen and the bronze specialists and sculptors Denière,
Matelin, and Roguier, after a design by the architect Charles Per-
cier, now in the Large Stables. The
imperial emblems were added in
1856 for the baptism of the prince
imperial. OPPOSITE: The "Victory" carriage, dating from the
First Empire. Its arms were re-
painted under Napoleon III.*

Chapter 4
THE GARDENS AND THE TRIANONS

LEFT: The Baths of Apollo. Horses by the Marsy brothers. OPPOSITE: The Marble Trianon or Large Trianon. The interior of the central gallery, or peristyle, with a view of the courtyard. The arcade openings were closed with door-windows in the Napoleonic period. Recent removal of these door frames would seem to have restored this feature to the state envisioned by Louis XIV.

Opposite: Bird's-eye view. Painting by P.-D. Martin (1724; Versailles Museum). The eccentric plan of the Large Trianon is due in part to retention and reuse of basic structural elements of the Porcelain Trianon. The large wing extending toward the horizon contains the gallery; its far end occupies the site where the Pavillion des Parfums, or Scent Pavilion, once stood. The wing diverging from this point to the right—the only portion of the building whose stone is not faced with marble—is known as the Trianon-sous-bois.

The close relation of garden design to the art of architecture is clearly demonstrated by the history of Versailles. The entire area encompassed by the Hunting Map (including both the Small Park and the Hunting Park) underwent a process of careful "architectural" restructuring until the end of the old regime. Not much can be said about the Hunting Park, so it often goes completely unmentioned; when we speak of the "Park of Versailles" today, the Small Park is generally meant. This latter is difficult to overlook: it contains two large bodies of water—the Grand Canal and the Pool of the Swiss Guards—as well as the Trianon complex. The gardens proper also contain some structures of real significance, such as the Orangery and the Colonnade.

Bird's-eye view, drawing by I. Silvestre circa 1690 (Louvre Museum). Note the correspondence between the gardens and the town, whose overall disposition echoes that traced by the fountains and bosquets.

THE GARDENS UNDER LOUIS XIII

Parterre du Chasteau de verssaille

The bounds of the gardens of Louis XIII were more or less the same as those of Louis XIV. The ensemble, which constituted a rough square, was divided into rectangles by a network of walkways. At the end of the central walk, which was given no more emphasis than the others, was a basin of water known as the Rondeau (later replaced by the Apollo Fountain) marking the western extremity of the gardens proper. Diagonal walks emanated outward from the central one. Little is now known about the bosquets situated within the rectangles. In front of the château was an area known as the Western Terrace, one of the first such in France to feature *broderie*: garden "embroidery" composed of shrubbery or flowers planted in ribbon patterns set off by sand or fine gravel and surrounded by low plant beds or hedges. "Embroidered" terrace designs were somewhat different from the geometric patterns used previously, being characterized by a greater amplitude and an emphatic, if sinuously elaborate, symmetry. Two gardeners working at Versailles have claimed the honor of inventing this design concept, Jacques Boyceau de La Baraudière and Claude Mollet. They are also the first theoreticians of the French pleasure garden: Boyceau wrote a *Traité de jardinage selon les raisons de la nature et de l'art* (1638, published after his death), while Mollet authored *Théâtre des plan[t]s et jardinages contenant des secrets et inventions incognuës* (1652, also published posthumously).

Work on the gardens of Versailles was begun in 1631, when Louis XIII began to transform his house into a château. The initial plans were formulated by Jacques de Menours, Jacques Boyceau's nephew, and probably by Boyceau himself: an illustration of the "embroidered" terrace realized at Versailles was published in his treatise. Boyceau, perhaps best known for having designed the gardens of the Luxembourg Palace, died in 1635. He was succeeded by the team of Claude Mollet and Hilaire Masson, who oversaw a first redesign in 1639.

Claude Mollet claimed to have invented "embroidered" plantings in the gardens for Saint-Germain-en-Laye by applying ideas proposed to him by Du Pérac, who had first designed its grounds. At the time these were the most celebrated gardens in France. Exploiting the exceptional site, beginning in the late sixteenth century Du Pérac had created terraced gardens there on the Italian model. It was also at Saint-Germain that Thomas Francini first emerged, forebear of the Francine dynasty, whose members would subsequently construct much of the waterworks at Versailles. But in 1630 the gardens there paled in comparison with those of Saint-Germain.

The Southern Terrace.

THE GARDENS DURING LOUIS XIV'S
FIRST CAMPAIGN

The greater part of the funds allocated for Louis XIV's first building campaign at Versailles (1661–68) was spent on the gardens, particularly on terracing the terrain and draining the low-lying lands. Along the east-west axis Le Nôtre extended the Western Terrace by construction of another, lower terrace (1664–65; the future site of the Latona Fountain). He also widened the central walk (1667; the future Royal Walk), which gently sloped down to the Rondeau; began excavation of the Grand Canal (1667); and established a crow's-foot configuration at the far side of the Rondeau that imposed a pattern on the park.

THE GARDENS OF THE GODS

Never have these banks been without zephyrs;
Here, where Flora basks in the music of their sighs,
Oft the surrounding nymphs, when the night is thick
Bathe together under its sheltering darkness.
The sites I have described, the canal, the rondeau,
The terrace with its design so pleasant and new,
The amphitheaters, fountains, all answer the palace,
But none of these beauties is lost or confused.
Happy are those capable of such invention!
Prior to this precinct such beauties were unknown.
All parks were orchards in the time of our ancestors,
And all orchards parks; the knowledge of these masters
Transforms simple plant beds into royal gardens,
As it makes of a king's gardens those of the gods.

La Fontaine, Les Amours de Psyché et de Cupidon, *1669*

In the process of creating the first Northern and Southern Terraces, Le Nôtre established a transverse axis passing through the château's court. To the north the natural slope of the terrain was retained, while to the south this was modified by construction of an Orangery (1663) that supported the Southern Terrace. This last was decorated with *broderie* composed of flowers and grass and was enclosed by an ironwork fence supported by terms—pedestals with emerging figures. The Northern Terrace (1664) was composed of large tracts of lawn. The area covered by these two terraces would subsequently be doubled, shifting the transverse axis farther to the west so that it bypassed the Envelope façade but allowed for basic retention of the original disposition. Green lawns were prominently used here. Could this reflect an early English influence on French garden design? In his *Dictionnaire d'architecture* (1693), Charles Daviler proposed one of these arrangements at Versailles as a typically "English" terrace. Curiously, however, he points not to the Northern Terrace, with its prominent use of lawns, but rather to the Southern Terrace. It seems likely that this designation was a simple error.

The history of the *boulingrin* (bowling green) of Saint-Germain, one of the first in France, lends support to this hypothesis. It was created in the 1660s, when Henrietta of England married Monsieur, the king's brother, on whom the new château there had been conferred. Its green was a large sodded area, slightly depressed, in principle designed for bowling (actually, the game of *boules*, a French variant); originally it was known as the *bouloir de gazon* or bowling lawn (A. Mollet, *Le Jardin des plaisirs*, 1651). The word *boulingrin*, documented in French usage from 1663, comes from the English "bowling green."

The first bosquets were installed in these same years. Those known as the Bosquet of the Waterspout (Bosquet de la Girandole) and the Bosquet of the Dauphin, to either side of the future Royal Walk, are documented from 1663 (in 1775 they were replaced by the two so-called Quincunxes). The idea of the maze had already been exploited in medieval gardens. The one at Versailles was a shaded labyrinth whose intersections were subsequently fitted out with thirty-two fountains illustrating various episodes from Aesop's fables. This idea was probably due to Charles Perrault, author of the famous *Mother Goose Tales.*

Full-grown trees were uprooted and brought to Versailles to adorn its walks and bosquets: elms and lindens from the forests of Compiègne, beeches and oaks from Normandy, green oaks from Dauphiné; many were transplanted from the greenhouses of Vaux-le-Vicomte, confiscated from Fouquet. It was in this period that Madame de Sévigné wrote of having seen on the surrounding roads "entire leafy forests on their way to Versailles."

During Louis XIV's first campaign the park and gardens were enriched by two structures whose fame was as great as their existence was ephemeral: the Menagerie and the Grotto of Thetis.

The Southern Terrace. In the background, the Pool of the Swiss Guards.

*T*OP: *The Menagerie, engraving by Pérelle. The Menagerie was constructed by Le Vau in 1662–64. The crossbar of the Grand Canal would be built to facilitate rapid waterborne passage between the Menagerie and Trianon. BOTTOM: Façade of the Grotto of Thetis (engraving by P. Le Pautre, 1672). Begun in 1664, the grotto was destroyed in* 1684 *to make way for the Northern Wing. The work was probably the result of a collaborative effort in which Claude Perrault, Charles Le Brun, Louis Le Vau, the waterworks expert Denis Jolly, and the rockwork craftsman Delaunay all participated. The Francine brothers may also have been involved. The grilles on the doors bear representations of the sun's rays.*

The Menagerie was built by Le Vau, at the point where the left arm of the Grand Canal would terminate, in 1662 or 1663 (the earliest known construction records concern the roofing and date from January 1664). The taste for such zoos dates back to antiquity and persisted through the Middle Ages. It has proved impossible to establish an exhaustive list of the species kept at the Ver-

sailles Menagerie, though we know there was an abundance of birds—pheasants, pelicans, ostriches—as well as many small mammals and members of the deer family, and dogs, horses, and cows. Thus it was simultaneously a kennel, a farmyard, and a place for breeding horses. More exotic animals would arrive toward the end of the century, but the principal attraction of the Menagerie was the building itself. It was composed of a central block with two prominent pavilions at either end; in its rear was an oblong extension with a second-floor gallery culminating in an octagonal rotunda. It has been noted that this plan is phallic in shape; although it cannot be proven that this was intentional, the observation facilitates comprehension of the complex plan. The rotunda was in the center of a court surrounded by radiating enclosures; a ring of second-floor balconies allowed for easy viewing of the animals. The ground floor was decorated to suggest a grotto. The central block with its end pavilions contained only two suites of reception rooms intended for daytime use. From the entrance located in this block, the courts and cages behind were invisible; when one arrived in the rotunda via the gallery, the effect was one of total surprise.

The Grotto of Thetis was placed near the château, thus necessitating its demolition to allow for construction of the Northern Wing in 1684. It was a small rectangular pavilion topped by a reservoir open to the sky. Access to the interior was through three arches whose grillwork gates were ornamented with depictions of the sun and its rays. "It seemed as though the sun was within the grotto and visible beyond its doors (Charles Perrault, *Mémoires*). Its interior, entirely covered with shells and multicolored stones, housed a water-operated organ and, most important, a sculptural ensemble representing Apollo attended by nymphs as well as the horses of the sun. Fortunately, the fame of these three sculpted groups saved them from destruction; moved several times, toward the end of the eighteenth century they would come to a final rest in the bosquet of the Baths of Apollo. The Grotto of Thetis was begun in 1664, and the original intention was to build nothing more than a *château d'eau*, or water tower; the sculpture was not installed until ten years later. The Perrault brothers claimed credit for both the idea and the design of the grotto. It was probably Charles Le Brun who designed its sculptural groups, as he did for

BELOW: The Baths of Apollo. In the center one sees Apollo attended by Nereids, by Girardon and Regnaudin. On the left are rearing horses by the Marsy brothers; on the right, horses at rest by Guérin.

FOLLOWING PAGES. LEFT: The Grotto of Thetis. Engraving by P. Le Pautre (1672). RIGHT: The Baths of Apollo. The grotto was begun in 1664; its sculptural elements were installed in 1674; it was demolished in 1684 to make way for the Northern Wing. The Baths of Apollo were created in 1776–78 by Hubert Robert as a setting for the sculptures from the Grotto of Thetis (1666–72). In the central group, Apollo and the two foremost Nereids are by Girardon; the remaining three Nereids are by Regnaudin; on the right are horses at rest by Guérin.

most of the park's sculpture. Le Vau was probably responsible for the final disposition of its façades. And the Francine family? Its field of expertise would seem to have determined its involvement with the project, for it is scarcely credible that these creators of the grottos of Saint-Germain, the models of the genre, would not have been consulted in planning the Grotto of Thetis. However, the only individuals mentioned in the documents are the waterworks specialist, Denis Jolly, and a rockwork craftsman named Delaunay.

"ON ONE SIDE A TRITON, ON THE OTHER A SIREN"

The grotto's interior is disposed in such a way
That all glances, confused, know not where to stay.
The ceiling and walls are preciously adorned
With rocks and shells that the sea has returned,
Or which enclose in their hearts minerals of earth
Rich in color, and arrayed in countless designs.
Above six pillars of like construction
Six masks of shell with grotesque expression,
Dreams of art touched with the bizarre,
Are visible above the principal niche.
This niche boasts a thousand things rare:
On one side a Triton, on the other a Siren,
Each holding a seashell in hands of stone;
From their breath a fountain leaps forth.
High in each niche a basin spreads the flow;
From deep in its throat the mask vomits it up;
It falls once again, composing a web,
And is as quickly gathered in another basin.
The rustle, the crash, and its clear transparency,
Which seems reminiscent of a crystal veil,
Excite a pleasure of a thousand pleasures mixed.
When the water stops and the crystal disappears,
There are mother-of-pearl and coral to delight:
Petrified stones, shells, and odd formations,
Infinite caprices born of chance and earth's waters,
Once more appear, yet more beautiful and brilliant.
In the depth of the grotto, embraced by an arcade,
Are marbles brought to life by art.
The god of these rocks, leaning on an urn,
Is in mournful repose, secure in his cavern.
Torrents fall, and the entire hollow partakes;
The waters form a river, leaving a trail of icicles.

La Fontaine, Les Amours de Psyché et du Cupidon, *1669*

Apollo attended by Nereids. Apollo and the two foremost Nereids are by Girardon; the remaining three Nereids are by Regnaudin. The figure of Apollo is directly inspired by the Apollo Belvedere, the celebrated antique work; but his identification with Louis XIV is effected by the depiction of the "Crossing of the Rhine" on the vase carried by one of the Nereids.

*A*BOVE: *Horses of the sun by the Marsy brothers. The horses of Apollo's chariot have just been unyoked. The majesty of the central Apollo group is in striking contrast with the agitation of these horses. The French school of sculpture can here be observed vacillating between emulation of the antique advocated by Le Brun, who probably provided drawings for these groups, and emulation of the baroque exemplified by Bernini. RIGHT: The horses of the chariot of the sun drinking water, a group executed by Guérin.*

THE GARDENS DURING LOUIS XIV'S SECOND CAMPAIGN

*T*he Water Walk or *Infants' Walk, created in 1670, realizing an idea suggested by Claude Perrault.*

During the second campaign, which saw construction of the Envelope (1668–78), sculpture was the main concern in the gardens. Le Brun's role as orchestrator and overseer was crucial here. The principal water basins were fitted out with their sculptural groups: the Latona Fountain in 1668, the Apollo Fountain in 1671, and the Fountains of the Seasons in 1672. In 1674 the so-called Great Commission (*Grande Commande*) was issued, whereby twenty-four statues were ordered to ornament the Water Terrace; in fact, the resulting works would be dispersed throughout the gardens. The Water Terrace was a set of water basins designed and built by d'Orbay (1672) on what subsequently became known as the Western Terrace, in front of the Envelope façade, from which it was separated only by a flight of stairs

that functioned visually as a kind of plinth for the façade. The Water Terrace would receive its definitive form and ornament only later under Mansart.

The Latona Fountain, below and beyond the Water Terrace, and the Apollo Fountain, which replaced the Rondeau, punctuate the central east-west axis, whose walk was widened once again (1674). The secondary walks of the initial grid were also ranked hierarchically, through their relation to four newly installed basins named after the four seasons.

The transverse axis was given new emphasis through creation of the Water Walk or Infants' Walk (Allée des Marmousets). This wide promenade gently sloping away to the north was composed of three parallel paths separated by two bands of lawn, each of which was ornamented with a series of seven fountains composed of small basins supported by children. According to Charles Perrault, credit for this idea is due to Claude Perrault. The fourteen fountains were installed in 1670; eight others were added in 1678, being distributed around the periphery of the semicircular area to which the walk led and which also contained the Dragon Fountain. Somewhat farther on, the Neptune Fountain would be installed (1676), though most of its sculpted ornament would be completed only in 1738.

Beginning in 1669, the Grand Canal was home for a fleet of boats whose great variety would have been worthy of a naval museum, replete as it was with dinghies, longboats, gondolas, hoys, yawls, yachts, feluccas, barges, half-galleys, galleys, and frigates. These craft were built in the shipyards of Dunkerque, Rouen, Marseilles, and Venice (the gondolas were given to Louis XIV by the Venetian Republic), or in Versailles's own "Petite Venise." This was a village, or rather an enclosed town, built in 1674 at the head of the Grand Canal and inhabited exclusively by sailors. These latter—Venetian, Genoese, or French—were legally incorporated, and the resulting community was governed as a kind of republic with its own rules. Membership

in the corporation was much sought after and was passed down from generation to generation, like most privileges and benefits under the old regime.

To accommodate this fleet, the Grand Canal was considerably enlarged (1671): at its far end a half-star of pathways radiated into the Hunting Park. Simultaneously, a perpendicular crossbar was added that had not previously been envisaged; its extensions allowed for waterborne passage between the Menagerie and Trianon, where the king built a residence.

THE PORCELAIN TRIANON

The Porcelain Trianon, as depicted by Aveline (before 1687). Built by Le Vau in 1670, the central building housed two apartments; the pavilions, of progressively smaller dimensions, were used to store and serve food and drink. To give the complex an à la chinoise look, all the walls were faced with blue faience and the roofs were decorated with vases, animals, and children.

The first royal house at Trianon, known as the Porcelain Trianon, was Le Vau's last building (at least, it is all but certain that he was its author). The village of Trianon was purchased in January 1668; the house was built in a few clement months in 1670. It became famous immediately, both for its conceit of imitating Chinese architecture and for the speed with which it was erected. In the words of André Félibien: "Everyone held this place to be an enchantment: begun only at winter's close, it was finished before the end of spring, as if it had sprung from the ground with the flowers of its surrounding gardens" (*Description de Versailles*, 1674).

Like the Menagerie, the Porcelain Trianon had been designed for day trips—gastronomic forays, judging from the kitchen and dining facilities that figured so prominently there. Since the Envelope had definitively changed the scale of the private house that had once been Versailles and allotted an equal prominence to the queen's quarters, Trianon became the choice locale for the king's pursuit of illicit pleasures. The oblong building contained, in addition to an entry hall and central salon, two symmetrically disposed reception rooms, one of which was often occupied by the beautiful Montespan. A cluster of detached pavilions of progressively smaller dimensions bordered a main courtyard and two subsidiary ones, accommodating various kitchen-related service facilities (maintenance, tableware, vegetables, appetizers, main dishes, desserts, fruit, jams and jellies). These pavilions were faced entirely with blue and white faience: the square tiles were from Delft, while Saint-Cloud, Rouen, Lisieux, and Nevers all contributed some of the more elaborate decorative elements—vases, birds, and cupids—ornamenting their upper reaches. "On the entablature," wrote Félibien, "there is a balustrade filled with numerous vases, and the entire roof is a kind of crown, its lower portion covered with young cupids armed with darts and arrows chasing animals. Above these, ascending rows of vases mount to the culminating peak, with many naturalistic representations of birds." From top to bottom, inside and out, all was covered with ceramic "in the style of works of Chinese origin" (Félibien). Even the furniture was painted blue and white in imitation of porcelain.

The use of such facing was not unprecedented in France, for the château de Madrid, built by Francis I in the Bois de Boulogne, had also used it. But the Trianon was inspired by a very different model. Mazarin had made China fashionable. Reports from missionary envoys had conveyed something of the character of Chinese architecture: *Chine illustrée*, ca. 1670, by the German Jesuit Athanasius Kircher, for example, included a depiction of the nine-story Tower of Nanking, entirely encased in porcelain. The market for porcelain, lacquer, and silk from

"Lachine" (as it was often designated in this period) was strong. An English and Dutch monopoly on such articles was broken by the establishment of a French import concern known as the Compagnie des Indes Orientales (1664). Sensitive to the challenge this represented, French artisans, furniture makers, and tile makers attempted to compete through use of substitute procedures until learning, in the eighteenth century, the Oriental techniques for production of porcelain and lacquer that had previously been a closely guarded secret.

The craze for things Chinese had considerable impact on the evolution of the decorative arts, but its importance for the development of architecture was even greater. The Porcelain Trianon, while not truly Chinese in character, marks the advent of an eclectic tendency that would have an enormous impact on architectural history; subsequently, imitation of exotic models would completely upset the established system of architectural references in Western Europe. Claude Perrault had proposed to Colbert that the Louvre should contain public rooms decorated "in the various styles of the world's most celebrated nations—Italy, Germany, Turkey, Persia, Mongolia, Siam, China." Such rooms would serve to demonstrate to visiting ambassadors from these countries that "France encapsulates the world." Doubtless the ambition was to emulate the palace of the empress of China, which constituted "a survey of all that the most famous nations of the universe have to offer that is beautiful, singular, or rare" (caption of a seventeenth-century engraving depicting the empress).

If one links the construction of the first Trianon with the fact that the most grandiose ambassadorial re-

ceptions in Versailles's annals were mounted for the Turks, the Persians, and the Siamese, an underlying political program is suggested. Louis XIV, whose emblematic device was *Nec pluribus impar* (literally, "not unequal to most"; more idiomatically, "equaled by few" or "matchless"), nonetheless regarded himself as without par on earth, save perhaps the emperor of China, East and West being different worlds. Contemporary descriptions of China, more or less fanciful, often drew the parallel between the Sun King and the "Great King of the Tartars."

Louis XIV had a passionate interest in flowers, and the Trianon gardens were given over to rare species. "The flowers in the beds of its terraces were changed every day," wrote Saint-Simon, "and I have been present when the king and the entire court were driven from their vicinity by the perfume issuing from the tuberoses, which was so strong that, despite the open site bordering the canal, no one could remain in the garden." There were three basic groups of plants deployed here: tuberoses (tulips, narcissi, hyacinths), small perennials (rocket plants, veronica, sweet william, knapweed, rose campion, violets), and larger perennials (chamomile, bluebell, gillyflower, white lilies, Greek valerian, anemone, Spanish jasmine, narcissi of Constantinople). It is believed that in the period of its glory Trianon boasted 96,000 plants in its beds and 2 million in pots. There was even a Perfume Room, at a slight distance from the pavilions, in which those plants with the strongest odors were assembled. The mastermind behind these wonders was the gardener-horticulturist Michel Le Bouteux. He even developed a method for cultivating orange trees in the ground, by enclosing them in portable greenhouses through the winter.

THE GARDENS DURING LOUIS XIV'S THIRD CAMPAIGN

The Bosquet of the Domed Pavilions. Engraving published by Mariette. The Bosquet of Fame, conceived by Le Nôtre in 1675, was transformed into the Bosquet of the Domed Pavilions (Bosquet des Dômes) following Hardouin-Mansart's addition of the two pavilions in 1677. The sculptural groups from the Grotto of Thetis were installed in this bosquet between 1684 and 1704. Note the trellis walls, or palissades de treillage, which, after Mansart's appointment, replaced the palissades of trees clipped into rectangular blocks.

In the course of the third building campaign (1678–88), Mansart put an end to Le Brun's dominance and entered into stiff competition with Le Nôtre in his own sphere of activity. As a result of Le Brun's disgrace, the statuary produced for the Great Commission was not installed on the Water Terrace as originally intended. Le Nôtre retained the king's favor until his death (1700), but Mansart, no doubt encouraged by the king's taste for novelty, seems to have done his best to remodel the bosquets he had designed. Mansart's first work at Versailles was construction of two domed pavilions (1677) that so altered the appearance of the Bosquet of Fame

(Bosquet de la Renommée) created by Le Nôtre in 1675, that its very name was changed as a result. This Bosquet of the Domed Pavilions was widely admired; its pavilions (now destroyed) introduced innovations of great importance in the history of the decorative arts that will be discussed in a later chapter.

It is not always easy to distinguish the respective contributions of Mansart and Le Nôtre during this campaign. The Tapis Vert, the band of lawn running down the center of the Royal Walk, which was widened yet again in 1680, is generally attributed to Le Nôtre by virtue of its consistency with his original conception of the central perspective. On the other hand, Mansart was essentially responsible for transformation of the southern arm of transverse axis. Le Vau's Orangery, whose destruction was rendered unavoidable by construction of the Southern Wing, was reconstituted farther to the west along more ambitious lines, entailing a complete recasting of the Southern Terrace. Outside the borders of the garden proper, in the park, the Pool of the Swiss Guards was excavated (1678–82), which was a sort of southern Grand Canal extending from the front of the new Orangery.

Construction of the latter (1684) would confirm Mansart's preeminence. Critics of Mansart's production, whose assessments have often been severe, are unanimous in their praise of the Orangery. Yet its originality is far from obvious. It is sited similarly to Le Vau's structure; the disposition of its façade, with an arcade cut into banded rustication, is a commonplace of French architecture; and the conception of its masonry vaults, superbly executed, geometric in their precision, powerful and naked like an athlete, builds upon the rich tradition of French stereotomy. Even the idea for the framing exterior Stairways of the Hundred Steps (Cents Marches) was appropriated from Le Vau. However, the dimensions of the new structure were considerably larger than those

The Royal Walk with
its lawn. In the foreground,
Cyparisse and Her Deer by
Anselme Flamen (1687–88),
probably executed after a design
by Girardon.

*T*OP: *View along the transverse axis from south to north. In the foreground, the façade of the Orangery and the Southern Terrace.*

*B*OTTOM: *View of the Southern Wing. To the lower left, the rue de l'Indépendance Américaine. In the center, the Southern Terrace with its two unadorned circular pools. To the upper left, the terrace in front of the Orangery and one end of the Pool of the Swiss Guards.*

*R*IGHT: *View along the transverse axis from south to north. In the foreground, the edge of the Pool of the Swiss Guards and the Saint-Cyr highway. Beyond, the terrace in front of the Orangery, flanked by the two Stairways of the Hundred Steps. Above the Orangery, the Southern Terrace.*

of the old (the new central gallery was 510 feet long and 69 feet wide), and this change necessitated a fundamental rethinking of the design concept as well as of technical procedures. In an account of the 1686 visit of the Siamese ambassador to Versailles, an author for the *Mercure galant* wrote as follows of the Orangery: "The interior is bare of all sculptural and architectural ornament, while, as is necessary in this kind of building, the contrivance of the vaults is of the greatest beauty. . . . It is this that provoked the first ambassador to remark that the magnificence of the king was indeed extraordinary, if he provided so superb a structure to house his orange trees." In the view of Jacques-François Blondel, the Orangery was "of a magnificence worthy of the Romans" and "one of Europe's marvels" (*Architecture française*, 1752–56).

Mansart's structure was all the more conspicuous, given the rarity of orange trees in seventeenth-century France, where an orangery on one's property entailed great social prestige. Louis XIV was quite enamored of orange trees; his collection of two thousand in box planters was unrivaled in Europe. Characteristically, he did not shrink from the use of force in assembling it; many of its plants had been seized from the collections of his subjects. The oldest and tallest of these orange trees, known as the High Constable (Connétable), dated back to the first ar-

LEFT: One of the Stairways of the Hundred Steps. BELOW: The Orangery, built by Hardouin-Mansart in 1684. It exploits and regularizes the sloping terrain, supporting the Southern Terrace above. It is framed by the two large Stairways of the Hundred Steps. It is entirely vaulted in fitted stone. Here, the vaulting underneath one of the stairways.

rival of such trees in France in the wake of the Italian wars. The first orange trees to reach France arrived at Blois in the fifteenth century. The High Constable was purportedly first planted in Pamplona, brought to France by the connétable de Bourbon, and confiscated by Francis I, who brought it to Fontainebleau. However, a variant history traced its origins to the collection of the connétable de Montmorency at Chantilly. In any case, in 1623 its presence is documented at Fontainebleau, whence Louis XIV subsequently had it transported to Versailles. Whichever of the two stories is accurate, the nickname "High Constable" remains appropriate. It is also sometimes called "le Bourbon," which is problematic, and sometimes "le Grand Condé," which is even less justifiable. Several trees have doubtless shared a common history.

The Bosquet of the Ballroom (Bosquet de la Salle de Bal, 1680), is one of the few bosquets by Le Nôtre that Mansart spared. This is a bipartite amphitheater, consisting of a tiered, sodded embankment to accommodate spectators and another of gritted millstone set with exotic shells down which water could be made to flow. Dancers moved through the intervening area, while musicians were placed above the artificial waterfall.

LEFT: The Orangery. Above, the Southern Wing is visible. BELOW: The terrace in front of the Orangery. During the warm months the palm trees are exposed to the elements.

*B*ELOW AND OPPO-
SITE: *The Orangery. Built entirely of fitted stone, this structure
is a masterpiece of stereotomy, an
art of central importance in France
since the Middle Ages. Its barrel
vault follows the basic disposition
of the Orangery's plan. The window bays are subvaults penetrat-
ing into the supporting walls of
the main vault.*

*F*OLLOWING PAGES.
LEFT: *A statue of Louis XIV by
Desjardins, given to Louis XIV by
the maréchal de La Feuillade. This
statue, though mutilated during the
Revolution, has survived in restored form, whereas its twin in the
Place des Victoires in Paris was
destroyed.*

Louis XIV first laid eyes on Bernini's equestrian statue of him in the Orangery. By a stroke of luck, the timing of the statue's recent, momentary return to this space allowed us to photograph it there. Commissioned in 1665 and completed prior to 1673, the statue reached Versailles only in 1685, when the king took an instant dislike to it and had it exiled to the far end of the Pool of the Swiss Guards.

PORTRAIT OF LOUIS XIV

He was very fond of fresh air and exercise, as much as he could take. He had excelled at the dance, at the game of mail [an ancestor of badminton], and at tennis. Old as he was, he still rode well. He loved to see all these activities executed with grace and style. . . . He was fond of archery, and no one could handle a bow and arrow with greater mastery or superior grace. . . . He was also partial to deer hunting, but from an open carriage, after having broken his arm in pursuit on foot at Fontainebleau soon after the death of the queen. He did this alone, in a kind of hooded carriage drawn by four small horses that were changed five or six times, and that he drove all by himself at full tilt, with a skill and dexterity surpassing that of the best coachmen, and marked by his habitual grace. His postboys were children between nine or ten and fifteen years of age whom he supervised personally.

Saint-Simon

VERSAILLES OR GUERMANTES

Between the last entertainment of the summer and winter's exile, one wanders anxiously in this picturesque realm of potential encounters and sentimental melancholy, and one would be no more surprised to discover that it was outside the geographic universe altogether than if, from the upper terrace at Versailles, an observatory around which clouds accumulate against a blue sky in the style of Van der Meulen, having thus transcended nature, one discovered that over there where her domain begins once more, at the far end of the grand canal, the villages discernible against a horizon as ravishing as the sea were called Fleurus or Nijmegen.

Marcel Proust, A la recherche du temps perdu:
Le Côté de Guermantes, 1920

With its shellwork reminiscent of the Grotto of Thetis, the Bosquet of the Ballroom had come to seem a bit outdated by the time Mansart built the Colonnade (1684), whose integral use of French marbles was in itself a rather "modern" gesture. The Colonnade is a ring of arcades with thirty-six columns, a kind of classical round temple, but roofless. Its white marble blends handsomely with its purple breccia and blue turquoise, all from quarries in Languedoc and the Pyrenees that Colbert had reactivated in view of providing an alternative to Italian marble. Among other things, the Colonnade was intended to promote usage of such indigenous material. "This work demonstrates that the king is the most magnificent of earthly princes and signals that marble is currently more easily available in France than in Italy," wrote the editor of the *Mercure galant* (1686). According to Saint-Simon, when Louis XIV asked Le Nôtre for his assessment of the Colonnade, he replied: "Well, sire, what would you have me say? You have made a gardener of a stonemason, and he has given you a straightforward demonstration of his craft." This anecdote is probably apocryphal, but it accurately reflects the rivalry of these two artists.

In any case, Le Nôtre did not lack for a motive to denigrate Mansart's Colonnade, for it had replaced the

Bosquet of the Wellsprings (Bosquet des Sources) that he had created in 1679. This bosquet, with its curving walks and sinuous interwoven streamlets, was perhaps the earliest indication of a turn toward a more natural, or rather, less rigorously geometric approach to garden design in France. One should probably dismiss the possibility of a precocious influence of Chinese gardens here. However, Le Nôtre managed to get even with Mansart by creating at Trianon—Mansart's domain—a new Garden of the Wellsprings that was essentially a re-creation of the earlier bosquet. Le Nôtre himself described it as follows: "Here streams follow serpentine courses without apparent order, tracing circles around trees, with waterspouts placed irregularly throughout." And he added: "This is the only garden . . . that I find pleasant to walk through, and the most beautiful. I leave the imposing and the grand to others." This last remark—an implicit criticism of the approach of the French garden largely formulated by Le Nôtre himself—is particularly revealing of the competitive tension between him and Mansart, who is reputed to have reintroduced "natural" effects into French garden design. At Marly, where the initial phase of construction coincided with the third building campaign, the gardens were designed by Mansart. In the eighteenth century they were often contrasted with those of Versailles: in the words of one commentator, "Haughty souls will frequent Versailles to loftily engage with their like, and to admire its artistic marvels and the magnificence surrounding them; more sensitive souls prefer the bosquets of Marly, ideal for dreaming and delicious conversation, where they can calmly indulge a taste for artistic beauty less remote from that of nature" (Bricaire de La Dixmerie, 1765).

Mansart had sensed the change in the wind earlier than Le Nôtre; but paradoxically, it was perhaps Le Nôtre himself who had initiated the change. In any case, he will remain forever identified as the creator of the classic French garden, which would be harshly criticized in the eighteenth century. These criticisms at least have the advantage of clarifying the originality of the gardens of Versailles, "whose magnificence astonishes, but which rebuff all possibility of casual use," in the words of Saint-Simon. "Areas of refreshing shade are accessible only by traversing a vast, sun-baked zone, at the far side of which one has no option but to go up and down ceaselessly." In effect, the shaded areas are all at a considerable distance

The Bosquet of the Ballroom, or Bosquet of the Shellwork (rocaille). Engraving published by Mariette. Created by Le Nôtre in 1680, this is one of a small number of his bosquets to survive. The open space in the center was for dancing; the orchestra was placed above the cascade.

from the château, being separated from it by terraces, and the slope to which Saint-Simon refers is still in evidence. "If nature constrained, buried under a dressing of excessive symmetry and magnificence, if all that is artificial, extraordinary, strained, and bombastic makes for a beautiful garden, then Versailles is without equal," wrote Laugier in his *Essai sur l'architecture* (1753). Laugier was responding to the "embroidered" terraces and, above all, to the *palissades* or rows of trees with greenery carefully clipped into rectangular blocks suggestive of architectural massing. As hornbeam (*charme* in French) was particularly receptive to such topiary manipulation, this gardening device came to be designated generically as *charmille*. When the trees of Versailles grew too high to allow such clip-

ping, it was abandoned, but the clearings in the bosquets were still bordered by a variant form of *palissades* involving trellises covered with greenery. It was apparently at Clagny that Mansart and Le Nôtre first made extensive, systematic use of such trellis work, which served to impose a crisp architectural frame on the bosquets. Such use of what was, in effect, "four walls" was not to the taste of Laugier, who found the result "too enclosed" and judged that "the alignment and height [of the *charmilles*] transform garden walks into tiresome streets."

However, it must be understood that the natural effects advocated by French garden treatises of the early eighteenth century were very different from those that would become prevalent in its later decades under English influence. In the first half of the century only substitution of architectural greenery for masonry was in question: green replaced white, and clipped lawns invaded areas formerly given over to stone terraces. We have seen that such lawns had become fashionable as early as the mid-seventeenth century, with Versailles leading the way. As for *charmilles*, they disappeared from Versailles only at the end of the eighteenth century.

To a remarkable extent the evolution of French garden design was consistent with evolving ideas and social practice. The monarchy, which aimed to impose conformity on both animate and inanimate worlds, found in Le Nôtre its ideal official portraitist. But he was not alone. The celebrated gardener Jean de La Quintinie was overseer of the king's kitchen garden, established in its present site in 1679, during the third building campaign. It is not surprising that its plant beds were rectangular, for the most provincial of kitchen gardeners had never proceeded differently. But there are many different ways to organize such a garden within a rectangular grid. La Quintinie informs us in his *Instructions sur les jardins* (1690) that his garden was cast as an extension of the overall design concept. "It is above all necessary that [such a kitchen garden] please the eye.... The handsomest form for a cultivator of fruits and vegetables is a beautiful rectangle, especially when its corners are carefully squared and its length is one and a half or two times its width.... Views of neatly squared, carefully tended beds of strawberries, artichokes, and asparagus or of chervil, parsley, and sorrel afford great pleasure."

*L*EFT: *The Colonnade in an engraving published by Mariette. This structure was erected by Hardouin-Mansart in 1684. OPPOSITE: The Colonnade as it appears today.*

In the center of the Colonnade, *The Rape of Proserpina* by *Girardon* (*a copy; original executed 1677–99*).

THE MARBLE TRIANON

The transformation of the Porcelain Trianon into the Marble Trianon was one of the principal events of the third campaign. Not only had cracks appeared in the ceramic facings; in addition, the favorite for whom it had been built had fallen in the king's esteem.

The Marble Trianon rose as rapidly as the Porcelain Trianon, between June or July 1687 and January 1688, when Louis XIV first took luncheon there. At that point the interiors were largely incomplete, but the basic structural work was finished before the next outbreak of war. The structural frames of the extant pavilions were retained, as only their ceramic facings had deteriorated. Their incorporation into the new structure goes some way toward explaining the unusual plan of the Marble Trianon, notably its long gallery, which joined the former Perfume

The Large Trianon or Marble Trianon, built by Hardouin-Mansart and de Cotte in 1687–88. The idea for the peristyle, or open central porch, came from Louis XIV himself.

PRECEDING PAGE AND LEFT: Views from the peristyle's interior. Its colonnade opens freely onto the gardens. In the background, the wing containing the gallery is visible.

Room to the main building. The plan of Mansart's first proposed design, which attempted to encompass all the old pavilions, was even more eccentric. It was much simplified in the wake of the king's insistence on the peristyle, or central portico, which bridged the gap between two lateral pavilions of the former complex, while the old central pavilion, left detached by this scheme, was demolished.

It is clear that the peristyle was the king's own idea; Mansart had gone to the springs of Bourbon for reasons of health, and the king had working designs drafted by Robert de Cotte. We know from Saint-Simon (see the anecdote of the window earlier) that the monarch kept a very close eye on the work there, and the marquis de Sourches further corroborates this: "As the season was quite advanced when construction of this edifice was begun, and he wanted it to be completed before winter, he did all he could to hasten the work, going so far as to spend many afternoon hours under a tent at the site, where he worked on his affairs with Monsieur de Louvois and at the same time closely observed the progress of the construction" (*Mémoires*, published 1882–93). The correspondence between Louvois and Mansart confirms that the basic design decisions were all the king's. The phrase "columns disposed in a peristyle" occurs in a letter of September 18, 1687; the term "peristyle," while technically inappropriate, has been used ever since to designate the portico that pierces the center of the Marble Trianon, making its gardens visible from the entry court. This portico is composed of an open arcade facing the court and a row of columns facing the gardens; the king was also responsible for this unorthodox choice (letter of September 22). It has been claimed that the original intention was that the openings in the arcade be closed; in effect, their edges are still equipped with fittings to receive door frames. But these probably date from the Napoleonic period, when the peristyle had been enclosed on both its sides. The addition of frames for glazed doors would have masked the peristyle and impeded the view of the gardens from the courtyard, this last being the king's principal motivation for building the portico in the first place. Such central openings had long been in his thoughts: as early as the competition of June 1669 for redesign of the château, he had vainly expressed his desire "that there be views from the central court in all four directions" (Colbert, *Mémoires de ce que le roi désire*, June 8, 1669).

The king determined not only the general disposition of the building but many of its details as well. He insisted on the doubling of the peristyle's columns (letter from Louvois, September 28). He gave very precise instructions concerning the selection of materials (letter from Louvois to Villacerf, October 19). He prohibited use of mansard roofs such as those used in the Porcelain Trianon, which Mansart had proposed to repeat in his original design; according to the king, this roof treatment

gave the Trianon a character too close to that of an "oversized conventional house." Nothing was to appear above the culminating balustrades, not even the chimney stacks necessary for proper functioning of the fireplaces. Even the pronounced horizontal emphasis, the new Trianon's most original feature, was the doing of this architect-king.

What is left to be attributed to Mansart? In all probability the systematic use of French doors—it was by way of Trianon that this design feature entered general currency—as well as the disposition of the façades, which was generally admired and widely imitated. Mansart found himself obliged to integrate the rhythms of the older pavilions into his elevations. Le Vau had employed rectangular bays topped by decorative plaques; Mansart adapted these by suppressing the plaques and increasing the height of the bays, just as he had done in the Envelope. To arrive at an accurate view of his design, the vases, trophies, and statues formerly punctuating the roofline above the cornices must be restored in the mind's eye.

The marble that determined the name of this Trianon (subsequent construction of the Small Trianon would lead to its being dubbed the Large Trianon) was still a fashionable building material. As in the Colonnade, only French marbles were used: pink from Languedoc and green from the Pyrenees. However, the so-called Trianon-sous-Bois, a wing extending outward from the far end of the building's northern gallery, was constructed entirely of building stone. This wing, which is indeed contemporary with the rest of the building, seems later in date, owing not only to its premonitory rejection of marble but also to its consistency with design tendencies that would flourish under Louis XVI. But this similarity is due precisely to the Trianon-sous-Bois's having been widely emulated by architects of the later period.

OPPOSITE AND BE-LOW: *The Trianon-sous-Bois is one of Hardouin-Mansart's neglected masterpieces. It is not clear why this final extension of the wing of the Large Trianon (or Marble Trianon) was built of stone. This wing, while contemporary with the rest of the building (1687–88), is astonishingly "modern": it anticipates the architectural style of 1750–70, the last years of Louis XV's reign.*

BELOW: The Large Trianon. The gallery leading to the Trianon-sous-Bois. It is decorated with twenty-four paintings representing the gardens of Versailles and Trianon, executed by Allegrain, Martin, and Cotelle (1688–90). OPPOSITE: The Salon of Mirrors, created sometime between 1688 and 1703 by Hardouin-Mansart or de Cotte. This is a remarkable early example of the "white" decors that would proliferate in the eighteenth century, with plaster ceiling and ornamental woodwork all painted in light colors. Gilding had been projected but was not carried out for lack of funds.

OPPOSITE: The Room of the Setting Sun (Cabinet du Couchant), also known as the Malachite Salon. Decorated in 1699 by Lassurance. The furnishings are those of 1811. Beneath the mirror, a table with a malachite surface by Jacob-Desmalter. Here Napoleon kept the collection of malachite given him by Czar Alexander I after their meeting at Tilsit. BELOW: The spacious Louis-Philippe salon in the Large Trianon. This was created under Louis-Philippe by the joining of two adjacent rooms; it is now furnished with pieces contemporary with his reign. The paintings, however, date from the Trianon of Louis XIV.

FOLLOWING PAGES. LEFT: The Large Trianon, bedroom. This room was remodeled several times, being occupied successively by Louis XIV, the Grand Dauphin, the empress, and Louis-Philippe. The alcove dates from Louis XIV. The bed (1809) was commissioned by Napoleon for the Tuileries. RIGHT: The emperor's bedroom. This room, also remodeled several times, has been restored to its state in 1809.

OPPOSITE: The Large Trianon's gardens. BELOW AND RIGHT: The Walk of the Ahahs. An ahah is a gap or opening in an enclosing wall intended to frame a perspective view. These openings do not provide access; at Trianon entry from the outside is precluded by small moats known as saut-de-loup or fox jumps. The Trianon park is surrounded by a fence with many such ahahs.

THE GARDENS AND THE TRIANONS UNDER LOUIS XV; THE SMALL TRIANON

BELOW AND OPPO-SITE: The French Pavilion. Erected in 1749 by A.-J. Gabriel, it is among the earliest manifestations of a revival of Louis XIV style. Its elevations are directly modeled after those of the neighboring Trianon-sous-Bois. Rococo elements are employed only in the decoration of its small rooms.

The reign of Louis XV left no mark on the gardens of Versailles, except for the remodeling of the Neptune Fountain and the completion of its ornamental sculpture in the monumental style of the preceding reign (1738). By contrast, within the Trianon precinct, where Louis XV could cultivate a style of life consistent with his tastes and inclinations, the modifications were significant, or at least became so after the Peace of Aix-la-Chapelle (1748). Here again the king, while assisted by A.-J. Gabriel, served as his own archi-

tect. But the stylistic coherence of the various works undertaken there probably owes much to Madame de Pompadour. Although widely regarded today as the reigning muse of the rococo, Pompadour—seconded by her brother, the marquis de Marigny, whose appointment as overseer of the king's buildings she had engineered—was in fact the instigator of a return to a "finer taste." Her campaign to achieve this was supported by many contemporary critics, who deplored the depravation of taste exemplified for them by the rococo idiom. In any case, this style scarcely left an imprint at Versailles, as will be evident from our later discussion of the decorative arts.

Jeanne Poisson became the royal mistress in 1745; this was officially announced the day after the victory of Fontenoy, when she was named the marquise de Pompadour. Beginning in 1750 passion was transmuted into friendship, but Pompadour continued to exercise great influence at court until her death in 1764. Her ability to generate the atmosphere of relaxed intimacy of which the king was so fond seems to have been matchless. She gradually acquired a set of simply appointed houses that she called *ermitages*, one of which was located at the entrance to the gardens of Versailles on the side of the Neptune Fountain (rue de l'Ermitage).

To groom him for his responsibilities, Madame de Pompadour sent the future marquis de Marigny on a voyage to Italy with the architect Soufflot. In the course of this trip the aesthetic doctrine justifying a new style of royal building—neither too severe nor too extravagant, fusing an antique nobility with the spontaneity of the rococo—was formulated. In fact, this was none other than the "style Gabriel"! But this did not prevent the overseer from seeking out less headstrong practitioners of the new style than the first architect himself.

The French Pavilion (1749) is typical of the Gabriel style. This is a pavilion for rest and relaxation built at Trianon close to a small zoo principally devoted to rare species of gallinaceous birds that was created by Louis

XV in the same year. It was initially known as the Menagerie Pavilion, and it is not surprising to find animals from the neighboring zoo depicted in its decoration. Its current name derives from the French garden in which it was set. Sometimes called the King's Garden, it included on its periphery sinuous pathways that were extremely unorthodox as well as a grove composed exclusively of evergreens, something of a novelty at the time. Thus its name was misleading, as the garden was less characteristically French than the pavilion set within it. The elevations of the building essentially repeat those of the nearby Marble Trianon and can be said to embody Louis XV's architectural ideal. While visiting the pavilion in the company of the duc de Croÿ, who was himself about to undertake some con-

struction projects, the king reportedly told him that "this was the style in which to build" (*Mémoires* of the duc de Croÿ, published 1906–7).

The Small or Petit Trianon, begun in 1760, was completed only in 1764, about the time of the death of Madame de Pompadour, for whom it had been intended. Its first occupant would be Marie-Antoinette, who received it as a gift from her young husband, Louis XVI (1774). In fact, it seems to be in what is known as the Louis XVI style. The Small Trianon was probably inspired by winning projects submitted to the competition of the Architecture Academy in 1758, which were among the first designs to reflect the reorientation of the French school under Marigny's guidance. Can it be claimed that its character is indebted to the growing taste for things

RIGHT AND OPPOSITE: The Small Trianon. Built between 1760 and 1764 by A.-J. Gabriel for La Pompadour, who would never use it (she died in 1764). Given to Marie-Antoinette by Louis XVI in 1774. This masterpiece of the Louis XVI style, executed under his predecessor, was manifestly inspired by the Louis XIV style.

Greek at the moment of its construction? We think not: commentators persist in praising the atticism of this building, but in fact the reserve, polish, and elegance of Gabriel's work has nothing in common with the rather brutal Doric order employed at Paestum. Like all Mansart's disciples, Gabriel here evidences a superb mastery of the architectural profile: sensitive use of detailing and insets creates a play of light and shadow that banishes all harshness, generating an effect of grace and luminosity that is altogether exceptional.

In addition, Louis XV created a botanical garden in the Trianon precinct that, overseen by the gardeners Claude and Antoine Richard and the botanist Bernard de Jussieu, would become one of the most beautiful and renowned in the world. It boasted some four thousand different plant varieties. Its destruction under Louis XVI provoked protests from the whole of intellectual Europe. This botanical garden, like the experimental profile of his zoo, bears witness to Louis XV's interest in major developments of his time, the age of Buffon, Jussieu, and the efflorescence of the natural sciences. As often as he could, Louis XV sought escape from government obligations and the constraints of court etiquette in the laboratory he had created at Trianon. In his view, the arrival of the first pineapple there in 1751 was a triumph of his reign, one comparable to the victory of Fontenoy.

BELOW: Ceiling of the theater in the park of the Small Trianon. RIGHT: The theater in the park of the Small Trianon, built by R. Mique for Marie-Antoinette in 1779.

THE TRIANON GARDENS AND THE HAMLET FROM LOUIS XVI ON

The English garden of Marie-Antoinette, which replaced the botanical garden of Louis XV, emulated the latter's great variety in selection of species, but to aesthetic rather than scientific ends, the goal being not assembly of typical representatives of certain plant families but maximal beauty and contrast. Likewise, the Hamlet or Hameau built for Marie-Antoinette at the extremity of the English garden brings to mind the *ermitages* of Pompadour; but these had been small châteaux or middle-class residences without any remarkable architectural character, while the Hamlet imitated peasant houses, at least as shown in contemporary painting. Thus while the rustic posturing of Marie-Antoinette may be said to owe something to her predecessor's modest tastes, its character was fundamentally different.

In July 1774 the new queen of France approved the plan for an English garden proposed by the comte de Caraman, who had already created a similar garden for his own pleasure. The gardener Antoine Richard had also proposed a plan. As executed, the Versailles English garden incorporated elements from both of these but was the work of two of the queen's protégés, Richard Mique and Hubert Robert, for whom the post of designer of the king's gardens had just been created. The famous painter of ruins and evocative landscapes was perfectly qualified to design picturesque gardens in this mode, which had been fashionable for thirty years and was indebted to the classical landscape tradition. In conformity with the rules of the genre, this concentrated dose of "nature" included several of the small ornamental garden buildings known as *fabriques*: a Temple of Love (1777–78),

a Belvedere (1778–79), and a theater (1779). The Hamlet, built in 1783–85, ten years after the one at Chantilly, originally included, in addition to the queen's house that made it famous, several rustic buildings that have only partially survived: a mill, a reception cottage, a billiard cottage, a small structure in which meals brought from elsewhere could be reheated, a dovecote, a gardener's cottage, a barn, and a dairy. The Marlborough Tower, inspired by a famous contemporary popular song, was built as a stand-in for the lord's château. An actual farm was also included, but some distance away.

The Hamlet has acquired the dubious reputation of being a kind of operetta version of a small village. In assessing the accuracy of this judgment, one should first jettison the names assigned these structures in the nine-teenth century (lord's house, mayor's house, vicarage, etc.) and acknowledge as well the disastrous effects of an early twentieth-century restoration. Even after these corrective adjustments, the buildings intended for the queen's own use must be judged precious and artificial, for hidden behind their rustic exteriors were interior rooms worthy of the Small Trianon. But the service buildings and the working farm were more accurately conceived than has generally been realized. The Hamlet was closely modeled after farming complexes characteristic of the region of Caux in Normandy, which had often been singled out by theorists as the ideal setting for a return to an earlier, simpler way of life. These were composed of small, detached, single-function buildings (lodgings, barn, storage, etc.) of timber-frame construction and thatched roofs clus-

Belvedere, in the park of the Small Trianon. Built by R. Mique for Marie-Antoinette in 1778–79.

The Hamlet, built by R. Mique for Marie-Antoinette in 1783–85. The fashion for hamlets composed of cottages reminiscent of those in the area known as Caux was initiated at Chantilly in 1774. BELOW: The only element drawn from the prestige architectural traditions is the gate to the farm, which is rusticated like that of a sixteenth-century French château; doubtless the architect was here proposing a visual pun on the word "rustic," which both refers to peasant architecture and provides the root of the term "rustication." OPPOSITE: The queen's house.

THE CHARM OF THE HAMLET

Later I resolved to revisit Trianon, that place so dear to the unfortunate queen. I returned to the Small Trianon, to what is known as the Hamlet. This consists of a farm, a dairy, a parsonage, a mill, a master's house, a bailiff's house, an overseer's house, and finally the Marlborough Tower. On certain days the court gathered at Trianon, in the Hamlet. Louis XVI was the master of the village; his two brothers were bailiff and schoolmaster, and the queen was the farmer's wife and held forth in the dairy, whose interior was dressed entirely in marble. Everyone wore appropriate costume. Louis XVI played these games with the greatest ease and good nature, with a simplicity that was admirable. All the thatched cottages had a rustic air, but their interiors were models of luxury and elegance.

François-Louis Poumiès de la Sibotie,
Souvenirs d'un médecin de Paris, 1847

tering around a meadow. The Hamlet, whose cottages were built by craftsmen brought from the provinces, duplicated its model even in its separation of functional facilities into discrete buildings.

On the accession of Louis XVI, the natural cycle that had decreed the end of Louis XIV's political system also condemned the trees of his gardens, which were cut down in 1774. Both the abbé Delille and Hubert Robert were melancholy witnesses to this devastation, which prefigured the revolutionary violence to come. "Oh Versailles! Oh grief! Oh ravishing glades / Masterpieces of a great king, of Le Nôtre, and of time! / The hatchet is at the ready, and your hour is come" (abbé Delille, *Les Jardins,* 1780). The singular spectacle of this deforestation occasioned two beautiful paintings by Hubert Robert, in which this connoisseur of ruins is well in his element.

The replantation ordered by Louis XVI deferred to the general disposition of the earlier design of the gardens, a point to be emphasized in light of the increasingly prevalent taste for more picturesque garden concepts. However, the *palissades* were suppressed and many exotic trees introduced: black walnut from America, juniper and tulip trees from Virginia, and sequoias from California. Most of these species had been known in Europe for decades, even as long as a century, which lends credibility to the theory that their incorporation may be a reflection of the ongoing war of American independence, which had made that country fashionable and in which France participated as an American ally. But other regions were represented as well, notably the Mediterranean basin, with silver linden trees from the Balkans, cedars from Lebanon, pines from Corsica, and so on. In any case it is difficult to determine with precision exactly what was done during these last years of the old regime. In 1775 it was estimated that two hundred thousand oaks would be needed over a three-

year period; ten years later it was recorded that the replantation of the park was complete.

Despite Louis XVI's expressed intention to preserve the gardens of Louis XIV, the oldest of its bosquets were sacrificed during his reign: those of the Waterspout and of the Dauphin were replaced by quincunxes, and the Labyrinth by the new Bosquet of the Queen. The new Baths of Apollo were created in 1776–78 under Hubert Robert's direction as a setting for the sculptural groups depicting Apollo attended by nymphs and the horses of the sun, which had been presented in surroundings unworthy of them since the demolition of the Grotto of Thetis. Hubert Robert has been much criticized for having compromised the scale of these marble groups by placing them in a gigantic artificial grotto that overwhelms them, making them seem like porcelain figurines; nonetheless, his work here created one of the most startling images in the whole of the gardens.

ABOVE: *Trees being trimmed in 1984. LEFT AND OPPOSITE: Paintings by Hubert Robert representing the felling of the mature trees in Versailles's gardens in 1774, preliminary to a complete replanting. In the first painting, the new Baths of Apollo are pictured under construction. In the second, note the* Castor and Pollux *by Coysevox, the* Milo of Crotona *by Puget, the Colonnade, and the Grand Canal.*

The Revolution spared the gardens of Versailles, partly because Antoine Richard cleverly planted crops on the terraces to preclude their destruction. Louis XVIII did no more than replace one of Louis XIV's bosquets with the charming King's Garden, which, with its variegated species, plant borders, clumps of trees, and picturesque character typifies early nineteenth-century garden design. By the time of Napoleon III another replantation was required, one whose results would prove sufficient for more than a hundred years: most of the trees destroyed by the storm of February 1990 had entered their second century.

IN SEARCH OF VERSAILLES

In the wake of so many others, I would prefer not to pronounce you here, Versailles, that grand name, tarnished and agreeable, that royal cemetery of greenery, with its vast expanses of water and marble, a site truly aristocratic and demoralizing, where remorse for the lives of so many workers sacrificed not so much to refine and augment the joys of another period as to increase the melancholy of our own, does not trouble us. In the wake of so many others, I would prefer not to articulate your name, and yet how often, at the reddish basins of your pink marble pools, have I drunk to the dregs and even to the point of delirium the intoxicating, bittersweet draft of these superb autumn days. The earth covered with faded and rotting leaves from a distance resembled a tarnished mosaic, yellow and purplish. Passing near the Hamlet, putting up the collar of my overcoat against the wind, I heard doves cooing. Everywhere the odor of boxwood, like that of Palm Sunday, left one intoxicated. How could I have managed to gather even a skimpy spring bouquet in these gardens ravaged by autumn? On the water, the wind crumpled the petals of a trembling rose. Amid the general falling of leaves at Trianon, only the fragile peak of an arch of white geranium lifted its blossoms, resilient before the force of the wind, above the icy water. To be sure, having breathed the strong winds and the salt in the sunken roads of Normandy, having seen the sea shimmer through flowering branches of rhododendron, I fully understand how proximity to water can enhance the graces of the vegetal world. But what a virginal purity there is in this sweet white geranium, bending with its gracious retinue above the icy waters edged by borders of dead leaves. On silvery decline of woods yet green, oh weeping branches, ponds, and pools placed here and there by pious gestures, like urns offered up to the melancholy of the trees!

Marcel Proust, Les Plaisirs et les jours. Les Regrets, rêveries, couleur du temps, *1896*

PART THREE

The Arts in Concert

Chapter 5 ～⌒⌐

INTERIOR DISTRIBUTION AND THE DECORATIVE ARTS

Left: Set of furniture executed by Georges Jacob for the château of Saint-Cloud (1787), currently in the Large Reception Room of the dauphin. OPPOSITE: The inner chamber of Madame Adélaïde, during restoration. The ground-floor apartments of the royal family were restored in 1984 with remarkable success.

*I*nterior distribution, namely the organization of interior spaces in view of their intended function, and interior decoration, which encompasses both furnishings and fixtures, are ephemeral modes of expression subject to the influence of passing fashion. Furniture functions simultaneously as distribution and decoration: in this period, for example, it was often created for specific placements and its presence could either complement or modify the established character of a given room, within which it also tended to establish subsidiary spatial units. Until the end of the old regime the words *meuble* and *ameublement*, usually translated as "furniture" and "furnishings," were also used to designate a coordinated ensemble of textile accessories or fittings for a room, including seat covers and wall decorations, which could be changed with the season ("summer furnishings" or *meuble d'été*, and "winter furnishings" or *meuble d'hiver*). One of the rare extant documents concerning the interior decoration of the château of Louis XIII describes a gift that the king received from his sister, Christine de France, duchess of Savoy: a set of four such *ameublements* bearing patterns in blue, gray, green, and nacarat, respectively, all of them of velvet fabric with a silver ground.

However, the difficulties encountered in attempting to reconstitute the later interiors of Versailles have less to do with this ephemerality than with a tendency to incorporate select older elements into new decorative schemes. Such reuse was pervasive, and as a result a given decor was rarely homogeneous. The extraordinary rapidity with which the palace interiors were successively recast is perhaps less remarkable than the parsimony evidenced by retention of older elements within schemes that were otherwise as sumptuous and fashionable as could be imagined.

One gets a sense of the difficulties involved in establishing successive dispositions within the château from the following unintentionally hilarious text dating from 1701, a set of instructions from Louis XIV regarding his new bedroom and the adjoining Council Chamber: "While diverting the flue of the chimney of the Council Chamber to the bedroom, have the said chimney itself reset into the wall against the Chamber of the Terms, and have it connected to the flue of the chimney of the Chamber of the Captain of the Guards, which is directly below. A new flue will then be built for the said chimney of the Captain of the Guards within the above-mentioned wall of the Council Chamber, while some of the space now taken up by the armoire behind the false door is to be reclaimed to add additional structural support for this wall." If, despite these difficulties, the history of the royal apartments has been more or less completely established, thanks to the determined research of several generations of historians, that of the various courtiers' lodgings often remains obscure.

The collective nature of creative work in the decorative arts further complicates the history of these interiors. The master craftsman who executed a given piece of work was not necessarily the one who signed the relevant documents. For example, it is known that a goodly portion of contemporary furniture production passed through the hands of dealers who commonly sold items fabricated by others, either without any identifying stamp at all or, in some cases, misleadingly with a stamp of their own. In addition, there is considerable confusion as to the respective contributions of three royal agencies concerned with Versailles: the Department of the King's Buildings, the so-called Garde-Meuble (literally, "furniture storage"), and the Menus-Plaisirs. We have seen that this last agency was responsible for all kinds of ephemeral manifestations, and thus it comes as no surprise that it played an important role in the history of Versailles's interior decors.

As a result of successive furniture sales, both during the revolutionary years and earlier—for there were important auctions during the reign of Louis XV—the greater portion of Versailles's furniture is no longer in situ; in fact, many major pieces are now in English and American collections. Those that remained or have since become part of the national collections are now kept at Versailles in observance of the Debré Decree (1962), which rendered their preservation at the château compulsory. Complemented by the gifts and acquisitions that, along with the reinstallation of the woodwork placed in storage under Louis-Philippe, have contributed so much to the restoration effort, the interiors of Versailles once more trace the historical development of French decors from the mid-seventeenth century to the end of the old regime, though allowances must be made for unfortunate lacunae in the château's holdings of seventeenth-century furniture.

Detail of the Bathing Room of Louis XV. Sculpted by Jules-Antoine Rousseau between 1770 and 1774.

THE INTERIORS TO 1684

As part of the first modifications effected by Louis XIV, the second floor of the old château, the greater portion of which had previously been set aside for Louis XIII, was evenly divided between the king and the queen, except for one room between their suites that much later became Louis XIV's bedroom. Very little is known of the original decoration of these rooms, which, after construction of the Envelope, would become known as the Appartements Intérieurs or Inner Rooms. During the second campaign the principal focus inside the château would be on completing the decoration of the Grands Appartements of the Envelope, which fortunately survive intact, notably their splendid Planetary Rooms. Each of these latter, which included all the ceremonial rooms of the Envelope with the exception of the Salons of War and Peace and the Hall of Mirrors, was dedicated to a classical deity associated with a particular planet. The decoration of these rooms was carried out between 1671 and 1680, but most of the work was completed by 1673, when the king officially took possession of those designated for his use. The Ambassadors' Staircase was decorated between 1676 and 1678, and the Queen's Staircase between 1679 and 1681. With the exception of the ceiling paintings, work on the Hall of Mirrors and the rooms at its extremities was carried out between 1678 and 1680.

The two royal suites were not equally extensive. The king's consisted of a vestibule (Salon of Diana), a guard room (Salon of Mars), an antechamber (Salon of Mercury), and a bedroom (Salon of Apollo), all of which were prefaced by the Salons of Venus and of Abundance (1683). The space in the queen's quarters corresponding to the Salon of Venus was occupied by the chapel. Each of the Salons of War and Peace in fact belonged to one of the two royal suites. But the Hall of Mirrors, while theoretically a "neutral" zone, in practice served for the king's receptions. Finally, on the ground floor beneath the Planetary Rooms the king maintained a Bathing Suite (Appartement des Bains) whose decoration, dating from the same period as the rooms above, was famous but of which almost nothing now remains.

The overall concept for the decoration of the Grands Appartements can be securely attributed to Le Brun, though the subsidiary roles of Mansart, who contributed several ideas from 1677 on, and Colbert, whose logistical mastery laid the foundations for this "peacetime effort," should not be overlooked. The official decree endorsing use of indigenous marble from Languedoc and the Pyrenees was issued in 1664. In 1662 the tract of land known as the Gobelins had been acquired, on which were merged the tapestry manufactories of Paris and Maincy. (This last had been established by Fouquet near his château at Vaux with an eye to its decoration.) The Gobelins Manufactory, intended to rival those of Flanders, was placed under Le Brun's direction, and in 1667 was given the impressive title Manufacture Royale des Meubles de la Couronne, to reflect its recent takeover of yet another factory at Savonnerie, site of a former soap factory at the foot of the Chaillot hill, which produced carpets "in the manner of Persia and the Levant." The *Visit to the Gobelins*, a tapestry belonging to the History of the King (Histoire du Roi) series dating from 1673, memorializes a visit made by the king in 1667. The Gobelins Manufactory established a style for such royal productions that would prove tenacious. Colbert's sponsorship of another tapestry manufactory at Beauvais in 1664 should also be mentioned, as should his establishment in 1665 of a mirror glass manufactory intended to rival Venetian production that, after several moves, finally put down roots in Saint-Gobain. The marbles, mirrors, textiles, tapestries, brocades, and velvets thus produced were the raw materials used in the interiors during the second campaign. The brocades and velvets in question were so prized that one Marcellin Charlier, a royal master weaver, became something of a contemporary celebrity.

Colbert's determination to use French materials did not, however, modify the style of these interiors, which remained within the Italianate idiom established in the apartments of Mazarin, Anne of Austria, and Fouquet. In fact, this extensive ensemble perfectly exemplified this prestigious decorative tradition. While each of the Planetary Rooms was located on the second floor and extended upward into an attic story (in the Italian fashion, as in the grand salon at Vaux), on the façade their upper portions, along with that of the Hall of Mirrors, were masked behind a false attic. However, the Grands Appartements featured elaborate painted vaulted ceilings that, since Mazarin, had come to be preferred to flat, compartmented French ceilings.

The rooms dedicated to Venus and Diana on the king's side, as well as the one corresponding to the Salon of Diana on the queen's—the first Planetary Rooms to be completed—were entirely faced in marble. The last-mentioned salon, now known as the Queen's Guardroom, initially served as a chapel; subsequently it received the decorative appointments originally intended for a Salon of Jupiter in the king's apartments, an ensemble that was orphaned when plans were drawn up for the Salon of War in its initially designated space. In the other rooms marble was used only for elements articulating the bays and for window reveals, as well as on a low strip of wall below the dado. From there to the ceiling cornices, the walls were covered with brocade. The original floors were of marble (only the door and window jambs remain). To make these rooms somewhat less forbidding—a goal already manifest in the introduction of brocade—wooden floors were eventually installed. These were of a special kind (since known as Versailles flooring) that followed a kind of diaperwork pattern, with a network of planks

The Visit of Louis XIV to the Gobelins Manufactory on October 15, 1667. From the series of tapestries known as the History of the King, executed after designs by Le Brun (Versailles Museum). The manufactory was established by Colbert in 1662; in 1667 it was officially designated the Royal Manufactory of the Furnishings of the Crown and was placed under Le Brun's direction. It would play a crucial role in the definition of a style versaillais. The vases and other vessels in the foreground belonged to the set of silver furniture created by the metalworker Claude Ballin.

outlining a grid of chevrons whose centers were filled in with other, interwoven planks. It was perhaps not inappropriate for the entry rooms to be entirely of stone; the Salon of Diana, with its integral revetment of multi-colored marbles in geometric shapes in the Florentine style, typifies this treatment. The Ambassadors' Staircase delivered the visitor into this salon and the Salon of Venus, whose handling was similar but whose wall elevations were eventually articulated by multiple columns, probably added by Mansart in 1683–84.

The novel mantelpieces, all but flush with the walls and extending only slightly into the rooms, were of Italian inspiration. They had no visible hoods, and paintings were placed on the walls above them. The bronze doors were the work of Philippe Caffieri, a carpenter and sculptor of Roman origin, most likely summoned to France by Mazarin and naturalized as a French citizen in 1665. His career was closely affiliated with that of Le Brun. Caffieri's doors were of three types. The first design, dating from 1672, featured attributes relating to the dedicatory deity of each room: lyre and sun for Apollo, helmet

and shield for Mars, bow and quiver for Diana. The second type, dating from about 1676–78, was created for the Ambassadors' Staircase; surviving examples are among the rare vestiges of this celebrated decor that have come down to us. The third type, from about 1681, was formulated for the Salons of Venus and Abundance.

The Grand Staircase, known as the Ambassadors' Staircase because ambassadorial missions were received there in the king's name before entering the Grand Appartement, was a double stair of a kind then rare in France; it perhaps owed something to those in Genoese palaces to which Rubens had devoted a publication in 1622, and that had already inspired Le Vau's stairway in the Hôtel Lambert. The final design of the Ambassadors' Staircase was the work of d'Orbay and Le Brun. Aside from nominal indirect light, the stairwell was lit only by an overhead skylight—not a completely novel idea, as this had been done previously at Chambord. The original iron grills by Nicolas Delobel, which closed off the entry vestibule from the stairwell proper, have recently been rediscovered and reinstalled in their original positions.

The Ambassadors' Staircase, or Grand Staircase. Designed by Le Vau, it was executed by d'Orbay between 1674 and 1680, decorated under Le Brun's direction, and destroyed in 1752. On its ceiling, elements drawn from mythology intermingled with evocations of Louis XIV's reign. The staircase was lit by a central skylight, one of the earliest in French architecture. Its doors, the only portions that survive, are the work of P. Caffieri (1676–78).

The Queen's Staircase provided access to the queen's apartments; with its polychrome marbles and illusionistic paintings of peopled loggias, it gives some idea of the effect of the larger, more majestic Ambassadors' Staircase, since destroyed. One of its paintings was sacrificed in 1701 to allow for construction of a real loggia providing access to the façade and admitting more natural light into the stairwell.

The decorative treatment of the Large Gallery (Grande Galerie), which acquired the name Hall of Mirrors only in the nineteenth century, can be attributed to Mansart, as many of its features are typical of his work—notably the use of pilasters. Neither the Gallery of Hercules in the Hôtel Lambert nor the Gallery of Apollo in the Louvre, both designed by Le Brun, included such pilasters; they figured prominently, however, in the gallery of the château of Clagny, which in its general disposition prefigured that of Versailles. Only the Hall of Mirrors' specially designed French-style capitals were the work of Le Brun. The sumptuous trophies of this gallery and of the Grands Appartements are typical productions of Mansart's Versailles workshop and would even reappear in the decor of the Chapel. Earlier precedents for them were visible in the pavilions of the Bosquet of the Domed Pavilions, whose gilded bronze trophies were widely admired. Mansart was not the author of this motif, which was previously used, for example, in the painted decoration, dating from 1672, of the Room of the Hocquetons or Guardroom (hocqueton is an archaic French term for a piece of armor or an armed man) on the ground floor beneath the Salon of Venus. But Mansart was responsible for its translation into bronze or stone relief work, which introduced it into the repertory of contemporary sculptors. It should be remembered that the château of Clagny and the bosquet pavilions were among Mansart's first works for the king. The bracketed entablature used in the gallery, so different from the cornice treatments employed in the Planetary Rooms, is also typical of the Mansart workshop: its consoles subdivide the frieze below the cornice into rectangular panels.

The use of mirror facings within the arches opposite the window wall was also probably the doing of the architect rather than the painter. Such a decorative treatment was not unprecedented: there was a mirror room in the Alcazar Palace in Madrid as of 1651, and the Council Chamber within the Old Château had replaced a Chamber of Mirrors dating from early 1665. In this period mirrors were manufactured only in small formats; coverage of large wall surfaces, in the Versailles gallery as elsewhere, was effected by use of thin bands of bronze.

Nothing now remains at the palace of the remarkable furniture production of Dominique Cucci and Pierre Gole, active at Versailles from 1660 to 1698 and from

Below and following pages: The Queen's Staircase. Built in 1679–81 by Hardouin-Mansart. The loggia was opened only in 1701; thereafter, one could air oneself on the façade balcony. This staircase, which symmetrically corresponded to the Ambassadors' Staircase on the king's side of the château but was much smaller in scale, features decorative elements that recall its larger twin: the use of polychrome marble revetment and illusionistic, peopled loggias.

OPPOSITE: The Salon of War. Realized by Hardouin-Mansart and Le Brun in 1678. Sculpture by Coysevox: in the fireplace, Clio composing the history of the king's reign; above the fireplace, Louis XIV Victorious over the Enemies of France.

FOLLOWING PAGES: The Hall of Mirrors was executed by Hardouin-Mansart and Le Brun between 1678 and 1686. Mansart was probably responsible for the overall design, with its pilasters recalling those of the celebrated gallery built by Mansart at the château of Clagny. In all likelihood he was also responsible

for the decision to use mirror revetments: such facings had been fashionable since the middle of the century, but Mansart may also have been drawn to them because they minimized the surface made available to the painter, his rival. Le Brun provided working drawings for the ceiling, which was largely executed by his studio. His first proposals for the painted decor focused, respectively, on Hercules and Apollo, gods he had already placed at the center of painted ceilings in the Hôtel Lambert and the Louvre. In the wake of the Treaty of Nijmegen, which marked the reign's apogee, he devised, in the course of several days, a design glorifying the king's reign to cover the entirety of the ceiling's 246-foot length.

1670 to 1680 respectively. The first was Italian and the second Dutch. Northern artisans generally dominated the field from the middle years of Louis XIV's reign on. Gole was the overseer of furniture production at Versailles and invented the prototype for the piece that, beginning in the nineteenth century, has been known as the Mazarin desk—a misleading appellation, as it was created after Mazarin's death.

The celebrated silver furniture, commissioned for the Grand Appartement of the king, was fabricated by the metalworker Claude Ballin, whom Charles Perrault included in his *Hommes célèbres* of 1696. "All was of silver, but the masterful craftsmanship was more wondrous than the extravagant material," wrote Piganiol de La Force (*Description de Versailles et de Marly*, 1701). This ensemble consisted of vases, basins, ewers, braziers, andirons, candelabra, and planters for orange trees of solid silver, as well as chairs and tables that were probably made of wood but faced entirely with silver, like the throne sculpted by Caffieri. Pieces of this furniture are visible today in a few paintings and tapestries from the period, notably the composition from the History of the King tapestry cycle and several weavings from the series known as the Royal Houses (Maisons Royales), as well as the painting by Claude Hallé depicting the reception of the Genoese ambassadors in the Hall of Mirrors on May 15, 1685.

A PALACE FOR DUPES

Louis XIV was great, without a doubt. But his palace gives no indication of this. It appears to be the work of a social climber advised by a pedant—the palace of a middle-class gentleman. Versailles is luxurious, perhaps even majestic, but not great; it could even be said to provide an object lesson in what makes the difference between majesty and grandeur. True grandeur requires a certain pomp, and a certain severity as well. There is pomp at Versailles, but no severity—not even seriousness.

Versailles is a palace for the frivolous, a palace for dupes: for those full of their own importance and wealth, but who see no farther than their noses.

. . . In this overwrought Versailles, an exercise in rhetorical flourish if ever there was one, meditation is not welcome. It appeals to the senses and to human vanity, nothing more; nothing here moves the soul.

Henri de Montherlant, Service inutile, 1935

PRECEDING PAGES: The Salon of Peace. Executed by Hardouin-Mansart and Le Brun in 1678. The oval painting over the fireplace, Louis XIV Bestowing Peace on Europe by Lemoyne, is later in date (1729).

BELOW: The ceiling of the Salon of Diana. In the center, Diana Overseeing the Hunt and Navigation by Blanchard. ABOVE: The painting above the fireplace is The Sacrifice of Iphigenia by Charles de La Fosse (1680). RIGHT: The Salon of Diana. Originally, this was the first in the sequence of Planetary Rooms. One entered it upon leaving the Ambassadors' Staircase. It is a particularly fine example of the style of these ceremonial rooms: polychrome marble, Italian fireplace, painting above the mantel, and painted ceiling in multiple compartments. On the pedestal is Bernini's bust of Louis XIV (1665).

*BELOW AND OPPO-
SITE: The room of the Queen's
Guard. This room in the Grand
Appartement of the queen, and the
Salon of Diana in the Grand
Appartement of the king, are similarly conceived. Originally, the
queen's Grand Appartement was
also to have been cast as a sequence
of planetary rooms. In fact, this
room was first used as a chapel
(1672); its present interior decor
was not installed until 1676–81,
using elements intended for a Salon
of Jupiter on the king's side of the
château that was never realized.
The paintings are by Noël Coypel.*

PRECEDING PAGES. LEFT: The Queen's Antechamber. RIGHT: The Salon of the Nobles. These two rooms of the Grand Appartement of the queen retain their Louis XIV ceilings (paintings by Vignon and Michel Corneille); the subjects depicted correspond to those of the Planetary Rooms of the Grand Appartement of the king. The antechamber retains its Louis XIV marble revetments and brocades; the ornamental woodwork of the Salon of the Nobles dates from a remodeling for Marie-Antoinette under R. Mique's direction.

OPPOSITE: The Salon of Abundance. Added at the head of the sequence of Planetary Rooms in 1683, this room served as a vestibule for the Room of Precious Objects (Cabinet des Raretés), in which Louis XIV kept a choice selection of objects from his collection. The figure of Abundance over the door is by Audran. The bracketed cornice, characteristic of Hardouin-Mansart's style, and the fictive view of the heavens on the ceiling diverge from the norms prevailing elsewhere in the Planetary Rooms. BELOW: The ceiling of the Salon of Abundance, painted by Houasse, depicts some of the most treasured objects in Louis XIV's collection.

THE INTERIORS FROM 1684 TO
THE DEATH OF LOUIS XIV

The 1689 melting down of the silver furniture, which marks the end of the decade of the third campaign, can be taken as the symbolic birth date of a new style, in part a response to austerity measures. But the appearance of this new idiom had been prepared by several events: in 1682, the official transfer of the seat of government to Versailles, which reinforced the public character of the Grand Appartement of the king; in 1683, the death of Queen Marie-Thérèse, which permitted Louis XIV to violate the principle of symmetrical quarters (as it no longer carried political implications) and reclaim the balance of the Appartements Intérieurs as his own in 1684; also in 1684, the disgrace of Le Brun, which gave Mansart full control over subsequent modification of these rooms. The latter would be transformed once again in 1701, in circumstances that had changed considerably: after the wartime decade of 1688–98, ending with the Treaty of Ryswick and with Mansart's appointment as overseer of the king's buildings, the decorative work was now placed under the direction of Robert de Cotte, and designers in the workshops, notably Pierre Le Pautre, assumed a new importance. In 1699 the Société pour les Bâtiments du Roy was established; this was an affiliation of the wood sculptors Jules Degoullons, André Le Goupil, and Pierre Taupin encouraged by Mansart, which facilitated expeditious work for a revivified royal patronage. The Degoullons corporation was occupied from 1698 on with design and execution of new decorations for the Menagerie that are now lost, but that were often cited as among the first manifestations of the new style, causing some confusion as to whether they should be dated to 1684 or 1699–1701.

By contrast, the general sense of stylistic evolution at this point is clear. Italian influence was on the wane. Marble was displaced by wood and bronze. The experience that sculptors had acquired in handling marble improved the quality of their woodwork and bronzework. White came to be favored over polychrome effects; painted vaults were replaced by white ceilings, and mural paintings by mirrors. In 1685 the invention of a process facilitating the manufacture of large-format mirrors would add a new impetus to the ongoing stylistic transformation. It is true that some rooms were painted a uniform white only provisionally, in anticipation of future ornamental gilding that never materialized for lack of funds. But it was increasingly understood that grounds, whether of ornamental wood panels or of masonry, were to be left white. The use of orders, whether of pilasters or columns, was frequent in these interiors. The columns added to the Salon of Venus date, in fact, precisely from 1684.

The most important of these new rooms in the Old Château were the Room of the Bull's-eye (Salon de l'Oeil-de-boeuf, named for its large oval windows) and the king's bedroom, whose decoration did not assume its definitive form until 1701. In 1684 the Appartements Intérieurs, now accessible by the Queen's Staircase, were still disposed as a pair of suites, one to either side of the central salon. The suite on the left, formerly the queen's lodgings, was now designated for the king's personal use. It included a vestibule, the guardroom, two anterooms, and the king's bedroom. The suite on the right included the Council Chamber, from which the king's council governed the realm, and a series of rooms in which Louis XIV kept his various collections, including, at its extremity and parallel to the Salon of Abundance, the Room of Precious Objects (Cabinet des Raretés). It was during the modifications of 1684 that the Small Gallery (Petite Galerie), adjacent to the Ambassadors' Staircase, was created for display of a choice selection of the king's paintings. In

The Room of the Bull's-eye. An antechamber constituted in 1701 by Hardouin-Mansart and de Cotte by joining two adjacent rooms, elements of whose 1682 decorative scheme remain. The treatment of the far wall dates from 1682: this is among the earliest examples of a large mirror installed above a fireplace. On the other hand, the high coving, necessary to mask the different ceiling heights of the two original rooms, with its frieze of children executed by Van Clève, Poulletier, and others, is a celebrated work dating from 1701.

1701 the central salon of the Old Château was transformed into the king's bedroom, and the Room of the Bull's-eye was constituted by fusing the second anteroom with the royal bedroom of 1684. The suite of rooms on the left and the centrally placed bedroom of 1701 would be left intact by Louis XV, but he would transform the suite on the right almost completely.

The essential disposition of the room of 1701, which would remain the ceremonial bedroom under both Louis XV and Louis XVI, dates from 1684, or even from 1679. In the latter year the central salon was joined to the Hall of Mirrors by the piercing of three arcaded openings, its windows were similarly enlarged, and the attic level, curiously emphasized in the room's interior elevations, was added to bring it into general conformity with the Italianate disposition of the other ceremonial rooms. Each of the walls was articulated into three bays by pilasters recalling those in the adjacent gallery; but the gallery's ornament was of marble, while that of the central salon was of wood. In 1701 the three arcade openings were closed to constitute an alcove for the royal bed. The painting above the fireplace was replaced by a large arched mirror, one of the first examples of an overmantel treatment that would come to be designated variously as "à la royale," "à la Mansart," and "à la Robert de Cotte." These three competing appellations nicely situate the milieu that saw initial formulation of this idea, which would be widely emulated. In 1701 there was but one fireplace in the king's bedroom. Louis XV would add another in 1758; the two mantelpieces currently in place were installed in 1761. Excepting the relief *France Watching over the King's Sleep* above the bed, by Nicolas Coustou, the 1701 decor was the work of the Degoullons corporation. This latter was responsible for the mirror settings, with their field of trelliswork behind culminating cupids, and the ornamental scheme for the windows and doors, with its tripartite divisions—a central rectangular decorative panel with two square ones above and below. Three textile *meubles* were fabricated for the 1701 bedroom: two for summer, of silver and flowered green respectively, and another for winter, of deep red velvet heavily embroidered with gold (132 pounds worth!). The *meuble* installed during the 1980 restoration, of silk embroidered with gold and silver, was inspired by one used by Louis XVI.

Traces of the earlier bedroom of 1684 still visible in the Room of the Bull's-eye reiterate several familiar features—triple bays articulated with pilasters, the bracketed entablature beneath the cornice—and thus aid in dating certain other motifs, such as the tripartite decorative panel disposition and the mirrored overmantel, with greater precision. Thus it can be said that the fireplace of 1684 was not treated exactly *à la royale*, for the pub-

The bedroom of Louis XIV. The central room situated at the juncture of the Appartements Intérieurs of the king and queen became the king's ceremonial bedroom only in 1701. Most elements of this room date back to 1684, or perhaps even to 1679, and were designed by Hardouin-Mansart. The alcove dates from 1701: it replaced the three archways by which the room was previously joined to the Hall of Mirrors. The mirror above the fireplace is characteristic of the treatment dubbed "à la Royale," which became fashionable after the invention of large mirrors in 1685. Louis XV had a second fireplace installed; the two mantelpieces both date from this addition. The ornamental woodwork was produced by the Degoullons studio. On the attic level, some of Louis XIV's most precious paintings are visible. Above the alcove, France Watching over the King's Sleep by N. Coustou.

lications of ornament designers that first proposed this appellation associated it with a repertory of ornamental motifs that appeared only toward the end of the century; but the actual fireplace disposition of 1684 seems to have constituted an interesting prefiguration of the *à la royale* treatment. To unite the two rooms constituting the Room of the Bull's-eye, which were of differing heights, it was necessary to extend the 1684 entablature and superimpose upon it the coved frieze into which the famous oval windows were pierced. This frieze, with its trellised ground and dancing children in gilded relief, is perfectly representative of the style of 1701.

In the rest of the building, notably in the right suite of the Old Château remodeled under Louis XV, elements from the decorative schemes of 1684–1701 can still be seen. The Princes' Staircase by Mansart, dating from the 1680s, has been preserved in the Southern Wing, in the vicinity of the former lodgings of the royal princes (destroyed under Louis-Philippe). This is a fine example of a cantilevered masonry stairway. Louis-Philippe, who unfortunately had it restored, apparently did little more than suppress one of its four ornamental niches to accommodate his monogram and replace the ceiling vault by a flat ceiling treatment.

The Large Trianon also retains significant traces of decorative schemes begun in 1688, unfortunately modified in the nineteenth century and even under Louis XIV, who, within a fifteen-year period, ordered three successive campaigns of decoration there: in 1688–91, decora-

tion of a suite in the right wing; in 1691–1703, decoration of a suite in the left wing; and in 1703, a return to the right wing. As a result the most noteworthy surviving room, the Salon of Mirrors, in which the king's council sometimes met, can be dated only very imprecisely, between 1688 and 1703. But there is no better example of the new style prominently featuring wood, mirrors, and white grounds (doubtless intended for eventual gilding), prefiguring so remarkably the Louis XVI style. But then, as already stated in the discussion of the façade elevations of the Trianon-sous-Bois, the Louis XVI style is in part a revival of this Louis XIV idiom.

Two important pieces of furniture delivered in 1708 by the celebrated cabinetmaker, chaser, gilder, and sculptor André-Charles Boulle for the king's bedroom at Trianon have fortunately been recovered and are now at Versailles. While designated as bureaux (desks) in the documents, these are more properly considered the first commodes ever made. The word commode was not used prior to 1714, but the drawers distinguishing such pieces from simple chests were already featured in Boulle's design. Its curious use of doubled feet suggests this was an idea still in the process of formulation. These *bureaux-commodes* with marquetry insets of copper and tortoiseshell and with bronze sphinxes perfectly exemplify Boulle's style of furniture design.

Also attributable to Boulle are two series of low armoires with bronze figures on each of their two doors, representing the seasons in the first set and a philosopher and Aspasia (the mistress of Pericles) in the second. Boulle did not mark his productions with an identifying stamp, and many pieces in his style were in fact the work of furniture makers like Alexandre Oppenordt and Aubertin Gaudron, active at Versailles into the second decade of the next century. To complicate dating of these pieces still further, Boulle's style became fashionable again in the late eighteenth century; some of the low armoires with Aspasia now in the Salon of Abundance bear stamps from this later period. Could these have been applied in the course of restoration work, or by craftsmen asked to supplement an extant set of furniture with additional, matched pieces, as was often done? We cannot say. It has been proposed that these low armoires belong to the set of twelve medal cabinets commissioned from Oppenordt for the Room of Precious Objects and delivered in 1684. In any case, it should be noted that both Boulle

Commode by Boulle (Versailles Museum). No trace now remains at Versailles of the furniture used at the château during Louis XIV's first years there. The oldest pieces now in the collection are the work of the furniture maker André-Charles Boulle, in particular a matched pair of pieces, designated bureaux *at their delivery in 1708, for the king's bedroom at Trianon, which are in fact the earliest commodes in the history of furniture. The marquetry work in copper, tortoiseshell, and rare woods that defines the Boulle style was practiced by the master's disciples and competitors, and reappeared after 1770, when this style again became fashionable.*

and Oppenordt were of Dutch origin (Boulle was born in Paris, but of Dutch parents). French eighteenth-century furniture would largely be the work of Dutch and German craftsmen.

In the decor of the Chapel and its two vestibules (one on the lower level and one above), attributable to Robert de Cotte, columns and trophies appear once more. The intervention of Degoullons and his team at a later stage is attested by several important decorative elements, notably the ornament on the Chapel entry doors and the case for the organ, whose workings were by Robert Clicquot. The motif of garlanded palm fronds, previously used in decorations for fêtes, made a first appearance at Versailles in less ephemeral form on this organ case; it would be frequently employed in decorative schemes of the 1730s.

THE DEATH OF LOUIS XIV OR "DID YOU BELIEVE ME TO BE IMMORTAL?"

On Sunday August 25, the feast day of Saint Louis, he passed an even worse night. No further efforts were made to disguise the extent of the danger, which was considerable and of great urgency. Nevertheless, he made it quite clear that no alteration was to be made in the accustomed procedures of the day; the percussionists and wind players assembled under his windows should play for him as soon as he awoke, and likewise the usual twenty-four violins should play in his antechamber during his dinner.

On Wednesday August 28, he made a kind remark to Madame de Maintenon, of whom he was scarcely fond anymore, and to which she did not respond. He told her that he was consoled for having to leave her by the hope that, given her age, the two of them might well be reunited soon. At seven in the morning he had Father Tellier summoned, and while he spoke to him of God, he saw, in the mirror over the fireplace, two of his servant boys seated at the foot of his bed, crying. He said to them: "Why are you crying? Did you believe me to be immortal? For my part, I never believed myself to be, and given my age, you had best prepare yourselves for my departure."

. . . On Saturday, August 31, he passed a horribly difficult night and day. He was only intermittently conscious, for brief moments at a time. The gangrene had spread to the knee and the entire thigh. He was given a medicine known to the late abbé Aignan, which the duchesse de Maine had sent, and which was an excellent remedy for smallpox. The doctors were receptive to any proposal, for they had lost all hope. Toward eleven in the evening he was so ill that last rites were administered. He recited the prayers with a voice so strong that it was audible above those of the many priests and others in attendance. He repeated several times "Nunc et in hora mortis" and then said: "O my God, come to my aid, give me relief quickly." These were his last words. He remained unconscious the entire night, and in great bodily distress, which came to an end on Sunday, September 1, 1715, at eight-fifteen in the morning, three days before the end of his seventy-seventh year, in the seventy-second year of his reign.

Saint-Simon

The Princes' Staircase. Built in the 1680s in the Southern Wing by Hardouin-Mansart, it was remodeled under Louis-Philippe (decorative details, flat ceiling to replace a vaulted one). This staircase, supported by virtuosic masonry vaults characteristic of French architecture, provided access to the princes' quarters.

RIGHT: The Salon of Hercules. The room was created in 1710–30 by Robert de Cotte on the site of the penultimate chapel, to house two paintings by Veronese: The Meal in the House of Simon *and* Eleazar and Rebecca. *The ceiling painting, which depicts the triumph of Hercules, is the work of F. Lemoyne (1736). The Salon of Hercules, situated at the head of the Planetary Rooms, marks a return to use of the polychrome marble revetments typical of these rooms. The ceiling is among the greatest examples of an illusionistic sky in French painting. BELOW: Detail of the fireplace, bronze work by Vassé.*

THE INTERIORS TO THE MID-EIGHTEENTH CENTURY

Transformation of the old chapel into the Salon of Hercules was the first project undertaken by Louis XV after his return to Versailles in 1722. It is now known that its construction began before Louis XIV's death, in 1712, under the direction of the design team led by de Cotte, who would return to the project ten years later. This room, situated at the head of the Grand Appartement of the king, is in the style of the Hall of Mirrors, with marble revetments and pilasters prominently featured. (This revival of an Italianate idiom raises certain questions regarding the significance of the innovations of 1684: was this latter really a new style, or is it better described as an adaptation of a decorative idiom to small, intimate quarters?) The fireplace, which would not be out of place in the Large Gallery, is an exceptional work of Antoine Vassé, a Toulon-trained disciple of Puget's who practiced in Paris in a rococo idiom. The latter style is present in the Salon of Hercules only in Jacques Verberckt's picture frames for the two splendid paintings by Veronese for which the Salon of Hercules had been created. The room was finally completed in 1736.

It was at this moment that Louis XV decided to remodel the royal living quarters. It would seem that nothing of importance was done prior to the birth of the dauphin in 1729, when the queen's bedroom was renovated. The Salon of Hercules aside, some traces of work that might predate 1730 have been found, but they cannot be dated with precision. In 1735 Louis XV began a series of remodelings that would completely transform the right suite of the Old Château. It was only in 1752, however, that he authorized demolition of the Ambassadors' Staircase and the Small Gallery, to accommodate lodgings for his daughter Adélaïde that he would reclaim for himself in 1769. At this point Adélaïde's quarters were moved onto the ground floor of the Envelope, which was entirely given over to the royal children. Louis XV's daughters shared the rooms under the Grand Appartement of the king, while their brother the dauphin and his wife resided under the Grand Appartement of the queen. The dauphin's suite was redecorated in 1747, on the occasion of his marriage to Marie-Josèphe de Saxe, his second wife.

Such are the basic facts, but more details will be required to trace a satisfactory account of the numerous alterations effected under Louis XV. It was certainly not during his reign that smaller rooms were sacrificed to create larger ones—on the contrary, since the king preferred suites composed entirely of small spaces with low ceilings, an arrangement most comfortably accommodated on the château's upper floors. It seems he was most at ease there, under the eaves or on the very roofs, where he had a "hanging" garden installed. The duc de Luynes has left us a curious description of the king's preferred routine: "For some time now the king has tended to mount to the roofs of the château after dinner, to take the air with his honored guests. . . . On several such occasions he has conversed with Madame de Chalais through a small window piercing the roof, and with Madame de Tallard through her chimney flue" (*Mémoires*, published 1860–65). Additional commentary from de Luynes goes some way toward explaining this most unroyal behavior, which was in fact characteristic of Louis XV: through Madame de Tallard's chimney, the king "spoke quite unaffectedly of his preferences and inclinations in relation to society."

As might be expected, it was Versailles's more intimate quarters that most easily assimilated the domestic comforts beginning to flourish in this period: faience heaters, calling bells, "elevators" (there was already a "flying chair" during the reign of Louis XIV), *chaises à l'anglaise* or pierced chairs, and Venetian blinds, which were invented at Versailles in 1727 by Antoine Duchesne, provost in the Department of the King's Buildings. Such blinds were installed in the rooms overlooking the château's interior courts.

The Louis XV style typified by the domestic rooms of Versailles is not to be confused with the decorative idiom (exemplified by the rococo salon in the Hôtel de

Soubise) that flourished in Paris under the Regency and, by the 1730s, had fully liberated itself from the constraints associated with Louis XIV. The bedroom of the young queen Maria Leszczynska was redecorated by a team active under Louis XIV consisting of de Cotte, who died in 1735; Jules Degoullons, who died in 1731; and André Le Goupil, who also died in 1735. Thus a certain continuity with the past, determined by respect for tradition and established workshop practice, was assured. As a designer of ornament de Cotte, all but blind, was essentially replaced from 1730 on by the young Ange-Jacques Gabriel, who would be named first architect only in 1742. He and Jacques Verberckt (who had married a daughter of André Le Goupil) were the true creators of the decorative idiom that flourished at Versailles in 1730–60, when the following elements were prominent: paneling of white

*T*he Chamber of the Pendulum Clock. An engraving published in Charles Gavard, Versailles, galeries historiques . . . (1838). Most of this room's decor dates from 1738 and was realized by A.-J. Gabriel and Verberckt. Note a trait characteristic of the 1730s: the disappearance of the cornice, replaced by ornamental work in the coving.

TOP: *The Gilded Chamber of Madame Adélaïde. This is one of the least homogenous rooms in the château. The cornice and the ceiling vault probably date back to Louis XIV. Most of the decor is the work of A.-J. Gabriel and Verberckt. The large panels date from 1753, when Madame Adélaïde, one of Louis XV's daughters, set up residence next to her father. In 1769, when Louis XV reclaimed Madame Adélaïde's rooms for himself, two panels with reliefs of musical instruments were added; these are somewhat inconsistent with the two panels bearing relief trophies composed of objects symbolizing earth and water, executed in 1753. BOTTOM: Engraving published in Charles Gavard,* Versailles, galeries historiques . . . *(1838).*

OPPOSITE: *Louis XV's office (the so-called Cabinet Intérieur). Remodeled in 1738 by A.-J. Gabriel and Verberckt to serve as the working office of Louis XV. Only the mirror dates from this time. In 1753 the same artists provided woodwork. In the center, the famous desk of Louis XV, begun in 1760 by Oeben and completed by Riesener.*

and gold; narrow pilaster-like panels ascending from a plinth or low dado to the cornice, subdivided into a large central decorative field and two smaller ones above and below; a mirror placed directly opposite the one above the fireplace, with a like pair on the two other walls; suppression of cornices; and white ceilings with narrow transitional coving adorned with gilded friezes. Thus the style formulated by Gabriel and Verberckt remained rather monumental in its effect; it featured none of the asymmetrical elements identified with the Parisian rococo.

The decor of Queen Maria's bedroom, which initiated this new series of renovations, was much too heterogeneous in character to be described as representative. The compartmented ceiling, similar to those in the Planetary Rooms, would seem to date from her occupancy. It is known that Vassé installed the mirror over the fireplace about 1725. Did its treatment inspire that used by Degoullons and his associates in 1730 for mirrors placed between the windows—the only elements of this decor left in place in the wake of alterations ordered by Louis-Philippe? Here one finds several motifs dating from Louis XIV: trellised grounds, interwoven palm fronds, and the winged, crowned medallions used in the overdoors of the Salon of Diana. On the other hand, the garland crossing directly over the mirror plate was new to Versailles, though it had been used in Paris since 1725. It was in 1734–36 that Gabriel and Verberckt provided the triple-framed panels and overdoors that completed the woodwork. Subsequent transformations did not fundamentally alter this 1730s scheme: new doors installed in 1748, sculpted motifs added in the corners of the ceiling in 1770, and a new mantelpiece in 1783. Recent restoration of the room returned it not to its state in 1735 but to that of 1789, so as to re-create its appearance during Marie-Antoinette's last days at Versailles. The wall covering was modeled after one delivered in 1787, a white fabric embroidered with bouquets of flowers.

The quarters of Louis XV, to the right within the Old Château, constitute one of the most remarkable decorative ensembles produced by Gabriel and Verberckt. The woodwork panels in the king's bedroom (1738) resemble those in the queen's, but here the ceiling is of plaster. The compartmented entablature probably dates from the Louis XIV period, but the small coved frieze in the alcove is altogether characteristic of the Gabriel-Verberckt style.

The adjoining room, the Chamber of the Pendulum Clock, which served as a gaming room, also features a remarkable decorative frieze on its slender ceiling cove. The two panels to either side of the mantelpiece date from 1738; in 1753 they were identically reproduced, again by Verberckt, to facilitate enlargement of the room.

In Louis XV's office or *cabinet intérieur* in this suite, only the mirror over the mantel and its companion across the room date from 1738. At that point the walls were covered with fabric. In 1753 the king asked that it be remodeled with woodwork, and it was then that Gabriel and Verberckt added the large decorative panels; one can judge from these that their style had not changed over the preceding fifteen years. Subsequent alterations to this room were of little importance: an overdoor by Jules-Antoine Rousseau in 1760, and the ceiling cove under Louis XVIII.

The first important works by the ornamental sculptor Jules-Antoine Rousseau (1710–82), who gradually overshadowed Verberckt, were the panels in the Chamber of the King's Council dating from 1755. Aside from their width, there is little to distinguish them from other relief panels designed by Gabriel. They were occasioned by a doubling of the room's volume; Louis XIV's Council Chamber encompassed only half the space of the present room. Many elements still remain from the 1701 remodeling, notably the mirrors, the window frames, the arches echoing those of the windows, and the bracketed entablature (which was extended in the course of the enlargement). The mantelpiece, with its gilded bronze ornament, dates from 1748.

One of the most remarkable rooms in Louis XV's suite has come to be known as the Gilded Chamber (Cabinet Doré) of Madame Adélaïde, because the most important portions of its decoration date from her occupancy of this and other rooms near to the king's own. The ceiling, whose character seems to date it to the Louis XIV period, was probably retained from a room originally adjoining the Small Gallery. The remainder of the decor is by Gabriel and Verberckt, but it is anything but homogeneous. The mirrors date from 1737. The vertical panels lacking central design motifs and crowned by medallions date from 1753, as do the two panels bearing trophies composed of attributes of Earth and Water. In 1769 this ensemble was completed by two panels with trophies of musical instruments. The 1753 panels are important, for they evidence both renewal by Gabriel-Verberckt of their decorative repertory and an unexpected revival of Mansart's trophy motifs.

Louis-Philippe's modifications severely damaged the first-floor rooms, but recent restoration campaigns have had remarkable success in some of them. Nothing of significance remains from the 1747 decor occasioned by the marriage of the dauphin and Marie-Josèphe de Saxe. The fireplace of the dauphin's room, with its fine bronzes by Jacques Caffieri, son of Philippe, dates from this time, but it was based on a design by Robert de Cotte from 1713; thus it is an interesting oddity, for it suggests that the beginning of the rococo style, also known as the *style rocaille*, should be dated to the final years of Louis XIV. The ornamental panels of the dauphin's library and the dauphine's chamber would seem to date from 1756; at least this is the year they were covered with Martin varnish. This last product, an invention of the Martin brothers that permitted convincing imitation of Chinese and Japanese lacquer on furniture and woodwork, was widely used in these years, but little or nothing of it now remains at Versailles.

As for the quarters of Mesdames, Louis XV's daughters, the large reception room of Madame Victoire has been partially reconstituted. Its woodwork and coving,

Engraving of the Chamber of the King's Council, published in Charles Gavard, Versailles, galeries historiques . . . (1838).

The Chamber of the King's Council. Constituted in 1755 by joining two adjacent rooms, one of them an office of the king in which the council had met under Louis XIV. The room retains some elements dating from Louis XIV: the mirrors, the window embrasures, and even the bracketed cornice, which was extended to encompass the newly doubled volume. The large decorative panels, by contrast, date from 1755 and are the work of J.-A. Gabriel and J.-A. Rousseau.

by Gabriel and Verberckt, are of superb quality, but they pose certain problems if the date usually assigned them, 1761–63, is accurate. The ornamental relief panels are in a tripartite configuration. The treatment of the coving, with its borders of horizontal moldings, makes it resemble a cornice. A similar transitional treatment is found in the bedroom of Madame Adélaïde, whose Gabriel-Verberckt decor dates from 1766: here the panels do not descend all the way to the dado and lack a central field.

Charles Cressent (1685–1758), the furniture maker most representative of the *style rocaille*, never worked at Versailles. If his career flourished in Paris under the Regency, it is tempting to attribute this to an absence of royal furniture commissions until 1735. But this explanation is not altogether satisfactory, as his contemporary and rival Antoine Gaudreau (c. 1680–1751), official royal furnisher, worked at Versailles, producing the medal cabinet for the king's office delivered in 1738. This piece, of violet wood, was designed by the Slodtz brothers, who also fabricated its bronzes. This cabinet retains something of the awkwardness of Louis XIV furniture and is less

representative of the *style rocaille* than are other works of Gaudreau, but more typical examples of his production for the château are not presently in its collections. In 1755 Gilles Joubert delivered two corner cupboards intended to make an ensemble with the medal cabinet; comparison of these pieces demonstrates the extent to which the rococo style, so discreetly evident in Gaudreau's work, was curbed even further by Joubert. The furniture for the office was completed by the celebrated desk of Louis XV, begun in 1760 by Jean-François Oeben, who died three years later, and finished after Oeben's death by Jean-Henri Riesener; the desk was delivered only in 1769, after eight years' work. Riesener, who would prove to be one of the most prolific and talented producers of Louis XVI furniture, here modestly adhered to the design begun by his senior colleague. Thus the famous Oeben can be considered the author of this, the most important example of *rocaille* furniture produced for Versailles. Such pieces full of hidden mechanisms and secret compartments, of which this desk is a splendid example, were one of his specialties.

Furniture was provided for the quarters of the dauphin and the dauphine by B.V.R.B., Bernard Van Ryssen Burg II. The most remarkable of these pieces is an armoire ornamented with Chinese red-ground lacquer panels. B.V.R.B. did much to make the use of such lacquer panels fashionable; like Martin varnish, they would be widely employed through the middle years of the century. Unfortunately the armoire is not dated, but it corresponds with the description of such a piece known to have been delivered to the dauphine Marie-Josèphe de Saxe.

OPPOSITE AND BE-
LOW: The library of the dauphin
and the small reception room of the
dauphine. These two rooms in the
quarters of the dauphin, son of
Louis XV, and the dauphine Marie-Josèphe de Saxe, are painted
with a varnish invented by the
Martin brothers that, when first
applied here (1755), had just been
invented. This Martin varnish creates the illusion of lacquer.

*B*ELOW AND OPPO-
SITE: *The queen's bedroom. The
decor of this room, restored to its
state at Marie-Antoinette's departure in 1789, is rather heterogeneous. The ceiling retains a
compartmented treatment dating
from Marie-Thérèse, Louis XIV's
wife. But Boucher added the grisaille paintings for Maria, the wife
of Louis XV (1735), and Rousseau created the corner reliefs bearing the arms of France and Austria
for Marie-Antoinette (1770). The
wall treatments, executed for Marie
from 1725 on, are the work of the
then venerable team of de Cotte,
Degoullons, and associates as well
as of the younger team of A.-J.
Gabriel and Verberckt. The overdoors are by de Troy and Natoire
(1734). The fabric is a reproduction of one used in the room during
Marie-Antoinette's residency.*

THE INTERIORS AFTER THE MID-EIGHTEENTH CENTURY

The decoration of the Small Trianon, executed between 1764 and 1768, is often said to have been decisive in the transition from the rococo to neo-classicism. Proponents of this view maintain that these decorative schemes, commissioned by Madame de Pompadour, are in the "Greek" taste advocated by her brother Marigny. But the reality is somewhat more complex. It was in 1758 that La Live de Jully commissioned the famous ensemble of rather massive furniture for his Parisian residence that set the standard for work in this style. Nothing comparable to this would be created for the Small Trianon. As regards Versailles, it would seem that the most significant innovations in this line must be dated either earlier or later. In the French Pavilion of the Trianon complex, decorated in 1750 by Gabriel and Verberckt, the rococo was allowed to surface only in its smaller rooms, while its central salon featured classical orders and the bracketed entablature last employed by de Cotte. Clearly this interior should be linked to contemporary calls for a return to the stylistic idiom associated with Louis XIV.

For the next comparable examples of stylistic revival, one must look to the decor of the Opera House, inaugurated in 1770, with its classical colonnade, and to the last interior of the reign, Louis XV's bathing room, with ornamental woodwork by Jules-Antoine Rousseau (and, in all probability, his sons Jean-Simon and Jean-Hughes). These splendid panels, which specialists date between 1770 and 1774, are only slightly later than the final productions of Verberckt. Here reversion to the straight line is systematic, and the motif of medallions suspended by cords already seems Louis XVI in style.

The library of Louis XVI, Gabriel's last interior, which was executed by Rousseau in 1774, immediately

Dressing Room of Louis XVI. Decor by R. Mique and the Rousseau brothers (1788).

following the young king's accession, marks the official advent of this style, which would predominate at Versailles until the eve of the Revolution, when the Rousseau brothers produced their masterpiece, the Dressing Room of Louis XVI (1788). Its design was the work of Richard Mique, who had also designed several rooms for the queen: her library, the Cabinet de la Méridienne (an intimate room for rest and repose, 1781), and above all the Gilded Chamber. There are many similarities between the king's Dressing Room and the queen's Gilded Chamber, notably their decorative panels bordered by delicate garlands, with one motif on their lower borders and another suspended above. But the Gilded Chamber, with its palmettes, sphinxes, and tripod motifs, is more self-consciously antique in character.

Much of the furniture commissioned by the crown in the 1780s is now at Versailles. In 1786 Marie-Antoinette ordered a complete set of new furnishings to replace those then in use, which dated from the preceding reign. But there are fewer pieces illustrating the transitional final years of Louis XV. Despite their celebrated accuracy, the two pendulum clocks built in midcentury by the mechanician Claude-Simon Passemant demonstrate the difficulties inherent in formulating stylistically innovative casings for clockwork. The clock with the spherical pendulum, whose mechanism dates from 1750, was a gift from the Academy of Sciences and was delivered to Versailles in 1754, when it was placed in the Chamber of the Pendulum Clock. It was also in 1754 that the king received the clock known as the Creation of the World, which Dupleix had ordered for the king of Golconda in India; it would remain in France, however, in the wake of Dupleix's recall from India that same year. The spherical pendulum clock is mounted in a rococo casing full of curves and countercurves, one of the last productions of Jacques Caffieri. The bronzes on the Creation of the World are the work of François-Thomas Germain, who would become as famous as his father, also a celebrated metalworker. Reminiscences of Bernini, delight in pure formal invention, and a fascination with the movements of the heavens—all were exemplified in this work and through the second half of the century were embraced by those of advanced taste.

The architect Jacques Gondouin was of this clan; he worked simultaneously on designs for the School of Surgery, one of the first neoclassical buildings in Paris, and for a series of *torchères* or candlestands for the Hall of Mirrors (1769). (Those now in the gallery are recent copies; a few of the originals are in the Salon of Apollo.) The commode commissioned from Etienne Levasseur by

the comte d'Artois, the king's brother, for his lodgings in the Temple in Paris is not dated, but it was probably produced in the 1770s, for the count began to remodel these rooms in 1776. Levasseur, who had worked under one of Boulle's sons, specialized in the production of furniture in the style of his famous predecessor, whose work, like things in the Louis XIV style generally, had again become fashionable.

The art of Jean-Henri Riesener is well represented at Versailles, notably by a commode of 1782 made for Marie-Antoinette's bedroom at Marly (now in the Gilded Chamber) and by an ensemble of two commodes and two corner cupboards made in 1786 for the Salon of the Nobles in the Grand Appartement of the queen, where these pieces are visible today. Riesener was fortunate enough to take over Oeben's prestigious workshop after his death; he practiced in its established idiom until 1774, when he

replaced Joubert as official royal furnisher. Thereafter he became one of the most representative practitioners of the Louis XVI style, producing pieces that were monumental and architectural in character with gilded bronze ornaments set off against unadorned fields of acajou.

In 1784 the crown decided to replace Riesener, whose prices had been judged too high, with Guillaume Beneman (or Benneman), though Riesener continued to work for the queen. Of Beneman's production, which is well represented today at Versailles, we mention only one exceptional piece predating Riesener's disgrace. This is a collector's cabinet ornamented with bird feathers and butterfly wings placed under glass, dating from 1774; it is not known whether this was made for Louis XVI or for Madame Adélaïde, or for that matter, whether it is Beneman's work at all, though it bears his identifying stamp.

BELOW: The Gilded Chamber of Marie-Antoinette, designed in 1783 by R. Mique for the queen. OPPOSITE: Louis XVI's library. This was A.-J. Gabriel's last interior, executed by the Rousseau brothers following Louis XVI's accession (1774). On the table, Sèvres porcelain reductions of figures from the Great Men of France series commissioned by d'Angiviller during the reign of Louis XVI.

TOP ROW, RIGHT: Medal cabinet in Louis XV's office (Cabinet Intérieur), executed by Gaudreau (1739). LEFT: Corner cupboard ordered for Louis XV's office (Cabinet Intérieur), executed by Joubert (1755).

MIDDLE ROW, RIGHT: Collector's cabinet incorporating bird feathers and butterfly wings attributed to Beneman (1779). LEFT: Armoire by Bernard Van Ryssen Burg II. Rosewood and violet, with lacquer ornament (undated). This piece corresponds to the description of an armoire delivered to the dauphine Marie-Josèphe de Saxe.

BOTTOM ROW, LEFT AND CENTER: Commode and corner cupboard by Riesener and Gouttière (1786), part of a set of two commodes and two corner cupboards intended for the Salon of the Nobles in the Grand Appartement of the queen (1786, in place). RIGHT: Commode by Riesener for Marie-Antoinette (1782, in the Gilded Chamber), intended for the queen's bedroom at Marly.

*B*ELOW LEFT: *Jewelry cabinet executed by Schwerdfeger for Marie-Antoinette's bedroom (1787, in place). RIGHT: Commode by E. Levasseur, ordered by the comte d'Artois for his rooms in the Temple (c. 1776). A fine example of the revival of the Boulle style under Louis XVI.*

Another exceptional piece is the jewelry cabinet made for Marie-Antoinette in 1787 by the furniture maker Ferdinand Schwerdfeger. Its acajou veneer is set with mother-of-pearl, painted panels, and plaques of Sèvres porcelain. This is perhaps the most neoclassical piece of furniture at Versailles. Its caryatids supporting Ionic capitals freely imitate those of the Erechtheum in Athens.

This is not the place to systematically survey all the identifying marks in the Versailles collections. But it would be unfortunate to overlook the eighteenth century's two most celebrated chairmakers, Georges Jacob and Jean-Baptiste-Claude Sené, both of whom were official royal furnishers. Of Jacob's work, we mention the ensemble created in 1787 for the king (for the Large Reception Room or Grand Cabinet of the dauphin at Saint-Cloud), consisting of a sofa, four armchairs, six chairs, and two small tables; originally, this set contained sixty chairs! An ensemble commissioned by the king from Sené, for Louis XVI's library at Compiègne, was executed in 1790–91. But the king had left Versailles in 1789, never to return.

Between August 23, 1793, and August 11, 1794, all the furniture at Versailles was sold; the sale catalogs contained some 17,000 entries!

MODIFICATIONS AND RESTORATIONS IN THE NINETEENTH AND TWENTIETH CENTURIES

The denuding of the royal residences caused by these revolutionary sales was corrected under the Empire, whose furniture makers, encouraged by Napoleon I, were exceptionally productive. Empire pieces remained in use at the château until the mid-nineteenth century. Jacob-Desmalter was Napoleon's favorite furniture maker.

The recent refurnishing of the Large Trianon, which was occupied throughout the entire nineteenth century, has properly given pride of place to Empire pieces. Some of its old-regime furniture that remained in public collections was moved by Louis-Philippe into the Grands Appartements, the only portions of the château that, in the context of his museum project, were to retain a domestic profile. The woodwork in these rooms was painted a uniform gray. Most of the woodwork in the remaining rooms was removed, but fortunately it was placed in storage and thus preserved. Many mezzanine levels were sacrificed in this period. The entire Marble Court was lowered to allow for renovations placing the ground floor of the surrounding château on a single level; it has only recently been restored to its original level.

Eighteenth-century furniture became fashionable again in France only in the 1860s; unfortunately, a marked taste for it had developed somewhat earlier in England. But Empress Eugénie, an admirer of Marie-Antoinette, did manage to acquire some fine pieces by Riesener and Weisweiler that had belonged to the queen.

By the end of the nineteenth century Louis-Philippe's museum had fallen out of public favor. Art of the postrevolutionary era no longer seemed at home in the château of the Hall of Mirrors, where, in 1871, the German Empire had officially been proclaimed. In 1887 Pierre de Nolhac,

recently appointed conservator, formulated a long-term plan to reconvert the museum into a château. This policy has been implemented by his successors over the intervening years.

The revival of interest in nineteenth-century art, so marked over the last few decades, has resulted in preservation of key elements of Louis-Philippe's museum: its arrangements in the Southern Wing have been integrally retained, while others of its holdings have been reassembled in the Northern Wing. Restoration of the eighteenth-century decors has been carried out only in the Old Château and the Envelope of the central block; after a century of work, this project can now be considered complete.

The key dates of this restoration history are as follows. 1925–28: the first contributions from the Rockefeller Foundation; 1953: legislation rendering preservation of Versailles compulsory; 1962: the Debré Decree ordering that the château be refurnished; 1978: budgetary legislation assuring five years of endowments for work at Versailles. Key restoration campaigns were focused on the Opera House (completed in 1957), the Large Trianon (1965), the queen's bedroom (1975), the king's ceremonial bedroom and the Hall of Mirrors (1980), and the lodgings of the royal princes and princesses, notably those on the ground floor of the Envelope (1986). The African Rooms still await restoration.

One cannot overpraise the results of all this work, scrupulously executed since the 1930s, in large part based on the solid research of Pierre Verlet. But is it justifiable to render a precious piece of furniture totally inaccessible so as to return it to its original placement? And the jewelry cabinet by Schwerdfeger, which Versailles compelled the Louvre to surrender: does it really belong next to the queen's bed, where it is far less visible? Was it really worthwhile to carefully reproduce period fabrics used on the walls, beds, and seating, when the extravagant cost of their manufacture dictated that they be protected under sheets of plastic? Should it not be remembered that

these fabrics were intended to intensify the stunning impact of the original decorative ensembles? Now they contribute to a sorry spectacle of royal furnishings covered with Fifth Republic plastic! Is such a gesture, motivated by thrift, appropriate for the palace of Versailles?

The recent construction of a grand staircase projected by Gabriel at the extremity of the right wing of the Royal Court poses for the restorer problems of another order altogether. Should the limited funds available for restoration projects have been spent on such a costly undertaking? Assuming this stairway was genuinely needed, as has been maintained (despite its still being inaccessible to tourists, whose circulation it was meant to facilitate), would not execution of a modern design have been more in the spirit of Versailles and its evolution? Response: architectural pastiche was pervasive in the old regime, as demonstrated by Mansart's appropriation of elevations by Le Vau, and Gabriel's own imitation of Mansart. Does not the design as executed have many flaws? Its railing, whose terminations resemble umbrella stands or plant holders, and its cramped landing hardly seem worthy of Gabriel. Response: its construction scrupulously conformed to a design duly stamped and unquestionably from Gabriel's own hand, though the areas intended for sculpture have not been carved. Very true, but while waiting for these blank areas of masonry to receive their sculptural ornament, the result is more reminiscent of Bofill than of Gabriel. In any case, the stairway pleases the general public, which perhaps even prefers it to the antiquated wonders to which it is intended to grant access, just as it often prefers contemporary pop paraphrases to the classical music on which they are based.

*T*he Louis-Philippe Staircase (in the space formerly occupied
by the Ambassadors' Staircase).

Two of the historical rooms bordering the gardens, on the ground floor of the Southern Wing. BELOW: The Room of the Estates General. LEFT: The Room of 1804.

*V*estibule in the center of
the sequence of historical rooms on
the ground floor of the Southern
Wing.

*B*ELOW AND RIGHT:
Stone Gallery on the ground floor
of the Southern Wing. The designation "stone gallery" is used for
all the galleries in the Northern
and Southern Wings bordering
their interior courts. Originally
they were open. FOLLOWING
PAGES: Staircase of the Northern
Wing, mounting from the Rooms
of the Crusades on the ground floor
to the African Rooms on the second
floor.

293

The Low Gallery, beneath the Hall of Mirrors, restored in 1986. Its decorative sculpture could not be re-created. OPPOSITE: In the portions re-created during the restoration, the blocks intended for sculpting were left uncarved, they will most likely remain in this state. The painting on the easel is by Hubert Robert (1733–1808). BELOW: In the eighteenth century, sculpture in some portions of the gallery was defaced when they were transformed into private rooms.

*T*he Low Gallery, be-
neath the Hall of Mirrors, restored
in 1986.

Quarters of the children of Louis XV: the Large Reception Room of Madame Victoire. Decorated by A.-J. Gabriel and Verberckt in 1763, it became part of the quarters of Madame Victoire, one of Louis XV's daughters, in 1769.

The library of Madame Victoire. Victoire, Adélaïde, and Sophie are the three of Louis XV's six daughters who figure in the history of Versailles's decoration. These three sisters occupied the set of rooms beneath the Grand Appartement of the king. Adjacent to the Large Reception Room of Madame Victoire (c. 1761) was her library. Here, the glazed doors of its bookcases are open.

THE INERTIA OF THE MINISTRY OF FINE ARTS AND THE TRIALS OF CONSERVATORS

The history of the old wing typifies the approach of official government architects. It was one of the oldest portions of the building, added by Louis XIV to his father's original hunting lodge. At first, traces of humidity appeared on one of its ceilings, indicating that a few of the roof slates had been displaced, and soon droplets of water began to fall, requiring the installation of wooden conduits to catch them through the winter. The architect who was informed could not be bothered to turn his attention to so small a problem, so the following winter it proved necessary to keep a bucket under the ceiling crack at all times. The following year a large tub was needed, but the architect continued to turn a deaf ear; before long, several such tubs arranged in a line following the leak were required, and we had to exercise care in crossing the room, which was now quite damp and full of obstacles. Each year the problem grew worse, and the maintenance authorities, finally obliged to deal with it, decided that the entire roof would have to be replaced, since work on a smaller scale was deemed useless. The Ministry of Fine Arts responded to my memoranda with a majestic inertia, but the rot in the ceilings had spread to such an extent that the architect could realize his secret desire: to rebuild the old wing from top to bottom. . . . A few of the symbolic statues on the second floor of the projecting bays had become corroded; though at a distance they retained their noble silhouettes, it seemed appropriate to have some of them remade. But why, in removing them, was it necessary to saw them into three fragments? . . . Once on the ground, their considerable beauty was all too visible, and these works, formerly of museum quality, had been irreparably damaged. . . .

A similar barbarism ravaged the ground floor. The finest artists of Louis XIV's reign had carefully adhered to a specific program in executing the keystone masks on the arcade. . . . I know that one of these, the smiling face of the garden deity that initially adorned the window of the dauphin's library, was removed solely because it lacked the tip of one of its ears. One can only wonder where this delicate visage, which if exhibited with proper lighting would have been the pride and joy of a private collector, ended up. Perhaps in a dusty storage room, or in the inner sanctum of an exclusive dealer.

P. de Nolhac, La Résurrection de Versailles; souvenirs d'un conservateur (1887–1920), *1937*

*O*PPOSITE: *Quarters of the children of Louis XV: Madame Victoire's bedroom. BELOW: The Large Reception Room of the dauphin.*

*O*PPOSITE: *Study of Madame Victoire, with woodwork restored in 1986. In conformity with late-twentieth-century restoration practice, the missing portions have not been reconstituted, but rather evoked. RIGHT AND BELOW: Marie-Antoinette's bathing room in the ground floor apartments.*

*A*ntechamber of the
Large Reception Room of the Captain of the Guard.

The first antechamber of Madame Victoire.

*O*PPOSITE AND BE-
LOW: *The southern attic. In this
room, situated above the seventeenth-century rooms, are objects
relating to Napoleon I.*

*T*he staircase in the Gabriel Wing, built in 1984 after an
unrealized design by A.-J. Gabriel. In the nineteenth century,
when the art of detailing was still
in hand—an art that attained a
sort of perfection with Gabriel—
such a reconstitution would have
been successful. Undertaken in the
twentieth century, the result is a
labored exercise in theatrics.

Chapter 6
PAINTING AND
SCULPTURE

LEFT: Marie-Antoinette with a Rose, *a portrait by Louise-Elizabeth Vigée-Lebrun (1783; Versailles Museum).* OPPOSITE: *Detail of a nymph by Le Gros, on the Water Terrace.*

A chapter on French painting and sculpture in which Versailles plays a central role could well be entitled "the years of Le Brun." The remarkable trajectory of this artist's career was propelled by an extraordinary set of fortuitous circumstances. He made the initiatory trip to Rome in the 1640s, just as French patrons were turning with a new urgency toward the Eternal City for inspiration. He studied the antique, Raphael, the Carracci, Domenichino, and Pietro da Cortona. He must be counted one of the most effective advocates for the Italianate decors, with their richly architectural marble wall treatments and illusionistic painted ceiling vaults, which would come to be favored over the prevalent French use of woodwork and exposed ceiling joists. Mazarin attempted to lure the most illustrious Italian painters of his day to Paris; unable to convince Pietro da Cortona, he had to make do with Romanelli. Le Brun, who had mastered the artifices of the painted ceiling while in Rome, applied his knowledge to splendid effect in the decorations he executed for the château of Vaux-le-Vicomte, which must be cited once more as a forerunner.

Le Brun was fortunate again in attracting the protective interest of Colbert, who facilitated his rise to a lofty position from which he long dominated French art. His preeminence was determined as much by his talent as by his doctrines, though the latter would be adopted by the Royal Academy of Painting and Sculpture. In his view, artistic creation was more a matter of intelligence than of impulse. Thus the importance for him of a thematic framework that bestowed meaning on artistic productions, and of drawing, which was preliminary to both the application of color and the evocation of volume.

In 1671 the team of painters then working at the Tuileries under Le Brun's direction was summoned to Versailles to execute decorations for the Grands Appartements of the Envelope. After Le Brun's disgrace, which followed closely on Colbert's death in 1683, these collaborators, many of whom had felt constrained working under Le Brun's close supervision, began to manifest their individual gifts more fully in the Large Trianon and the Chapel. Le Brun's active intervention in the domain of sculpture began in 1666, with the Grotto of Thetis. Prior to his disgrace he produced designs for all sculpture intended for Versailles. However, his role in this area became less predominant as of about 1678, as a result of the rise of Mansart.

The chronological breakdown employed in our discussion of the château's construction can serve for painting and sculpture as well, if allowance is made for a few significant discrepancies. These fields of activity are less expensive than architecture and thus less closely tied to the effect of war on the state budget. On the other hand, execution of  works in these media often consumes considerable amounts of time: several years or even an entire decade can elapse before a commissioned statue is delivered. Finally it should be noted that, in comparison with architecture, individual destinies have a more direct influence on realization of works of painting and sculpture.

LEFT: The Pyramid Fountain, as realized in lead by Girardon (1668–70). Originally, it was gilded. OPPOSITE: A preliminary design for the Pyramid Fountain by Le Brun (Bibliotheque Nationale, Cabinet des Estampes).

PAINTING

Little is known of the painted decorations at Versailles prior to construction of the Envelope. Fragments of mural and ceiling paintings have been found within the walls of the Old Château, but it is not clear whether these date to Louis XIII's occupancy or to Louis XIV's first campaign. In any case, they are evidence of a period in which the rooms still featured conventional French-style ceilings.

The painted decorations of Louis XIV's first campaign are mostly the work of Charles Errard and Noël Coypel. Charles Errard was a formidable rival for Le Brun, who outflanked him in the most elegant way imaginable: in 1666 he used his influence to procure Errard's appointment as director of the newly founded French Academy in Rome, which put him out of the running for royal commissions. Noël Coypel is the patriarch of a famous dynasty of painters who would work at Versailles. Though initially a protégé of Errard, Le Brun would take him under his wing. The ceiling and mantel paintings in the Queen's Guardroom are fine examples of his work. As already noted, this decor features elements originally intended for a Salon of Jupiter in the king's apartments.

Although begun only in 1672, the decoration of the Room of the Hocquetons was carried out in an idiom close to that of the first half of the century and can thus be taken to reflect the decorative mode predominating in Louis XIV's first Versailles.

The Grand Appartement of the king, on the second floor, is the decorative ensemble most representative of the years 1670–80 now remaining at Versailles; it is basically intact, though damaged by some unfortunate nineteenth-century restoration work. Here all of Le Brun's principal collaborators left their mark: René-Antoine Houasse (ceiling of the Salon of Venus); Claude Audran

II (a portion of the ceiling of the Salon of Mars); Jean-Baptiste Jouvenet (a portion of the ceiling of the Salon of Mars; and Charles de La Fosse (a portion of the ceiling of the Salon of Diana and the entire ceiling of the Salon of Apollo). Charles de La Fosse was perhaps the most gifted of this group and also the most independent. His *Sacrifice of Iphigenia* (1680), above the fireplace in the Salon of Diana, is a characteristic example of his work. His style was closer to Rubens than to Poussin, these two masters being the stylistic opponents cited in the Academy's debate over the primacy of color versus drawing.

Le Brun was mainly responsible for the painted decors of the Grands Appartements, even though he scarcely applied his brush there: he himself painted a good deal of the Salon of War but very little of the Hall of Mirrors ceiling and, in all probability, nothing at all in the Planetary Rooms. However, Le Brun supervised the overall conception, set the general style, and provided compositional drawings for the various decorative ensembles. The use of elaborately compartmentalized fields and foreshortened ceiling figures above, and of grisaille figures evocative of sculpture below, reflects Italian influence, notably that of Pietro da Cortona's Planetary Rooms in the Palazzo Pitti in Florence, which served as the model for those at Versailles.

The Salon of Venus retains two perspective views painted by Jacques Rousseau (1683), a specialist in this genre who was in great demand. The illusionistic tapestries of the Ambassadors' Staircase, now destroyed, were the work of Antoine-François Van der Meulen, another genre specialist who was appointed painter of the king's campaigns in 1664.

The Salon of Abundance, added at the beginning of the sequence of Planetary Rooms in 1683, features a painted ceiling by Houasse whose conception is rather novel. The room's name is a reference to the Room of Precious Objects, where Louis XIV kept the most precious items in his collections. The Salon of Abundance adjoined this room, which was technically part of the Appartement Intérieur. The ceiling of the Salon of Abundance features the earliest illusionistic sky now preserved at Versailles. It is not broken down into compartments, but rather opens unhindered onto a fictive view of the

heavens framed by a painted cornice, replete with objects intended to evoke those on view in the room beyond. Le Brun had earlier sketched such an illusionistic sky composition for the ceiling of Versailles's fourth chapel, but this was never realized. In fact, this idea had originally

The Room of the Hocquetons. The Provost's Room (1672). Hocquetons are an archaic kind of arms, here represented in the trophies painted on the walls, meant to evoke the room's function. The provost was the head of the palace guard.

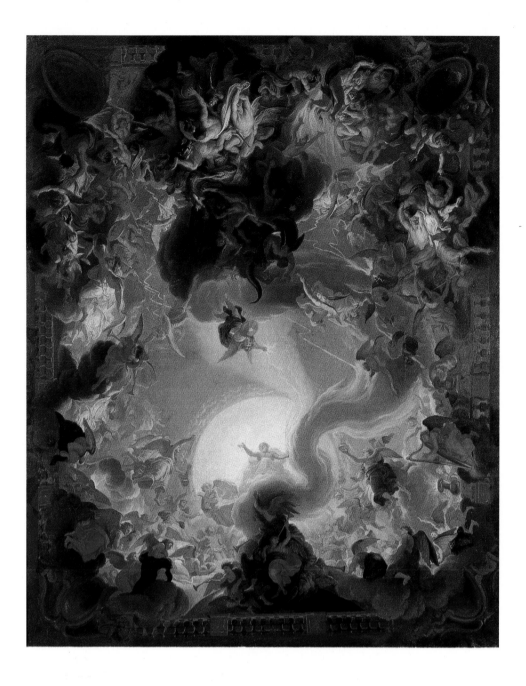

The decoration of the Large Trianon also made full use of more specialized painters: Jean-Baptiste Blain de Fontenay, the flower painter; Jean-Baptiste Martin, who succeeded Van der Meulen as official battle painter; and Jean Cotelle and Etienne Allegrain, who depicted the royal gardens.

The central portion of the Chapel ceiling (1708–9), by Antoine Coypel, is a fine example of pierced-roof illusionism. Coypel was undoubtedly influenced here by Pozzo, but the work's light palette and airy compositional scheme also evoke Venetian painting. Some vestiges of compartmentalized structuring remain, however: the *Resurrection* by Charles de La Fosse and the *Pentecost* by Jean-Baptiste Jouvenet function quite distinctly, as if fending off Coypel, who was in fact hopeful of appropriating their portions of the ceiling for himself. As for the Bon brothers and Louis de Boullogne, their contributions were relegated to the ceiling above the tribune.

The *Apotheosis of Hercules*, one of the largest fictive skies and one of the most famous painted ceilings in French art, was executed in the Salon of Hercules between 1733 and 1736 by François Lemoyne, using a palette imitative of the works by Veronese exhibited there. This masterpiece led to Lemoyne's being appointed first painter.

The collections at Versailles include many important eighteenth-century French paintings, but few of them are monumental in scale. For a renovation of the queen's bedroom under Louis XV, Natoire and De Troy executed overdoors of children, while Boucher contributed monochrome depictions of the queen's virtues for the ceiling. Paintings by Boucher, Carle Van Loo, Lancret, De Troy, Pater, and Charles Parrocel commissioned for a Gallery of Foreign Hunts—a short-lived decor on the third floor (1735–36)—are now in the museum in Amiens. The ceiling painted by Charles Durameau for the Opera House merits no more than a passing mention, for it is thoroughly mediocre.

In truth, the *Apotheosis of Hercules* was the last notable large-scale composition executed at Versailles prior to the ensembles commissioned by Louis-Philippe for his museum. These last were long held to be of interest exclusively because of works by a few consecrated artists, notably David and Delacroix. In recent years, however, there has been a revival of interest in painters more rep-

been formulated for a sacred context: the church of Sant' Ignazio in Rome, where the Jesuit priest Andrea dal Pozzo had executed a spectacular fictive depiction of an opening into the sky.

Le Brun's disgrace cleared the way for an old rival, Pierre Mignard, to take his revenge: Mignard immediately rose to a position of preeminence where he remained for the rest of his life. In the king's apartments at Versailles he painted the ceiling of the Small Gallery, which was much admired by contemporaries; this work is known to us today only through engravings.

The decoration of the Large Trianon, most of which was carried out in 1688–89, was chiefly the work of Le Brun's former disciples, notably Noël Coypel, who remained in favor until Mansart's appointment as overseer of the king's buildings in 1699. Mansart would favor the more innovative artists formerly in Le Brun's entourage—Charles de La Fosse, Louis de Boullogne, and Antoine Coypel, the son of Noël—and preside over the victory of the colorists. Roman models were displaced by Venetian ones, and many French artists began to employ a much lighter palette in emulation of Veronese.

resentative of Louis-Philippe's reign whose work is visible at Versailles, notably Ary Scheffer, Léon Cogniet, and Horace Vernet. If some reservations remain concerning the importance of these decors in the history of French painting, this is because many of the museum's most admired paintings were not created expressly for it. Such is true, for example, of the three large works by David: *The Tennis Court Oath*, begun in 1791 and left unfinished; *The Distribution of Eagles*, commissioned in 1810 by Napoleon for the Tuileries; and the *Sacre* or *Coronation*, a copy of the painting now in the Louvre executed between 1808 and 1822. *The Battle of Aboukir* by Gros had been commissioned by Murat and exhibited at the 1808 salon. The two works by Gérard (*The Battle of Austerlitz* and *Henry IV Entering Paris*) were first exhibited, respectively, in the 1810 and 1817 salons. *The Battle of Bouvines* and *The Battle of Fontenoy* were painted by Vernet for the Tuileries by order of Charles X. On the other hand, two celebrated compositions by Delacroix, *The Battle of Taillebourg* and *The Crusaders Entering Constantinople* (sent to the Louvre in 1889; the version now at Versailles is a copy) were indeed commissioned for the museum, as was Vernet's enormous work *The Taking of Smalah* (1843).

LEMOYNE AND THE CEILING OF THE SALON OF HERCULES

A few days ago I was told by a well-informed man that when Lemoyne undertook the Salon of Hercules, he intended to achieve a state of finish comparable to that of a cabinet picture to be viewed at close quarters. When his work was nearing completion, he wanted to judge of its effect. Descending the scaffolding, he noted that, seen from below, the large gilded cornice obscured part of his composition and some of his figures. He was so struck by this that he defaced the whole thing. He then executed the same work all over again, but in a broader, more generalized way; while the result was not as finished as his first effort, he found that the effect succeeded. Monsieur d'Antin named him first painter to the king and awarded him 10,000 écus for the Salon of Hercules. But his expenses totaled 29,000 livres, 24,000 having been spent on the blue tints alone. Reflection on this state of affairs weakened Lemoyne's mind and was the cause of his tragic demise. [He committed suicide.]

duc de Luynes, Mémoires

SCULPTURE: LOUIS XIV'S FIRST CAMPAIGN

Aside from engravings, nothing now remains of the first sculptural decor of Versailles's gardens, dating from the first building campaign (1660s). Its preferred material was stone and its style was mannered, hieratic, and architectonic. Terms were widely used as boundary markers and decorative accents. They evoked the gods of Greco-Roman mythology.

This decor was similar to that at Vaux, which is not surprising, as both were designed by Le Nôtre. By a curious chance, when architectural form was once more becoming a central concern in the gardens under Mansart's guidance, several terms originally intended for the gardens at Vaux belatedly found their way to Versailles: in 1683 Louis XIV purchased a set commissioned by Fouquet in 1656, executed in marble by Italian craftsmen after designs by Poussin.

As no archival records survive prior to 1664, the names of most of the sculptors of the first campaign have not come down to us. Only a few who also worked on the teams employed by Mazarin and Anne of Austria have been identified. Some of these are older artists, such as Philippe Buyster and the celebrated Michel Anguier. Others like Louis Lerambert and Jacques Houzeau, while somewhat younger, would be identified with the older generation by their contemporaries allied with Le Brun. Sphinxes ridden by children are the only surviving works that might be assigned to the first campaign, but then again both their date and their materials tend to assign them to the second campaign: the sphinxes themselves are of stone and the children of bronze, while the first campaign was limited to stone. On the other hand the sphinxes, sculpted by Lerambert and Houzeau, could not really be described as architectural in character. In any case, the children were cast in bronze rather late, but the model for them was sculpted by Jacques Sarrazin in 1660, the year of his death. This might be taken as evidence that Sarrazin, Lerambert's master and the most distinguished sculptor of the older generation active during Louis XIV's minority, was a creative presence at Versailles in these years.

The vases by Claude Ballin, creator of the silver furniture, should also be dated to the first campaign, for the earliest of them was executed in 1665, and its design

Busts of Louis XIV by Jean Warin (1665; eighteenth-century rooms) and Bernini (1665; Salon of Diana). Warin and Bernini competed in executing their portraits of Louis XIV; both busts were accorded places of honor. RIGHT: Warin's bust, placed in the Ambassadors' Staircase; it was replaced by a work by Coysevox in 1681. OPPOSITE: Bernini's bust in the Salon of Diana, from which it has never been moved.

is fully consistent with Le Nôtre's original conception. Most of these objects were cast between 1665 and 1669 (Southern Terrace), though many of those now visible at Versailles are nineteenth-century copies (Northern Terrace). These vases, of bronze with elaborate ornamentation, fall into the category of precious metalwork. Overall, it would seem that only the most precious works from the first campaign, those in marble and bronze, have survived.

Two contemporary busts not originally intended for Versailles are now preserved there. In 1665 both Jean Warin and Bernini were commissioned to create portraits of the twenty-year-old king. In this competition Warin, who was not of French origin (he was probably born in Liège) but who was fully integrated into the French artistic community, participated as the leader of the French school, in opposition to the formidable representative of the Italian school. When their two works were exhibited together in the Louvre, contemporaries were extravagant in their praise of the Warin; in fact, it is the finest non-relief work of this sculptor, who was known above all for his medallion reliefs and was not fully at ease working in three dimensions. His bust was cited as proof that

French art was no longer inferior to that of Italy; its author was compared to Praxiteles and was accepted into the Academy that very year.

Such partisan assessments to the contrary, Bernini must be said to have carried the day. On his arrival in France he had been greeted by a lavish reception more suitable for a foreign prince. If his project for completion of the Louvre was never carried out, his bust remains as proof of his magisterial superiority as an artist. Whatever the merits of Warin's work, in our view the palm clearly goes to Bernini, whose visit coincided with a transitional moment in French sculpture, between the death of its most eminent elder practitioner, Jacques Sarrazin, and the emergence of Girardon. The two busts make for a striking contrast, an emblematic demonstration of the opposed notions of classical and baroque. Warin's work was nonetheless preferred to Bernini's; in 1679 it was placed in the center of the Ambassadors' Staircase, while its rival was accorded an honorable but less prestigious installation in the Salon of Diana. But appearances can be deceptive. Bernini's bust would never be moved from this emplacement of 1684, whereas in 1681 Warin's bust was replaced by a more recent one by Coysevox.

SCULPTURE: LOUIS XIV'S SECOND CAMPAIGN

The arrival on the scene of French sculptors directed by Le Brun is the major event of the second campaign (1670s), which would see the gardens adorned with masterpieces. These sculptors are to be distinguished from their contemporaries, with whom they collaborated on many projects elsewhere, more on the basis of talent than style; they constituted less a distinct school than a clique, one whose members championed the newly formed Royal Academy of Painting and Sculpture against the old guild, with its privileges and distinctly craft-oriented agenda.

However, under Le Brun's guidance they adhered to principles that conferred a certain unity on their collective production. The firm distinction established between conception and execution, and the acknowledgment of the preeminence of design that this implied, permitted Le Brun to dominate in a medium that technically was not his own. Le Brun the painter is clearly visible, however, in the designs he produced for his sculptors, which, when not based on classical statuary, are often paraphrases of groups from contemporary Italian painting. Le Brun's sculptor collaborators were François Girardon, the brothers Balthazar and Gaspard Marsy, Etienne Le Hongre, and Pierre Le Gros, all of whom were born in 1628–29, as well as the somewhat older Thomas Regnaudin (1622) and the slightly younger Jean-Baptiste Tuby (1635). Except for Tuby, who was Roman, they came from the provinces. They were all accomplished artists as well as distinguished craftsmen: on the one hand, they performed skillfully when assigned decorative projects whose modesty might have seemed unsuitable for such prestigious members of the Academy; on the other hand, comparison of their more significant completed pieces to the drawings from which they worked clearly indicates that they were far more than simple executants.

The first productions of this circle of sculptors were the marble groups produced for the Grotto of Thetis. It is possible that these were based on a design by Claude Perrault that Le Brun subsequently elaborated and refined. Girardon created the Apollo and the three nymphs in the foreground of the central group, while Regnaudin executed the three nymphs farther back; the Marsy brothers were responsible for the rearing horses. The horses drinking water are by Gilles Guérin (born 1609), an artist of the older generation, others of whom also received occasional commissions for less important works, as for example the reliefs for the grotto by Buyster, now lost. Tuby was the author of the figures of Acis and Galatea that were originally in the grotto and subsequently installed in the Bosquet of the Domed Pavilions, while the other groups would eventually find their way to the Baths of Apollo. These marbles, begun in 1668, were essentially completed by 1672.

Girardon's work is antique in inspiration, but the sculptor sought to surpass his ancient models. First among these last was the *Apollo Belvedere*, the celebrated antique sculpture in the Vatican, which was well known in France through copies made for Fontainebleau under Francis I and for Versailles under Louis XIV; in fact, two copies remain in the gardens today. The *Acis* by Tuby was also directly inspired by a classical work, a flute player now in the Louvre. The Olympian serenity that Girardon successfully evokes in his *Apollo* is in marked contrast with the impetuosity and nervous agitation of Marsy's rearing animals, more suggestive of Bernini. The superior capacities of Le Brun's protégés were clearly in evidence here, where their works outshone Guérin's contribution. Girardon was the dominant personality of the circle, perfectly incarnating the ideal of French classicism formulated by and under Le Brun. But it is clear that the group was not totally immune to the attractions of the Roman baroque.

As for Guérin, his work is the most traditional element of this commission, evidencing his training in an older, mannerist idiom.

The Latona Fountain (1668–70) is the work of the Marsy brothers. Originally, its group of Latona and her two children was installed at water level, but in 1680 Mansart elevated it and had it turned 180 degrees as well. Recently the original marble was placed under cover and a copy was substituted. The original gilt-lead batrachian peasants, replaced later in the seventeenth century by bronze copies, are also now in the museum's storage rooms.

Lead, an alloy, was the principal material for the sculpture of this second campaign. Its malleability made it ideal for works in which delicacy was a central concern, all the more so as it could be gilded or painted. But it is fragile, and beginning in the 1680s many of the works created during the second campaign were remade in bronze, a material then deemed more noble. In all probability the intention was to carry out this change for all these works, a plan thwarted by mounting financial problems—fortunately, since those that escaped this transformation let us picture in our minds the impact of the gardens when much of its statuary was gilded and painted.

The Apollo Fountain group (1668–71), of gilt lead, is the work of Tuby, who here seems to reveal himself as Bernini's compatriot. In fact, however, it was Le Brun who selected the models in Italian painting from which he would work, and which were easily identifiable by contemporaries: Raphael's *Galatea* and Guido Reni's *Aurora*.

The Pyramid Fountain, placed at the beginning of the northern branch of the transverse axis, was executed in lead by Girardon after a design by Le Brun (1668–70). Its subsequent translation into bronze necessitated a simplification of many elements, notably the rockwork reminiscent of the nearby Grotto of Thetis. The two subsidiary Fountains of the Crowns, works by Tuby and Le Hongre that frame the Pyramid Fountain, have lost the large crowns for which they were named. The Nymphs' Bath, set into the slope just below the Pyramid Fountain, was designed by Le Brun, probably after an idea of Claude Perrault. Its secondary reliefs are the work of Le Gros and Le Hongre, but the central relief is a masterpiece by Girardon. Here again Italian paintings served as models,

*T*he Nymphs' Bath. *Fountain with ornamental reliefs. The largest of these reliefs, originally gilded, was executed in lead by Girardon (1668–70).*

OPPOSITE: The En-
celadus Fountain. Begun in 1675,
completed in 1677. The giant figure of Enceladus, in lead, is by
G. Marsy. Enceladus was one of
the Titans who warred against the
gods and were crushed beneath the
falling rocks they had piled up in
hopes of reaching the heavens. The
Fall of the Titans, painted by
Giulio Romano in the Palazzo del
Te in Mantua, was the inspiration
for this work.

Sculptures produced for the Great Commission of 1674. Two works from the series depicting the Hours of the Day. LEFT: Aurora, or Daybreak by G. Marsy. RIGHT: Diana, or Evening by Desjardins.

this time works by Domenichino, the Carracci, and Al-
bani. Girardon ostensibly adhered to the antique rule,
endorsed by the Academy, stipulating use of three levels
of relief to represent progressive planes of depth. Close
examination of Girardon's work, however, makes it clear
that the rule was not rigorously applied; classical models
exercised less influence on this production than did the
French relief tradition, notably the work of Jean Goujon,
which was much admired by Louis XIV's contemporaries.

The Water Walk or Infants' Walk is the work of
Lerambert, Le Gros, and Le Hongre. The fourteen fountains along the walk proper were completed in 1670, while
those of the hemicycle came somewhat later (1678). The
entire ensemble was replaced by bronze copies in 1688,
not without compromising, as at the Pyramid Fountain,
some of the ornamental details. The Dragon Fountain,
at which the northern axis came to an end prior to construction of the Neptune Fountain, was executed by Gaspard Marsy (1667), but it was seriously damaged by
nineteenth-century restorers. One hundred fifty animals
of gilded, painted lead were produced for the Labyrinth

by a number of sculptors, including Le Gros, Tuby, Le
Hongre, and the Marsy brothers; most are now lost, but
a few survive today in the storage rooms of the museum.
The four Fountains of the Seasons, also of painted and
gilded lead, are largely intact; they have lost only the
single figures of children formerly distributed around the
central groups, themselves composed of children surrounding a god or goddess. All were executed in 1672;
their sculptors were Tuby (Spring), Regnaudin (Summer),
Marsy (Autumn), and Girardon (Winter).

The Enceladus Fountain, a joint production of the
Marsy brothers, represents an episode from the Titans'
defeat at the hands of the Olympian divinities: the crush-
ing of the Titan Enceladus beneath the boulders he had
amassed in hopes of reaching the dwelling of the gods.
Here again, by way of Le Brun as intermediary, Italian
painting is evoked, this time the celebrated murals by
Giulio Romano in the Palazzo del Te in Mantua representing the fall of the Titans.

The sculpture for Le Vau's façades was executed by
the same artists who worked in the gardens, but it is

339

consistently mediocre. This marked difference in quality derives from the need for most such productions to conform to architectural prerogatives and to "read" from a great distance. Proof is provided by the series of masks for the façade arcades; these are clearly visible, and their exceptional quality is manifest even after rather crude nineteenth-century restoration work.

The Great Commission of 1674, consisting of twenty-eight works by various sculptors, should also be ascribed to the second campaign. A depiction of *Winter* as an old man (1675–86), the most beautiful of a set of the four seasons, is the work of Girardon. Le Gros's *Water* (1675–81) and Le Hongre's *Air* are the most successful in a parallel set of the four elements. The model for *Water* was probably Jeanne Marsy, the Marsy brothers' sister and Le Gros's wife, whose limpid, serene beauty left its mark on several of Le Gros's works. In this case the viewer senses the allegorical intent immediately: while *Water* is calm and pure, *Air* manifests a baroque agitation.

Notable in the Hours of the Day series are the *Aurora, or Daybreak* (1676–80), with her identifying star, by Gaspard Marsy, the more talented of the two brothers, and *Diana, or Evening* (1675–80) by Desjardins, a paraphrase of *Diana and the Doe*, one of the most famous ancient statues in the royal collections. The ancient work, now in the Louvre, was exhibited in the Hall of Mirrors during Louis XIV's reign. *Noon*, as the hottest hour of the day, is represented by a *Venus and Cupid* (1676–80) by Gaspard Marsy that has now been moved to shelter and replaced by a copy. The set representing the Four Corners of the Globe is of relatively inferior quality, but Guérin's *America* (1675–78) and the *Africa* by Georges Sibrayque and Jean Cornu have a certain exotic allure. A further decline in quality marks the Temperaments and the Poems sets, whose abstract conceits clearly left the participating sculptors unmoved. Houzeau's *Choleric* (1675–80), however, is worth mentioning, as it perfectly illustrates Le Brun's concepts regarding expression of the passions and the analogies to be drawn between animal and human physiognomies. It is rather curious that this exemplary demonstration should have come from an artist who, while affiliated with Le Brun, was nonetheless a member of the old school. Four Rapes were also envisioned, of which only three were executed. Those by Marsy and Regnaudin, long visible in front of the Orangery, are now in the Louvre. The *Rape of Proserpina by Pluto*, a masterpiece by Girardon begun in 1677, was installed in the Colonnade in 1699 (it was recently replaced by a copy). Such themes, evoking violent movement, had long been favored by Italian sculptors from Giovanni Bologna to Bernini. Girardon's *Rape* is quite close to Bernini's treatment of the same subject; in our view, analyses discerning a French classical impulse here, as opposed to Italian baroque influence, are oversubtle and unconvincing. This is a relatively late work by Girardon, formulated when Le Brun's unchallenged ascendancy was coming to a close. As this work might suggest, Bernini's influence was to increase, despite the fact that the celebrated sculptor's equestrian statue of Louis XIV was to be poorly received at Versailles.

The Rape of Proserpina by Pluto, by Girardon (1677–99). This work, placed since 1699 in the center of the Colonnade (now replaced by a copy), was produced for the Great Commission of 1674, which envisaged four such groups. Two others are in the Louvre; the fourth was never executed.

The King's Renown
by Guidi (1680–85). Renown is
depicted composing the history of
the king's reign in a volume carried
by Time. This work was executed
in Rome (save for the medallion
portrait of Louis XIV, carved by
Girardon, destroyed during the
Revolution and since restored). It
is characteristic of the baroque
style that flourished at Versailles
in the 1680s.

SCULPTURE:
LOUIS XIV'S THIRD CAMPAIGN

The equestrian statue of Louis XIV that arrived at Versailles in 1685, twenty years after having been commissioned from Bernini, was, in the eyes of contemporaries, unworthy of the artist. One should view with skepticism those later admirers who, exploiting the work's notorious history, would see in it the testament of a tormented, misunderstood genius. Clearly this freestanding work does not "turn" as one would like, and from some points of view its silhouette is decidedly strange. This is largely due to the fact that Bernini, following Colbert's instructions, modeled this work on his own *Constantine* in the Vatican, conceived for display against a wall.

The statue, commissioned during the sculptor's 1665 visit and completed before 1673, the year of his death, had acquired its reputation as a failure even prior to its arrival in France, which is why, despite the considerable pressure exerted on the artist to complete it, its delivery was so delayed. Its arrival at Versailles was, nonetheless, reported in the contemporary press. These reports do not consistently describe the location of the presentation to the king, some specifying in front of the Orangery and some within it. The *Journal* of Dangeau, dated October 9, 1685, reports that the work "is currently installed in the Orangery, where it is expected to remain." But another entry of November 14 reads as follows: "The king walked through the [just completed] Orangery, which he found truly magnificent; seeing the equestrian statue by the cavaliere Bernini that had been placed there, he found both horse and rider so badly executed that he resolved not only to have it removed from there, but to have it broken into pieces." Fortunately, in the end Girardon was asked simply to efface Louis XIV's likeness, and the work was exiled to the far end of the Pool of the Swiss Guards. Recently defiled by vandals, it was placed in the museum's storage rooms after a brief sojourn in the Orangery. But all of this is purely anecdotal. One should resist the temptation to view the work's exile as an expiatory gesture by which the king sacrificed, at the symbolic altar of French classicism, a Roman beauty with whom he had too long maintained dubious relations—a decision that, along with his marriage to Maintenon and the Revocation of the Edict of Nantes, has been said to reflect his turn toward religion around 1685! *The King's Renown* by Domenico Guidi (1680–85), delivered with Bernini's statue, was placed quite advantageously in front of the Neptune Fountain, so that the two works were symmetrically disposed at either end of the transverse axis.

The preceding year the bust of Louis XIV by Bernini had been installed in the Salon of Diana, and the *Milo of Crotona* and the *Perseus and Andromeda* of Pierre Puget, the most baroque and Italianate of French sculptors, were exhibited to general admiration at the entrance to the Royal Walk. These two major works, begun in 1670, were delivered only after Colbert's death. The minister had nursed a grudge against this sculptor from Toulon, who had worked for Fouquet and had not, like Le Brun, conspicuously transferred his allegiance in the wake of Fouquet's disgrace. Here, too, care should be taken not to confuse career vicissitudes with evolution of taste, though the importance of personal rivalries should not be underestimated. The arrival of Bernini's equestrian statue coincided with a marked effervescence in the production of royal portraits in French studios. In 1683 Desjardins, creator of *Evening* for the Great Commission—an artist of Dutch origin who, like Warin, was completely integrated into the French artistic community—completed a statue of Louis XIV commissioned by a courtier, the maréchal de La Feuillade, who wished to honor the king. By chance this work, badly damaged, ended up in the Orangery and so was spared the fate of its double, which, installed in the center of the Place des Victoires in Paris, was destroyed by revolutionaries. The years 1683–85 saw a profusion of proposals for royal squares, all of which presupposed a sculptural centerpiece. The intention may well have been to place Bernini's work in one of these squares. Among the French sculptors put to work in this campaign was Antoine Coysevox. He produced two fine busts of Louis XIV now at Versailles; the first, in the king's bedroom, dates from 1679, and the second, in the Room of the Bull's-eye, from 1681. Judging from these works, the intervening victory of Nijmegen had considerably bloated the king's features. In any case, the second of these busts replaced that by Warin in the Ambassadors' Staircase.

Coysevox was the most gifted French sculptor active in the third campaign (1680s), which unfolded under Mansart's direction, and he was among the principal beneficiaries of the redistribution of roles entailed by Le Brun's disgrace. The latter's function as overseer of sculptural design was assumed by Mignard and, perhaps to a greater extent, by Girardon, who as a result would have much less time for actual sculpting. Mansart was preoccupied

Bust of Louis XIV by Coysevox (1679; bedroom of Louis XIV).

with establishing general design priorities, and his preferences were formalist and architectonic in nature. As a result, sculpture became subservient to architectural considerations, with the basic forms of vases and terms heavily favored. This approach is illustrated by his handling of the works produced for the Great Commission of 1674: he had them distributed throughout the gardens in a way that totally disregarded the commission's iconographic program. The original plan to carefully place these pieces in coherent groups around the pools of the Water Terrace was abandoned; instead, they were sited before the *palissades* of greenery haphazardly, being treated with no more respect than the sculptures executed for the façade.

In several respects, the sculpture subsequently executed for the Water Terrace (1685–94) is the most remarkable and most characteristic ensemble of the third campaign. Bronze was the favored material in these years, during which bronze copies replaced many of the lead pieces from the previous campaign. This increased use of bronze was rendered viable by the Keller brothers, Jean-Jacques and Jean-Balthazar, from Zurich, who worked in the Royal Arsenal; their founding technique, perfected

in the manufacture of cannon, reached an exceptional level of sophistication. The works composing this second ensemble for the Water Terrace were representations of French rivers and their principal tributaries, the main rivers being male figures and their tributaries female figures. Each of these couples was treated by one sculptor: Regnaudin did the *Loire* and *Loiret*, Coysevox the *Garonne* and *Dordogne*, Tuby the *Rhône* and *Saône*, and Le Hongre the *Seine* and *Marne*. Preliminary drawings for figures visibly inspired by two celebrated ancient works, the *Tiber* and the *Nile*, then in the Vatican Belvedere, are generally attributed to Girardon. A bronze copy of the *Tiber* (the antique original is now in the Louvre) was ordered for Fontainebleau during the reign of Francis I, and Girardon himself owned a smaller version. The set of rivers is supplemented by eight nymphs and eight groups of children of uneven quality, which were not cast by the Keller brothers; the most successful of these last pieces are those by Le Hongre, Le Gros, and Corneille van Clève, a sculptor of Coysevox's generation, that of the 1640s.

According to some authors, a still more elaborate sculptural decor by Le Brun had been envisioned for the Water Terrace, featuring in the center of its two pools two gigantic groups depicting the triumphs of Venus and Tethys. According to other sources Mansart, who gave these pools their definitive form, insisted on reclining figures that would defer to the horizontal orientation of the façades.

Aside from the figures for the Water Terrace, Puget's groups, and a few other pieces such as *France Triumphant* by Coysevox and Tuby (1682–83), most of the standing figures installed in the gardens during the third campaign were ancient works or copies of them. This emphasis was unique to the third campaign, but was in fact the delayed result of Le Brun's classicizing agenda. He had initiated a requirement that French students in the Academy in Rome produce such copies. At the time these works were as highly esteemed as originals: speculative investment and the art market, which tend to fix the value of a work in its authenticity, had not yet done their nefarious work. These French copies were so freely executed that in some cases they could be deemed superior to their models. In any case, the few original antique works installed in the gardens of Versailles are of extremely mediocre quality. The surprising thing is not that modern copies should

From the set of French rivers on the Water Terrace: The Rhône by Tuby.

*O*PPOSITE: *A nymph by Magnier. RIGHT AND BE-LOW: From the set of French rivers on the Water Terrace:* The Loire *by Regnaudin.*

The Water Terrace.

From the set of French rivers on the Water Terrace: The Garonne by Coysevox.

The Water Terrace: a
nymph by Le Hongre.

have figured so prominently there, but that antique copies of lost originals should have been so prevalent.

The terrace immediately at the foot of the garden façade and dominating the Water Terrace received four copies cast in bronze by the Keller brothers: *Bacchus, Apollo, Antinous* (originals of the last two being then in the Vatican Belvedere, and still today in the Vatican collections), and a *Borghese Faun* known also as *Silenus Carrying the Infant Bacchus*, after a work then in the Borghese collection and now in the Louvre. In fact, there are several copies of the *Apollo*, the *Antinous*, and the *Faun* at Versailles; there is even a restored ancient copy of the *Faun*. The *Castor and Pollux* in the Prado was reinvented by Coysevox (1685–1712). Other copies include the Vatican *Cleopatra* or *Sleeping Nymph* by Van Clève (1684–85); the Vatican *Laocoon* by Tuby (1696); the Vienna *Crouching Venus* by Coysevox (his marble is now in the Louvre, having been replaced in the gardens by a bronze cast by the Keller brothers); the Louvre *Nymph with a Shell* by Coysevox (1683–85; this marble is also now in the Louvre, having been replaced by a copy); and the Vatican *Commodus as Hercules* by Nicolas Coustou. Nicolas and Guillaume Coustou, Coysevox's nephews, had Mansart's complete confidence. The copy of the *Commodus* was executed in Rome during Nicolas Coustou's sojourn there as pensioner at the French Academy. Less celebrated artists produced fine copies of the *Arrotino* in Florence, the *Farnese Hercules* in Naples, the *Arius and Poetus* in Rome, and the *Callipygian Venus* in Naples. The *Richelieu Venus* was produced by Le Gros (1685–89), partly after an antique torso in Richelieu's collection that has since been lost. The famous *Medici Venus* in Florence was copied for Louis XIV no less than five times.

With vases once more widely used in the gardens of Versailles, the most celebrated ancient ones, the Medici vase in Florence and the Borghese vase of the Louvre, were copied three times, with small changes that allowed for their display as pendants. The contemporary Vases of War and of Peace imitated their overall form. The Vase of War, outside the salon of that name, is the work of Coysevox; it bears a relief representing *French Supremacy Acknowledged by Spain after the French Victory over the Turks in Hungary*. The Vase of Peace, outside the corresponding salon, is the work of Tuby; it carries allegories of the treaties of Aix-la-Chapelle and Nijmegen. Thus these pieces are iconographically consistent with the programs in the Grands Appartements and the Hall of Mirrors.

However, most of Versailles's vases boast no more than simple floral or animal motifs. The two Vases of the Sun (1687) are a case in point; they are the work of Jean Degoullons, forebear of the dynasty of ornamental sculptors whose most illustrious representative was Jean's son Jules. The rather astonishing lead vases featuring aquatic animals—the Louis XIV contribution to the Neptune Fountain—are the work of Regnaudin, Coysevox, Van Clève, and Le Gros (1682–84).

The commissioning of twenty-four terms in 1685, as well as the above-mentioned purchase of those after designs by Poussin, signals a return to the design concept formulated by Le Nôtre, in which vases and terms played a dominant role.

In the new sculptural decor for the Marble Court (1679–80), *Mars* (by Gaspard Marsy) and *Hercules* (by Girardon) preside over a cornice supporting emblems of the four corners of the globe as well as virtues of the king and attributes of his power. More successful, perhaps, are

The Medici Venus. *Bronze copy in the Bosquet of the Queen.*

*O*PPOSITE: Crouching Venus, also known as the Pudic Venus or the Venus with a Tortoise. Bronze reproduction by the Keller brothers of a marble executed by Coysevox (1684–86), freely paraphrasing an antique work known through several ancient copies.

*B*ELOW: The Knife Grinder. A marble copy of this celebrated antique work in the Uffizi (Florence) was executed for Versailles in 1684 by Giovanni Battista Foggini. This version was replaced by a bronze copy cast by the Keller brothers in 1688.

*F*OLLOWING PAGE: Laocoon and His Sons. Copy by Tuby (1676–80), after the antique work in the Vatican representing a famous episode from the Trojan War: Laocoon, the high priest of Apollo, having provoked this god's anger, is carried away with his two sons by serpents that have emerged from the sea.

359

*P*RECEDING PAGE. TOP LEFT: Ganymede. Copy by Pierre Laviron (c. 1684–85), after the ancient work in the Uffizi (Florence). Jupiter transformed himself into an eagle to seduce the young Ganymede.

TOP RIGHT: Castor and Pollux. A very free copy by Coysevox (1685–1712) of an ancient group in the Prado (Madrid).

BOTTOM LEFT: Abundance. One of a series of terms that Fouquet commissioned from Poussin for Vaux-le-Vicomte. Executed in Rome under the master's supervision, it was purchased for Versailles by Louis XIV in 1683. These terms recall the first gardens of Versailles, the design of which closely resembled that of the gardens of Vaux.

BOTTOM RIGHT: Ceres by Jean Poulletier, after a design by Girardon (1687–88). This was produced as part of the 1685 commission for a series of terms. The reappearance of terms at Hardouin-Mansart's instigation signals a return to the style of Le Nôtre's earliest garden designs.

Antique works and copies of them, more or less free, invaded the gardens beginning in 1680. There are several copies of some of the most famous ancient statues, such as the Apollo Belvedere and the Medici Venus.

*B*ELOW: Minerva. Polychrome marble statue in the Bosquet of the Queen. RIGHT: Nymph with a Shell. Sculpture by Coysevox (1683–85), freely paraphrasing an ancient work. Coysevox's original, now in the Louvre, has been replaced by a recent copy.

FOLLOWING PAGES. PAGE 366, TOP: Vases from the Neptune Fountain. These lead vases, poorly documented, date from the end of the seventeenth century and were produced for Le Nôtre's Neptune Fountain (1678–82). BOTTOM: The Neptune Fountain. This fountain was created by Le Nôtre in 1678–82 but was left unfinished. An engraving by Pérelle illustrates a stage or plan of the work dating from the end of the seventeenth century. The fountain was refurbished by J.-A. Gabriel in 1738. It received its sculpted figures in 1740. In the center, Neptune and Amphitrite by L.-S. Adam; on the left, Proteus by Bouchardon; on the right, Ocean by Jean-Baptiste Lemoine; at either end, dragons by Bouchardon. PAGE 367: Vases, along with terms and copies of antique sculpture, are characteristic of the decor of the gardens after 1680. These vases were executed after designs by the metalworker Claude Ballin, creator of the silver furniture, and were cast between 1665 and 1669. They figured in the first decor of the gardens.

the ornamental elements on the roof; these are the work of Coysevox, Girardon, and Tuby, whose masterful handling of such appointments was also visible in the decorative ensembles for the Ambassadors' Staircase and the Hall of Mirrors.

Especially fine examples of such sculptural detailing are to be found on Mansart's two most original productions, the Stables and the Colonnade. The successful design of the Stables' portals, with their trophies and advancing horses, is clearly Mansart's work. This motif would be widely imitated in eighteenth-century stables, as for example at Chantilly. The carving is not of the highest quality; clearly the sculptors were more at ease in executing the grotesque masks for the keystones, whose function is more purely decorative. On the other hand, the keystones and the spandrels of the Colonnade (1685) are manifestly the work of highly accomplished sculptors—Coysevox, Regnaudin, Van Clève, Tuby, and Le Hongre. In both style and subject matter, they look forward to the decorative idiom subsequently employed in the Chapel.

BELOW: Aristaeus and Proteus. *Commissioned from Sébastien Slodtz after a design by Girardon in 1688, it was delivered only in 1723. One of the latest examples of the baroque style in the gardens of Versailles. To extract his predictions from him, Aristaeus, the son of Apollo, binds Proteus, who is gifted with the powers of divination.*

OPPOSITE: Ino and Melicertes. *Carved by Pierre Garnier after a design by Girardon (1686–91). Pursued by the vengeful Juno, Ino and her son Melicertes throw themselves from a cliff into the sea.*

SCULPTURE AFTER 1688

Two great artists are absent from the list of sculptors who contributed decorative elements to the Chapel: Girardon, who was too old to work on the project, and Coysevox, who was otherwise occupied at Marly. For this reason, perhaps, the Chapel's sculpture is often held to be of lesser quality—but such a judgment is unwarranted. It is true that the preeminent role accorded architectural elements here tended to reduce sculptural components to decorative accents. But with what verve and originality the Coustou brothers, for example, executed their ornamental plaques! The high altar, with its frontal relief and its glory (but not its tabernacle, a nineteenth-century restoration), is the work of Van Clève, perhaps with the collaboration of Vassé. It is possible that the overall design was formulated by de Cotte; whoever created it, the conception is decidedly baroque and Berninesque. The retables of the secondary altars were provided with ornamental reliefs of exceptional quality under Louis XV, the work of a new generation including Lambert-Sigisbert Adam, Edme Bouchardon, Sébastien Slodtz, and Jacques Verberckt.

This new generation completed both the Chapel and the gardens of Louis XIV. The *Aristeus and Proteus* by Slodtz, commissioned in 1688 but delivered only in 1723, recalls the idiom of Bernini or Puget, which would also dominate the work for the Neptune Fountain, completed in 1738 by Adam, Bouchardon, and Jean-Baptiste Lemoine. In 1746 Bouchardon produced his famous *Love Carving His Bow from Hercules' Club*, formerly exhibited in the Salon of Hercules and now in the Louvre. A replica of this work made by Bouchardon himself for Madame de Pompadour is now installed in the Temple of Love on the grounds of the Small Trianon. Some statues from the Great Men of France series (also known as the Illustrious Frenchmen), produced for an ongoing commission

The terrace of the Latona Fountain. In a manner characteristic of those portions of the gardens designed by Mansart, it features both terms and copies of ancient works: on the left, the Dying Gaul and the Apollo Belvedere; on the right, Castor and Pollux.

initiated in 1776, are now at Versailles. These are, however, not directly related to the palace, having been moved there in the nineteenth century; they were originally intended for the Large Gallery of the Louvre. Pajou, creator of the *Turenne* (1783) in this series, was also responsible for the sculptural appointments in the Opera House, which introduced a new classical vocabulary to the palace. The equestrian statue of Louis XIV by Petitot and Cartellier (1834), now in the Court of Honor, is the only significant sculpture dating from the Louis-Philippe period.

WHEN THE GARDENS ARE MELANCHOLY

Why is one so moved by these gardens spread out like an ancient dream? Ah! how one would like to plumb the meaning of this sweet melancholy that soothes our latent despair. The breath of centuries has swept from this place a brilliant society foolishly intoxicated with its power. We will be swept away in turn. . . .

However, the shadows are deepening. The park begins to retire slowly into its bed of glory. A few dreamers remain, persistent in the hope of grasping something of its mysterious secrets, of deciphering a few of its troubling messages, but gradually the relentless advance of the evening hours convinces them to depart, one by one.

Only the marble statues will hear, in the course of the night, the silent hymn, overwhelming in the intensity of its nostalgia, that hovers over this ground on which so many men did everything in their power to fabricate an immortal symbol of grandeur.

Jean des Vignes Rouges, L'Ame d'un parc, 1946

Chapter 7
FROM MYTHOLOGY TO HISTORY

*L*EFT: *The Baths of Apollo. Apollo and the Nereids, group by Girardon and Regnaudin.* OPPOSITE: The Death of Marat, *a copy of the painting by David.*

The subjects treated in painting and sculpture at the Versailles of Louis XIV were many and varied, but they were organized around a few basic thematic ideas that rendered them coherent, and they functioned within a larger concept whose framework was architectural. The evolution of the iconographic program was thus closely tied to the architectural development of the palace. During the reign of Louis XIV, form always conveyed meaning. Under Louis XV, the pace of construction slowed and thematic questions received less attention; as a result, in this period the decorative arts shone with particular brilliance. This shift of emphasis was not limited to Versailles. The decline of monumental imagery was a generalized phenomenon determined by many factors. As its name suggests, the century of Enlightenment was enamored of light, and of the white ceilings that reflected it. Representational imagery, having been forced to abdicate these upper regions, took refuge in small, eccentrically shaped fields that ornamental woodworkers inserted into their decors. Soon, furnishings followed suit: the typical Louis XIV cupboard, in which narrative elements were as richly present as in a cathedral, yielded to commodes ornamented with bronze elements of largely abstract design. Under Louis XVI, however, there was a surprising revival of iconography, one prefiguring the Museum of French History created by Louis-Philippe, in which, as under Louis XIV, representation served a specific political agenda.

*F*OLLOWING PAGES: *The Apollo Fountain. Placed at the site of the old Rondeau or fountain created in 1639. Its sculpture of gilded lead was executed by Tuby in 1668–70. It was inspired by the Aurora of Guido Reni.*

however, diverged from this tradition: at Versailles, Winter is represented not by Pluto, god of the underworld, but by Saturn-Cronus, an elderly figure personifying both time and death. This substitution had already been proposed in the work of Poussin, its initiator.

The sculpture of Le Vau's façades reiterated the same themes. The most original of these elements was the series of masks on the keystones of the ground-floor arcades, illustrating the aging of the human face; deplorable nineteenth-century restoration work scrambled their original order, thus obscuring their meaning. The statues above the columns represent the twelve months of the year and are placed to either side of the central figures of Apollo and Diana. The inclusion of these two deities could be viewed as an ingenious reference to the Latona Fountain, where they are depicted as children.

The iconography of Versailles is more respectful of the claims of earthbound reality than of the pantheon of the gods. Perhaps its mythological references, edging toward the abstruse only to avoid the burlesque, should not be taken too literally; they are the common currency of the theater, of play, and of fancy-dress. Is Nocret's painting of the royal family in Olympian garb to be taken seriously? It calls to mind a family on a pleasure spree captured behind the headless flats of a carnival photographer, or a group of actors striking a final tableau in an Offenbach operetta.

Both the Great Commission and the Ambassadors' Staircase date from 1674; they mark the apogee of mythological representation at Versailles and simultaneously signal its imminent marginalization. The Great Commission consisted of seven groups of four sculptures each: the seasons, the hours, the four corners of the earth, the elements, and the temperaments, as well as four poems and four rapes. Only the rapes called for more than one figure (at the least, abductor and abducted) and, by the very nature of their subjects, were inspired by ancient myths; it is difficult to see how these groups would have functioned meaningfully within an ensemble of isolated figures representing the physical and moral world, even if some of these assumed the guise of ancient deities. A few gods and goddesses appear among the seasons and hours of the day. Flora, Ceres, and Bacchus are mobilized once more to evoke three of the seasons, while the fourth, Winter, is personified as an old man. This last figure

OPPOSITE: The Fountains of the Seasons. Winter, or Saturn by Girardon.

BELOW: Africa by Georges Sibrayque and Jean Cornu (1682).

FOLLOWING PAGES: The Great Commission of 1674. The Seasons. PAGE 386, TOP: Spring, or Flora by Philippe Magnier (1675–81). BOTTOM LEFT: Summer by Pierre Hutinot (1675–79). BOTTOM RIGHT: Autumn, or Bacchus by Regnaudin (1680–99). PAGE 387: Winter by Girardon (1675–86).

extends a venerable national tradition, that of the months as depicted in French cathedrals, where February is represented by an old man shivering from the cold and warming himself at a brazier—a tradition persisting through the Renaissance, since the Hôtel Carnavalet features four seasons not very different from those of Versailles. In devising the other sets of figures, Le Brun depended more heavily on Ripa's *Iconologia* than on the mythological tradition. On occasion he turned directly to contemporary reality: America, for example, was represented by a be-plumed Indian, and Africa by a Negro. But Ripa is most helpful in deciphering many of these figures. While use of an overturned vessel to signify Water and an eagle for Air pose no problems, without this sourcebook the viewer would hardly grasp the rationale for including a chameleon in the figure of Air: Ripa informs us that, according to Pliny, the chameleon's sole nourishment was the air it breathed!

On the façades of the Southern and Northern Wings there are muses, arts, sciences, and virtues on one side, and on the other more sciences, arts, and muses, along with seasons, gods, and poems. It proved necessary to invent attributes for some of the more recondite sciences, much as chorography, altimetry, and horography, all unknown to the ancients. In designing these interminable façades, Mansart exploited the procedures developed by Le Brun and Le Vau, even to the point of exhaustion.

The most up-to-date events found echo in the decorative scheme devised for the Ambassadors' Staircase, executed between 1676 and 1678 under Le Brun's direction and completed prior to the signing of the Peace of Nijmegen. The third campaign, which began at this point, would be marked by a passage from mythological to historical imagery. The antique gods did not entirely abandon Versailles, but they retired to Trianon in pursuit, like the king, of a renewed youth. In the château and its gardens, two works begun late in Louis XIV's reign and completed during that of his successor remained under the spell of Greco-Roman mythology: the Neptune Fountain, a masterpiece of sculpture terminating the northern axis, and the Salon of Hercules, a masterpiece of painting at the beginning of the Planetary Rooms. These works were not Apollonian in theme, and thus deviated from the iconographic focus on the god of the sun established early in the reign.

CONTEMPORARY HISTORY DURING THE MIDDLE YEARS OF LOUIS XIV'S REIGN

On the ceiling of the Ambassadors' Staircase, the triumph of Louis XIV was once more evoked by means of mythology, allegory, and solar emblems. Four wall frescoes depicted groups of contemporaries observing the room from illusionistic loggias: skin color, attire, and attendant details clearly identified them as emissaries from the four corners of the globe. Four illusionistic tapestries painted by Van der Meulen pictured Louis XIV's most celebrated battles. Tapestry had been turned to the purposes of historiography at a very early date. The famous tapestry series known as the History of the King, based on designs by Le Brun, had been initiated in 1662; although in theory it should have continued until the king's death, its execution required only ten years. Along the Ambassadors' Staircase the king's history was represented in tapestry so as to render it visible to the world's emissaries; but the woven images were in trompe l'oeil, a concession to diplomatic prudence.

With the triumph of Nijmegen, however, the moment for rhetorical restraint was past; ambassadors were received in the Hall of Mirrors, where Louis the Great's exploits were depicted over the 246-foot length of the ceiling. Colbert had advised that on this ceiling "nothing should figure that is not consistent with the truth, nor anything that might prove overly offensive to the foreign powers involved." However, visiting ambassadors were obliged to humbly traverse the new Salon of War, whose ceiling depicted France triumphant over Spain and Holland. As for the Salon of Peace, at the opposite end of the gallery on the queen's side, it was not included in the usual ambassadors' itinerary! In any case, decoration of this last room was completed only during the reign of Louis XV. The great oval medallion in the wall of the Salon of War represents Louis XIV as a victorious warrior, while in the Salon of Peace Louis XV offers peace to Europe—an assignment of roles that, while haphazard, is basically consistent with the historical facts.

In the triad of rooms composed of the gallery and these two salons, history has displaced mythology, and quite literally, for the Salon of War occupies the space originally assigned to a Salon of Jupiter in the corner of the Envelope, while the envisioned Salons of Saturn and Venus were abandoned to accommodate the new gallery. Le Brun's original design for this room focused in turn on Hercules and Apollo, two gods who already figured prominently in his oeuvre (in the Hercules Gallery in the Hôtel Lambert and the Apollo Gallery in the Louvre). Finally, during the negotiations for the Peace of Nijmegen and under the sway of unfolding events, Le Brun within a few days produced sketches for a cycle glorifying the king's accomplishments. He drew his subject matter exclusively from the ten-year period between the Peace of Aix and the Peace of Nijmegen. The king's minority was not included, as Mazarin was responsible for all its finest moments; as for the history of the post-Nijmegen period, the king had yet to write it.

The first text advocating contemporary historical subject matter was Charles Perrault's poem *La Peinture* (1668), written in praise of Le Brun. Perrault advised that Le Brun no longer

> *. . . return to the century of Alexander*
> *In search of matter worthy of your hand*
>
> . . . .
>
> *The exploits of Louis, painted in their true colors,*
>
> . . . .
>
> *Provide still more brilliant subjects.*

The themes of the various images in the gallery are identified by accompanying texts. These had first been drafted in Latin, in accordance with tradition, but in 1685 Louis XIV commanded that they be rewritten in French. This constituted an important victory for the Gallicans, who since the Renaissance had battled for the increased use of French. Louis XIV had been swayed by François Charpentier, who addressed him as follows in his 1683 publication *De l'excellence de la langue française*: "The marvelous events of Your Majesty's reign have brought the French nation to the height of its glory. . . . Must she seek out the best words in which to express her happiness in a foreign tongue? [Why should we borrow] expressions from the an-

cient Romans to convey our gratitude, when your brilliant actions easily surpass all those of ancient Rome?"

Military victories alone would not have sufficed to effect this iconographic mutation in the decors of Versailles; it must also be understood in another context, the ongoing quarrel of the Ancients and the Moderns, which ended in a victory for the latter party, in whose front ranks the Perrault brothers fought. As a consequence, not only the deities of antiquity but its languages and heroes fell temporarily out of favor. Yet in 1685–88 Joseph Parrocel, a rival of Van der Meulen's, decorated the

Detail of France Triumphant, *a group created in 1682–83 for the Bosquet of the Arch of Triumph.*

*V*anquished Nations, *figures from the group known as* France Triumphant. *LEFT:* Spain *by Tuby. RIGHT:* The Empire *by Coysevox.*

first antechamber of the king's quarters in the Old Château, which served as Louis XIV's dining room, with a series of paintings of famous ancient battles.

Le Brun's contribution to the Hall of Mirrors was not restricted to its painted ceiling; he also designed for it a special French order recognizable by the Gallic cock and the Bourbon lily in its capitals. In 1671 Colbert had initiated a competition to formulate such a French order, which in principle would surpass the five orders of the ancient world. Clearly, the intention was to signal the important role of France in the development of classical doctrine.

Nijmegen had a less significant impact on the gardens, for sculpture, a less narrative medium than painting, is more resistant to novel subject matter. However, the

group representing *France Triumphant*, dating from 1682–83, reiterates the theme of the ceiling of the Salon of War: France victorious over Spain and Holland. But its three figures are allegories, not historical personages. Would the personification of France be recognizable without its cock-helmet, its sun-bearing shield, and its lance ornamented with fleurs-de-lis? As for the Water Terrace, it was not the realm's history but its geography that displaced the allegorical figures designed as part of the Great Commission: the rivers and tributaries that replaced them, so handsomely displayed around the terrace pools, are generic allegories for which attributes distinguishing the Rhône from the Garonne, and the Seine from the Loire, were not even provided.

Detail of The Empire.

RELIGION DURING THE LAST YEARS OF LOUIS XIV'S REIGN

*I*n the end, events of the post-Nijmegen period would figure neither in the History of the King tapestry series nor on the château's ceilings. The decade of peace was not to be pictured there, and the history of the subsequent, last decades of the reign were not so glorious. On the other hand, the new Chapel provided ample opportunities for Christian iconography. Its decorative program was ostensibly devised by Fathers La Chaise and Le Tellier, the king's confessors. While they could plausibly have authored it, no known documentation supports this claim, and one can regard their proposed involvement with a certain skepticism: this attribution could well derive solely from an overhasty assimilation of the style of the Chapel's decorative elements with the baroque idiom sometimes called the "Jesuit style." But whoever the program's formulators may have been, they were clearly well informed as to medieval traditions as well as Renaissance precedents.

The importance of the Sainte-Chapelle in Paris as a model, which is suggested by a comparison of the two structures, is further confirmed by iconographic analysis. The Crown of Thorns and the fragment of the True Cross, the monarchy's holiest relics for which Saint Louis had ordered the Parisian chapel built, no doubt inspired the theme of the Passion, which is developed in the sculptural reliefs of the arcades. The paintings on the ceiling of the tribune galleries are devoted to the lives of the apostles, who are likewise present in the Sainte-Chapelle, where sculptural depictions of them ring its upper sanctuary. The spandrels of the tribune windows are ornamented with virtues, selected for their correspondence with the saints on the ceiling compartments above them.

The ceiling of the central space is devoted to the Trinity. Here, the inspiration seems to have been the Chapel of the Trinity at Fontainebleau. At Versailles, the central portion of the ceiling is devoted to a depiction of God the Father reigning in majesty. At either end of this section are Saint Louis and Saint Charlemagne, patron saints of the monarchy; on the sides, the four Evangelists appear in as many lunettes. The Holy Spirit is included in a representation of the Pentecost; situated above the royal tribune, it evokes the sacre, the French coronation ritual in which consecration with sacred oil of supernatural origin (putatively brought to earth by the dove of the Holy Spirit) elevates the monarch to the level of the apostles. The Son is depicted in a scene of the Resurrection, directly above the high altar at which his sacrifice is ritually celebrated. The secondary altars are dedicated to the patron saints of the various members of the royal family, who are represented in their sculpted retables. The large room outside the entrance to the royal tribune is adorned, in its four corners, with depictions of the four corners of the globe; presumably these evoke the universality of the Gospel.

Overall, one has a sense that the Chapel was built in conformity with a coherent iconographic program that was scrupulously followed. Some exceptions, however, should be noted. The large statues along the exterior of the tribune walls are a confused set of apostles, Evangelists, fathers of the church, and saints; architectural considerations determined the placement of these figures, whose identities would seem to have been selected rather haphazardly. It might be proposed that such apparent negligence is of little consequence, as the statues are visible only from a great distance. But there are other, more flagrant inconsistencies. In principle the series of arcade reliefs illustrating the Passion constitutes a way of the cross, but it is difficult to identify many of its subjects with the stations identified in the liturgy. One of these reliefs was originally obscured by the pulpit, which no longer exists but whose early presence is documented. The representation of these scenes is extremely summary, when not wholly replaced by a few attributes culled from the repertory of the decorative arts: angels on the spandrels and trophies on the piers. It is fair to say that the Chapel's decoration, completed quite late, evidences a certain decadence in its iconography, even while providing us with the last such ambitious, coherent decorative program prior to the Christian revival of the nineteenth century. The decline it embodies was a phenomenon not limited to Versailles. Witness the spare white glazing of the Chapel's windows: stained glass, the church's most characteristic mode of painting, was gradually emptied of its content as the seventeenth century advanced.

Ceiling of the Chapel.

*B*ELOW: The Fox and the Head *by Le Hongre, after La Fontaine's fable in "The Fox and the Bust." This is one of the few surviving groups from the Labyrinth, which was decorated with lead groups inspired by Aesop's fables and was contempo-* rary with the first edition of the Fables of La Fontaine (1668). *OPPOSITE: Fighting animals. Four such groups, created in 1687, are symmetrically placed near the Fountain of Evening and the Fountain of Daybreak. Here,* Lion Overcoming a Fox *by Jean Raon.*

NATURE AND CHILDHOOD DURING LOUIS XIV'S REIGN

Mythology, history, and religion succeeded one another as dominant preoccupations of Louis XIV's reign. There was, however, another important theme woven through its entire length: nature. This prince, who in his château and gardens was said to have "mastered nature" (marquis de Sourches)—in other words, to have enslaved and disfigured it—was particularly fond of flowers. Their presence was everywhere apparent at Versailles. Artists who specialized in flower painting were constantly given commissions. The château gardens also had their painters, and evidence of the king's affection for them is plentiful, notably in a series of works now in the gallery of the Large Trianon. This building, most of whose interior decoration was completed in 1688–89, was conceived as a temple of Flora where myth, exiled from the château, could encounter the world of flowers, which were very sparingly used in the formal garden terraces. One of the most representative paintings executed for the Large Trianon is *Clytie Transformed into a Sunflower* by Charles de La Fosse. Clytie is one of the nymphs La Fontaine had thought he recognized in the grotto of Thetis. Her violent affection for Apollo resulted in her transformation into the sunflower, which always faces the sun. That such a theme was tailor-made for Versailles should be readily apparent.

Animal life, which would seem a natural focus of interest for a hunter like Louis XIV, is in fact not prominent in the iconography of Versailles, but it is not altogether absent. The Labyrinth, of which little survives today, featured a rich assemblage of animals in its many sculptural depictions of Aesop's fables. Each of these fountains was accompanied by a versified text written by the poet Benserade. The moralizing intent that underlay this concept should be clear, and in fact Bossuet, the tutor

of the Grand Dauphin, used it in educating his pupil. The Animal Room (Cabinet des Animaux) also exemplifies the animal painting of 1687.

As already noted, the oldest surviving garden sculptures from Versailles depict children astride sphinxes (1668), and an entire walk was devoted to children (1670). Boisterous infants appear on the Water Terrace (1684–95) and in the celebrated coved frieze of the Room of the Bull's-eye (1701). Playful youngsters appear again, in charming disarray, in the Fountain of the Children's Island, a late work of 1710.

Are the children of Versailles more numerous and more natural than the putti so prominent in the Italian Renaissance? There are real differences between these two related motifs; the temperament of French artists accounts for them in part, but they derive above all from

the king's sensibilities, which determined all choices of subject. The famous instructions given to Mansart regarding projected alterations in the decor of the Menagerie should be cited here: "It seems to me that some changes must be made. . . , that the subjects are too serious and that childhood should figure prominently in whatever is done there. . . . Childish things should be everywhere apparent" (September 10, 1699). These remarks are relatively late in date, it is true; they were extracted from the old king by the mischievous charm of the duchesse de Bourgogne, for whom these decorations in a new style were created. But these circumstances render the remarks all the more precious. Louis XIV inspired the iconographic program of Versailles in all its manifestations save perhaps the Chapel, the authorship of whose program remains in doubt.

*F*OLLOWING PAGE. TOP: *The Water Walk or Infants' Walk. The Water Walk is ornamented by seven pairs of fountains supported by groups of children. Matched pairs are disposed to either side of the walk. Here, hunters by Mazeline. Originally these fountains, installed in 1670, were of realistically painted lead and the children supported baskets of flowers and fruit. In 1688 the baskets were replaced by basins of Languedoc marble, and the children were recast in bronze.* BOTTOM: *Fountain of the Children's Island by Jean Hardy (1710).*

PRECEDING PAGE: Child Riding a Sphinx. There are two such groups, whose origins date back to Louis XIV's first building campaign. The model for the children was provided by Sarrazin in 1660 but the bronzes date from 1668. The sphinxes are by Lerambert and Houzeau.

BELOW: Tourville (1781) by Houdon. The subject, who lived from 1642 to 1701, was a famous marshal in the French army. OPPOSITE: The Stone Gallery with statues from the Great Men of France series. In one of the galleries bordering the courts of the Northern Wing, several figures of military men commissioned for this series have been brought together. This patronage initiative was launched by d'Angiviller in 1776. The works from this series, ordered between 1776 and 1789 and originally intended for exhibition in the Louvre, are now distributed among the Louvre, the Institut de France, and Versailles. The presence of some of these figures at Versailles is consistent with the consecration of the château "To all the glories of France" under Louis-Philippe, who distributed the sculptures among these three venues.

NATIONAL HISTORY FROM LOUIS XVI ON

During the reign of Louis XV, monumental imagery went through a fallow period. The Gallery of Foreign Hunts, decorated in 1735 with bear, leopard, and tiger hunts (among others), would merit more than a passing mention if it still existed: it initiated a marked proclivity for exotic subjects that would prove important in the development of French painting. However, it might be maintained that at the Versailles of this period it was not themes but rather specific genres that were refined and developed. Portraiture, for example, attained a notable degree of perfection. But these works were later perceived as mere decorative elements; since they did not belong to the tradition of monumental imagery, they were dispersed in the revolutionary period like the rest of Versailles's furnishings. This was the fate even of the portraits of Louis XV's daughters, commissioned by their brother the dauphin, which depicted them in the guise of the seasons and were intended to serve as overdoors—works now in an American museum. For the same suite, the dauphin in 1750 commissioned Oudry to paint *The Farm*, a work conceived "in the Flemish mode" and representing a subject previously scorned in France, the rustic house. This gesture is worth noting, for it is the first evidence at Versailles of an incipient taste that would eventually lead to construction of the Hamlet. But Oudry's *Farm* is now in the Louvre.

The statues of the Great Men of France, intended for exhibition in the Large Gallery of the Louvre, were in the end shared by the Louvre, the Institute, and Versailles. They would not be mentioned here but for the fact that, with its set of these figures, Versailles inherited

productions shaped by the last patronage initiative of the old regime. The ideas that shaped this commission were pervasive in the eighteenth century, but they were advocated with particular urgency by the comte d'Angiviller, Marigny's successor, an enterprising overseer of the king's buildings whose ambitions would be compromised only by a lack of time and money. He set out to establish a museum; his many other projects were tied to this goal, which was his principal focus. The intention was to make the royal collections accessible to the public, and the Louvre was selected as the ideal locale. The museum was to function not only as a repository but also as a school for artists.

The commission of 1776, a self-conscious gesture of innovation and renewal, set out to encourage sculptors to take up subjects from French history. The historical genre had always been exalted by the Royal Academy of Painting and Sculpture as a prestigious form of imagery, but only the history of monarchs had received anything like sustained attention. Monumental depictions of the king remained among the commissions most coveted by sculptors. The commission of 1776 entailed representation of a national history, one not conventionally monarchical in its focus, a history made by great men and not by the king alone. From one point of view this was a neoclassical commission: it coincided with a pervasive revival of things antique, and the works were conceived in the spirit of Plutarch's *exempla virtutis*. But the agenda of the Moderns still exerted certain claims: the great men were obliged to dress in appropriate clothing of their respective periods, so that in most cases classical togas yielded to armor. Thus the Middle Ages and the Renaissance were permitted entry into the repertory of classicizing art.

The 1776 commission called for two statues annually, and the resulting works were presented at the salon exhibitions between 1776 and 1789. Reduced versions made of biscuit porcelain were also produced by the Royal Manufactory of Sèvres. Should this gesture be viewed as a salutary exercise in patriotism or as commercial exploitation? The porcelain reductions did not sell very well; several of these statuettes are visible today in Louis XVI's library, reminding us that those honored included men of letters and thinkers. Their presence in the château's collections is particularly useful, for all the life-size originals sent to Versailles represent men of war.

Under Napoleon, in fact, Versailles was very nearly converted into an army museum. Napoleon regretted that "the Revolution, which destroyed so much, [did not] destroy the château of Versailles"; the revolution that had made the Emperor should have left a ruined Versailles, the only monument worthy of this great conqueror. Napoleon seriously envisioned a grandiose plan to transform the gardens into a most peculiar memorial. "I would banish all these nymphs in bad taste from their beautiful bosquets, and all their exotic ornaments, replacing them with stonework panoramas representing the capital cities we entered in victory, and the famous battles demonstrating our martial superiority. This would have created a series of eternal monuments to our triumphs and our national glory on the doorstep of the capital of Europe, an obligatory pilgrimage for the entire universe" (Las Cases, *Mémorial de Sainte-Hélène*).

A memorial, a pantheon, a refuge for great men in retirement. For a brief period the Royal Court played host to another series of great men, the monumental statues created under the Empire and the Restoration to decorate the bridge leading to the Place de la Concorde in Paris; but they proved so unsightly there that Louis-Philippe reclaimed them for his Museum of French History. It was during this period that the inscription now visible on the pediment to the right of this court was added: "A toutes les gloires de la France" (To all the glories of France).

Since Louis-Philippe, the heroes of the 1776 commission have occupied the second-floor gallery of the Northern Wing, while its first-floor gallery shelters casts of diverse statues of kings and queens of France from various locales (churches, châteaux, and tombs).

The Museum of French History was the idea of Louis-Philippe, who could not have resided at Versailles without irritating the legitimists and alarming the republicans. As noted above, the Revolution had already caused assembly at Versailles of French works from the royal collections. The resulting exhibition was intended to function didactically. In 1816, amid general reflections on the goals of public education, Laurent-Pierre de Jussieu, a relative of the famous botanist, had proposed the creation of a museum of paintings intended for instruction. While pretending to espouse similar goals, Louis-Philippe in fact created a museum that was above all a masterpiece of political propaganda, designed to demonstrate that the nation had been forged by the mutual actions of kings and the people, and that the Orléans family, the subsidiary line of the Bourbons that had actively supported the Revolution, had embraced the goal of achieving national unity. The basic structural work for the museum was completed between 1833 and 1837 under the architect Frédéric Nepveu. We will not dwell on the destruction carried out with the sole intention of making the rooms suitable for exhibiting works selected for their historical subject matter, not their aesthetic value. So as to obtain a consistent, well-ordered installation, many older works were removed from their stretchers, enlarged or reduced, and hung together with copies in frames fixed to the walls.

The interest of the permanent decors created in the Northern and Southern Wings, however, is sufficient to make us forget the earlier marvels sacrificed during their construction. On the ground floor of the Southern Wing, the epic of Napoleon's campaigns is pictured year by year, room by room. The emperor's coronation is glorified in another room on the second floor.

To cover these walls, Louis-Philippe assembled the paintings that Napoleon had commissioned for his own residences. Additional rooms were also created: the Room of 1792, the Gallery of Battles, and finally the Room of 1830. In 1792 the duc de Chartres (the young Louis-Philippe) had enlisted in the revolutionary armies and participated in the battles of Valmy and Jemmapes. The paintings in the room dedicated to this year depict these two battles and the enlistment of volunteers. The Room of 1830 commemorates the events that brought Louis-Philippe to the throne. The choice of battles to be represented in the gallery's paintings, ranging chronologically from Tolbiac to Wagram, was made by the king himself. A few of these are of particular significance. At Bouvines, Philip Augustus returned his crown to the people, asking that they designate the leader most likely to carry the day in battle. Farther along Joan of Arc, who for Michelet incarnated the ideal of populist patriotism, is pictured entering Orléans. The battle of Taillebourg was won by a king who was also a saint: Louis IX, a prestigious ancestor in the Orléans family line. Still farther along, Henry IV is shown entering Paris acclaimed by his people. Bourbon rulers are rather well represented, even though Louis-Philippe was not a descendant of Louis XIV. But far more space is devoted to Napoleon. All things considered, the republicans and Bonapartists were better treated in the Southern Wing than the legitimists. On the other hand, the latter were presented in a favorable light in the Northern Wing. The Rooms of the Crusades consist of four rooms and a gallery, in the center of which was placed a relic of sorts, the Gothic portal from the fortress of the knights of Saint-John-of-Jerusalem in Rhodes, which the Turkish sultan sent to Louis-Philippe as a gift. Families whose ancestors took part in the Crusades were invited to place their coats of arms on the friezes of these rooms. In this instance a wide net was thrown for political reasons: little or no effort was made to verify the qualifications of the submitted family names, and this gesture flattered the vanity of many minor officials pretending to such ancestry. This program, while a bit forced, nonetheless engendered exceptional interiors composed of troubadour painting and decorative appointments. Colonialist painting was also born in this wing, in its African Rooms devoted to foreign conquests in which members of the Orléans family had figured prominently. Finally, in the Room of the Estates General, benchmark events in the history of French representative government are depicted, from the first meeting of the Estates General in 615 to the meeting called in 1789.

This ambitious program was carried out rather rapidly: the Room of 1792, the Gallery of Battles, and the Room of 1830 were all completed in 1834; the Rooms of the Crusades were completed in 1838; the Room of the Estates General in 1839; and the African Rooms in 1842.

All in all, and despite appearances to the contrary, the iconography of the Louis-Philippe period has a deeper affinity with that of Louis XIV than with the initiatives of the late eighteenth century exalting native heroes. The latter figures were held up as testimony to the superiority of the French nation and, in a sense, as examples for the edification of other nations. By contrast, the focus of Louis-Philippe's agenda was exclusively internal: in dem-

onstrating the continuity of French national history, this self-proclaimed king of the French intended only to bolster his own legitimacy, a legitimacy bestowed directly on Louis XIV by the dove of the Holy Spirit soaring above the royal tribune on the ceiling of the Chapel.

If the large crowds it attracted are any indication, the Museum of French History was a great success. The underlying political maneuver failed, however, and after 1846 the museum lost its protector. But in the eyes of posterity, Louis-Philippe's project should be viewed as having brought that of Louis XIV to a logical conclusion.

The Stone Gallery on the ground floor of the Northern Wing. Under Louis-Philippe, casts of statues of the kings and queens of France were displayed here.

Museum storerooms. A diverse collection of statues of great men was assembled at Versailles for exhibition in the historical museum established by Louis-Philippe in 1837 and dedicated "To all the glories of France." As a consequence of the twentieth-century restoration of the château's rooms to their original state, these works have now been relegated to storage.

HYMN TO VERSAILLES

The ceremonial chariots, the royal marvels,
The guards keeping nocturnal vigil,
All are gone, you are no longer home to grandeur;
Slumber and solitude,
Gods formerly unknown, and the arts of reflection
Today compose your court.

André Chénier, Hymne à Versailles

View along the main axis, from east to west. From foreground to background: the Water Terrace with the Fountain of the Dawn (left) and the Fountain of the Evening (right), the Latona Fountain, the Royal Walk and the Tapis Vert, the Apollo Fountain, and the Grand Canal.

*V*iew along the main axis, from east to west. From foreground to background: the Royal Walk and the Tapis Vert, the Apollo Fountain, and the Grand Canal.

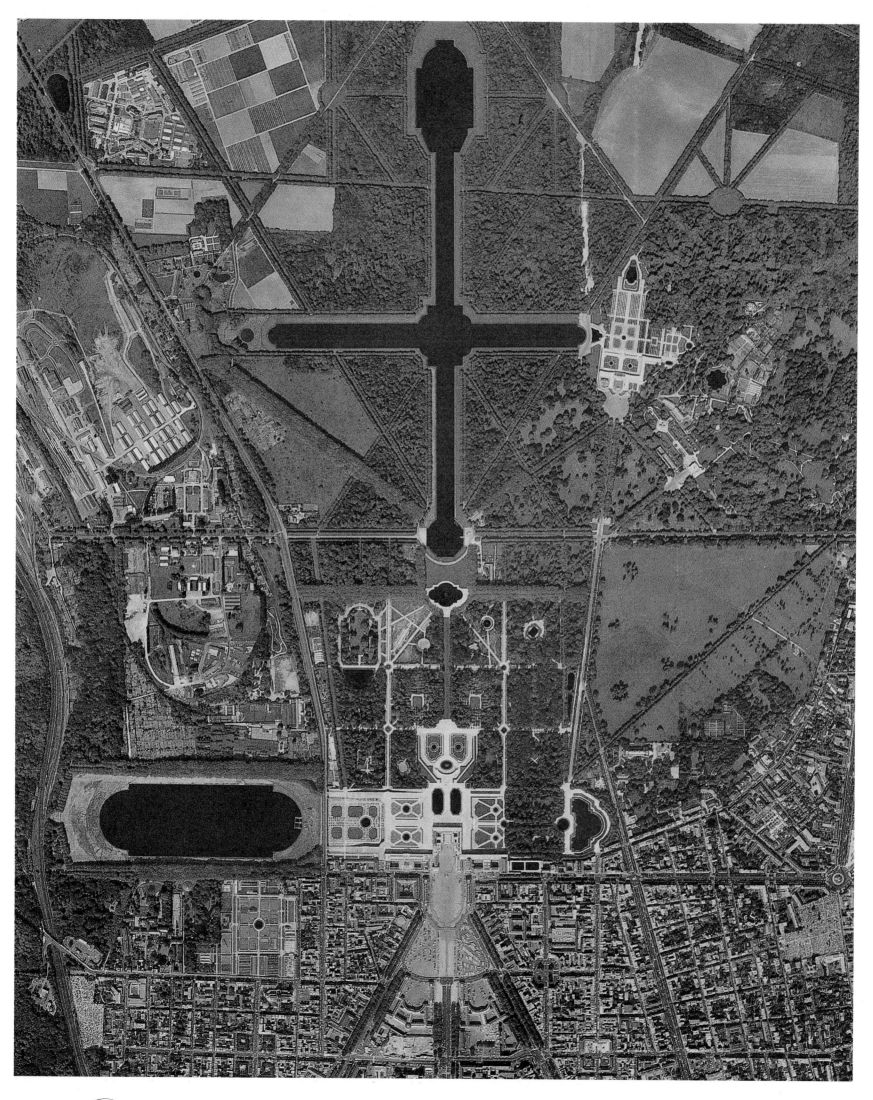

PLANS OF VERSAILLES

THE GARDENS, THE PARKS, AND TRIANON

Fountains and Pools

1	The Grand Canal	C1
2	The Apollo Fountain	C4
3	The Enceladus Fountain	C4
4	The Mirror Pool	B5
5	The Saturn Fountain	B4
6	The Flora Fountain	D4
7	The Bacchus Fountain	B5
8	The Ceres Fountain	D5
9	The Latona Fountain	C5
10	The Water Terrace	C6
11	The Pool of the Swiss Guards	A6
12	The Pyramid Fountain and the Nymphs' Bath	D6
13	The Dragon Fountain	D6
14	The Neptune Fountain	D6

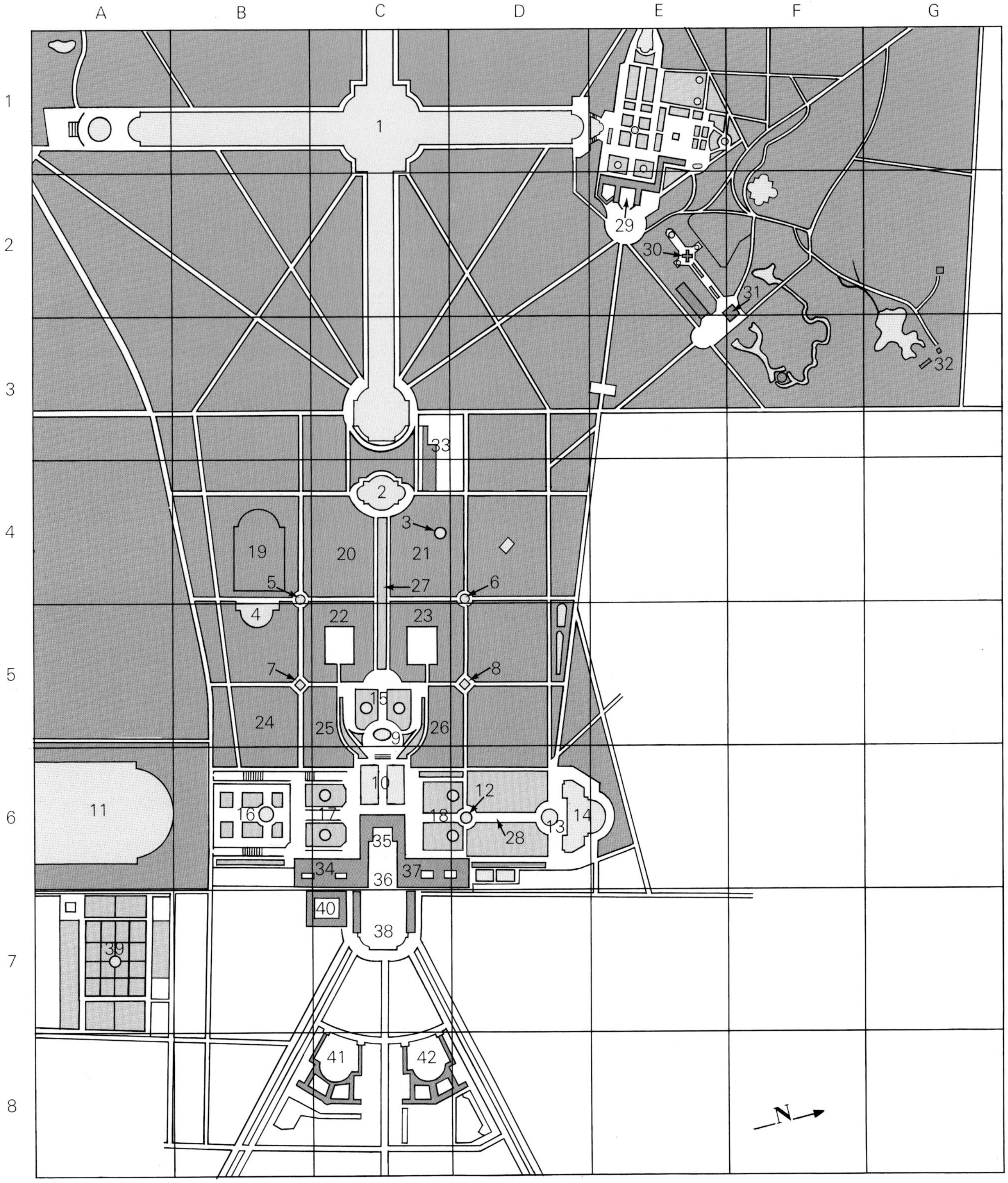

Terraces

15	The Latona Terrace	C5
16	The terrace in front of the Orangery	B6
17	The Southern Terrace	C6
18	The Northern Terrace	C6

Bosquets

19	The King's Garden	B4
20	The Bosquet of the Colonnade	C4
21	The Bosquet of the Domed Pavilions	C4
22	The Southern Quincunx	C5
23	The Northern Quincunx	C5
24	The Bosquet of the Queen (formerly the site of the Labyrinth)	B5
25	The Bosquet of the Ballroom	C5
26	The Bosquet of the Baths of Apollo	C5

Walks

27	The Royal Walk and the Tapis Vert (lawn)	C4
28	The Water Walk, or Infants' Walk	D6

Courtyards and Buildings

29–32	Trianon	
29	The Large Trianon	E2
30	The French Pavilion	E2
31	The Small Trianon	F2
32	The Hamlet	G3
33	Petite Venise	C3
34–38	The château	
34	The Southern Wing	C6
35	The Marble Court	C6
36	The Royal Court	C6
37	The Northern Wing	C6
38	The forward court and the Ministers' Wings	C7
39–42	Subsidiary structures	
39	The kitchen garden	A7
40	The Grand Commun	C7
41	The Small Stables	C8
42	The Large Stables	C8

Central Block

1 The Salon of Peace
2 The Large Gallery (Hall of Mirrors)
3 The Salon of War
4–8 The Grand Appartement of the queen
4 The Queen's Bedroom
5 The Salon of the Nobles
6 The Queen's Antechamber
7 The Room of the Queen's Guard
8 The Queen's Staircase
9 The former chapel, former Large Guardroom (in the Grand Appartement of the queen), and current Room of the Sacre, or Coronation (as arranged for the Museum of French History)
10 The Cabinets Intérieurs of Queen Marie-Antoinette
11–14 The Appartement Intérieur of the king (under Louis XIV)
11 The Room of the King's Guard
12 The Antechamber of the Grand Couvert, or ceremonial meals
13 The Room of the Bull's-eye

14 The King's Bedroom, known as Louis XIV's bedroom
15–22 The Appartement Intérieur of the king (under Louis XV and Louis XVI)
15 The Chamber of the King's Council
16 The King's Small Bedroom, known as Louis XV's bedroom
17 Dressing Room
18 The Chamber of the Pendulum Clock
19 The King's Office (Cabinet Intérieur)
20 The Gilded Chamber
21 The Bathing Room

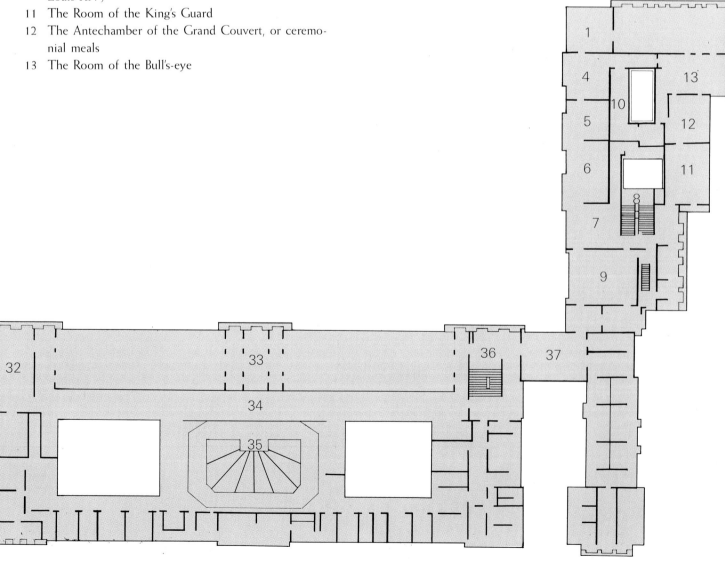

FLOOR OF THE CHATEAU

22 The King's Library
23 The Dining Room
24 The King's Staircase (as decorated under Louis-Philippe)
25 Space formerly occupied by the Room of Precious Objects
26–31 The Grand Appartement of the king (under Louis XIV)
26 The Salon of Apollo
27 The Salon of Mercury
28 The Salon of Mars
29 The Salon of Diana
30 The Salon of Venus
31 The Salon of Abundance

Southern Wing

32 The Room of 1831
33 The Gallery of Battles
34 The Stone Gallery
35 The Assembly Room
36 The Princes' Staircase
37 The Room of 1792

Gabriel Wing

38 The Grand Staircase (twentieth century)

Northern Wing

39 The Salon of Hercules
40 The Salon of the Chapel
41 The Chapel
42 The Stone Gallery
43 The African Rooms
44 The Opera House

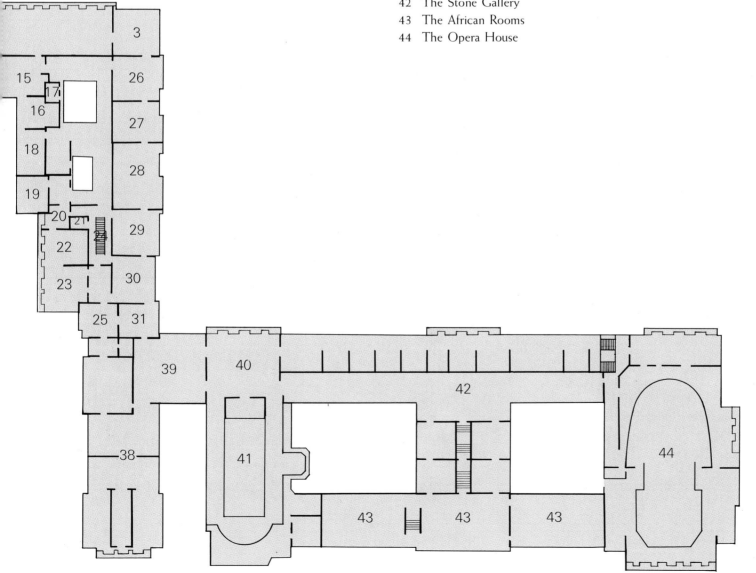

PLAN OF THE CHATEAU'S CONSTRUCTION HISTORY

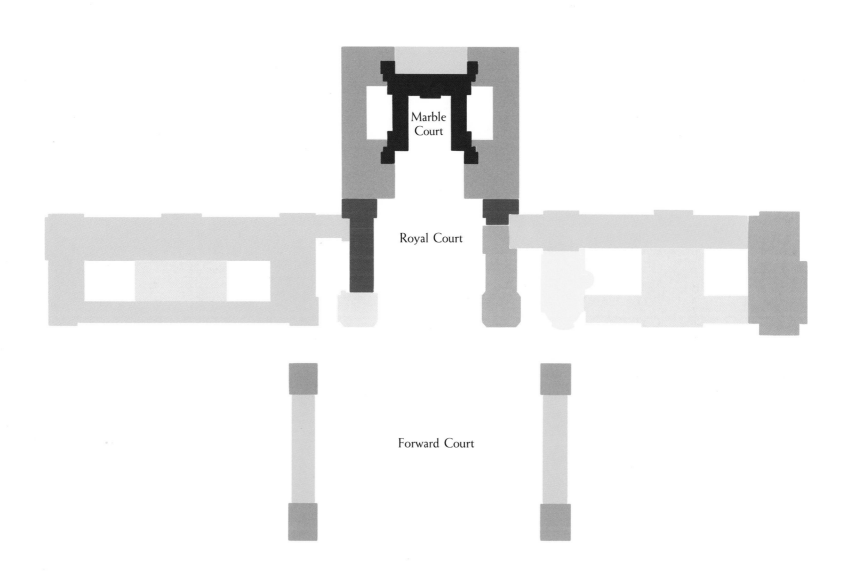

Marble Court

Royal Court

Forward Court

Louis XIII (1623, 1631)

Louis XIV and Le Vau. First building campaign (1661; portions reconstructed in the twentieth century)

Louis XIV, Hardouin-Mansart, and R. de Cotte (1699)

Louis XIV, Le Vau, and d'Orbay. Second building campaign (1688)

Louis XV and A.-J. Gabriel (1765 and 1771)

Louis XIV and Hardouin-Mansart. Third building campaign (1678)

Nineteenth- and twentieth-century construction

BIBLIOGRAPHY

While the bibliography of works dealing with the château of Versailles is quite extensive, the essential sources are the ten volumes of *Versailles et la cour de France* by Pierre de Nolhac (1925–30) and *Le Château de Versailles* by Pierre Verlet, which has recently been republished (Paris: Fayard, 1985).

Historical research on Versailles must begin with Pierre de Nolhac, whose publication is a major work of scholarship that has not been superseded by recent discoveries; the beauty of its literary style should further assure its continued interest. The above-cited work by de Nolhac is not illustrated, however, so we would also like to mention three other publications by the same author that do contain illustrations: *Le Château de Versailles sous Louis XIV* (1898); *La Création de Versailles* (1901); *L'Histoire du château de Versailles* (1911–18).

Pierre Verlet's book (with only a few schematic illustrations) is today the fundamental reference on Versailles; it skillfully summarizes research carried out over more than a century, and its bibliography is quite exhaustive.

We would, however, like to mention a few additional works published after 1980 that are of interest.

Berger, Robert W. *Versailles. The Château of Louis XIV.* University Park, Pa., and London: Pennsylvania State University Press, 1985. Berger is a specialist on the Versailles of Louis XIV.

Bottineau, Yves. *Versailles. Miroir des princes.* Paris: Arthaud, 1989. An exploration of the origins of Versailles and its influence by a former head conservator of the château.

Constant, Claire. *Versailles. Château de la France et orgueil des rois.* Paris: Gallimard, 1989. A provocative confrontation of images and texts, by the conservator who prepared the catalogue of paintings in the château collection.

Gaehtgens, Thomas W. *Versailles. De la résidence royale au musée historique.* Paris: Albin-Michel, 1984. Focuses exclusively on Louis-Philippe's historical museum, but on this subject it is excellent.

Himmelfarb, Hélène. "Versailles, fonctions et legendes," in *Les Lieux de mémoires*, collaborative publication edited by P. Nora, part 2, vol. 2. Paris: Gallimard, 1986. A remarkable study of the political and operational functioning of the château.

Hoog, Simone. *Le Bernin. Louis XIV. Une statue déplacée.* Paris: Adam Biro, 1989. On Bernini's equestrian statue of Louis XIV, by the conservator responsible for the château's sculpture.

Le Guillou, Jean-Claude. *Versailles, histoire du château des rois.* Paris: Deux Coqs d'Or, 1988. A history of the château, illustrated by a specialist who is also a remarkable draftsman.

Pons, Bruno. *De Paris a Versailles, 1699–1736. Les sculpteurs ornemanistes parisiens et l'art décoratif des bâtiments du roi.* Strasbourg: Université de Strasbourg, 1986. The basic reference work on the team of ornamental sculptors who worked at Versailles under Jules Hardouin-Mansart and Robert de Cotte.

Souchal, François. *French Sculptors of the 17th and 18th Centuries. The Reign of Louis XIV.* Oxford: Cassirer, 1977–87. Organized as a biographical dictionary, this is the basic source of information concerning French sculptors active during the reign of Louis XIV.

Waltisperger, Chantal. "La Clôture du grand parc de Versailles," in *La Revue de l'art*, 1984. On recently discovered documents concerning the boundaries and initial enclosure of the hunting park.

Walton, Guy. *Louis XIV's Versailles.* Chicago: University of Chicago Press, 1986. More an extended essay than a book, but by one of the most distinguished current specialists on the château of Louis XIV.

Weber, Gerold. *Brunnen und Wasserkünste in Frankreich in Zeitalter von Louis XIV.* Worms: Wernersche Verlagsgessellschaft, 1985. Includes important chapters on Versailles by the leading specialist on waterworks in French seventeenth-century gardens.

INDEX

Italic page numbers refer to captions and illustrations.

PHOTOGRAPHY CREDITS

All photographs by Robert Polidori, except for the following: Bibliothèque Nationale-Estampes: pages 32, 69, 72, 89, 90, 91 (top right), 106, 148, 155, 234, 328, 365; Dagli-Orti: pages 25, 44, 45, 49, 74, 78, 79, 84, 252, 262, 283 (right), 335; Giraudon: pages 31, 61; Lauros-Giraudon: pages 60, 68, 70 (top left), 375; Telarci-Giraudon: page 332; Institut Géographique National: autorisation no. 90 10 11, pages 29, 414; Réunion des Musées Nationaux: pages 22, 23, 24, 58, 59, 66, 70 (top right), 87, 128, 146, 147, 218, 219 (bottom), 231, 233, 244 (top left), 246, 253, 258, 276, 278, 279 (right), 282, 283 (left), 326, 333, 334, 343; Pérouse de Montclos: pages 39, 76 (top left), 88, 91, 113, 116, 152, 160, 162, 180, 182, 265, 266, 268, 378; Saint James's Palace, London: page 47.